D0053927

PRAISE FOR *THE CONFIDENT WOMAN*

"*The Confident Woman* is well supported by findings from social science research, but is delivered in such an open, human voice that you feel the author is sitting across from you in your living room (over tea) and speaking directly to you. Shaevitz is compassionate and funny—and among the wisest women I know."
—Laura L. Carstensen, professor of psychology,
Institute for Research on Women and Gender, Stanford University

"Reading *The Confident Woman* is like being with your dearest, wisest, most loving friend." —Dale Steele, founder and copresident of the
As We Change catalogue and *Internet Marketplace*

"Marjorie Shaevitz has done it again! *The Confident Woman*—like *The Superwoman Syndrome*—provides needed advice that 'hits the mark' for today's women leaders. I will recommend it to all the women executives I work with. Even more, *The Confident Woman* needs to be read by all leaders of the future, both women and men!" —Marshall Goldsmith,
coeditor of *The Leader of the Future* and *The Organization of the Future* and
a *Wall Street Journal* "Top 10" executive development consultant

"*The Confident Woman* has it all—poetry, thought-provoking facts, humor and humanity, generous suggestions, personal stories of success and learning. What a gift to the reader who realizes that a fulfilling life is an inside-out job and the best gift we can give ourselves (and others) is to truly know ourselves…and then go for it!" —Ken and Margie Blanchard,
authors of *The One-Minute Manager*; Blanchard Training and Development

ALSO BY MARJORIE HANSEN SHAEVITZ

The Superwoman Syndrome

Making It Together as a Two Career Couple
(with Morton H. Shaevitz, Ph.D.)

So You Want to Go Back to School
(with Elinor Lenz)

THE
CONFIDENT
WOMAN

How to Take Charge and Recharge Your Life

MARJORIE HANSEN SHAEVITZ

THREE RIVERS PRESS
NEW YORK

For permissions, see page 343.

Copyright © 1999 Marjorie Hansen Shaevitz

All rights reserved. No part of this book may be reproduced or transmitted in any form or by any means, electronic or mechanical, including photocopying, recording, or by any information storage and retrieval system, without permission in writing from the publisher.

Published by Three Rivers Press, New York, New York.
Member of the Crown Publishing Group.

Random House, Inc. New York, Toronto, London, Sydney, Auckland

www.randomhouse.com

THREE RIVERS PRESS is a registered trademark and the Three Rivers Press colophon is a trademark of Random House, Inc.

Originally published in hardcover by Harmony Books in 1999.

Printed in the United States of America
Design by Susan Hood

Library of Congress Cataloging-in-Publication Data
Shaevitz, Marjorie Hansen.
    The confident woman /
Marjorie Hansen Shaevitz. — 1st ed.
    1. Women — Psychology.   2. Assertiveness in women.
    3. Self-confidence.   I. Title.
HQ1206.S465   1999
305.42 — dc21
                                                99-34390
                                                   CIP

ISBN 0-609-80534-7

10   9   8   7   6   5   4   3   2   1
First Paperback Edition 2001

To Geoff and Marejka

For who you are.
For what you have done in your young years.
For being the sunshine in my life.

CONTENTS

PROLOGUE

That's the way things come clear. All of a sudden. And then
you realize how obvious they've been all along.

Madeleine L'Engle

One Saturday afternoon not long ago, Kate Karpilow, a friend and colleague from Berkeley, California, was visiting relatives in San Diego and
stopped by my house to say hello. I had not seen Kate in many, many
months even though I am on a number of boards with her. As we sat in
my living room chatting about her work and this book, Kate stopped me
in the middle of a sentence and said, "Marjorie, you've changed. Not that
you were such a wimp before, but I've noticed as we were talking that you
seem much stronger, more certain, so assured about yourself. What's
going on?"

With no time for reflection, I found myself saying, "Really? I hadn't
noticed any change, but now that I think about it, I have never felt better
about myself, more powerful, or more in control of what happens to me.
Writing this book has literally (forgive the pun) changed my life."

Kate and I then went on to talk about other things. After my friend left,
I began to think about my comment that writing *The Confident Woman*
had changed my life. For the first time I began to appreciate how true that
statement was. (Isn't it interesting how personal truths have a way of pop-
ping out of your mouth when you least expect them.)

Then I began to reflect on why writing this book had been such a life-
changing experience. I thought about the hundreds of hours I had spent
scouring research papers and books looking for new materials on the issue
of confidence. I recalled how people had told me to stop wasting my time
doing all of this research. They kept saying, "Write a KISS book [Keep It
Simple Stupid]. People don't care about research. Give them sound bites

like they get on radio and TV. Just tell women what to do in the simplest possible terms. And for God's sake, don't use footnotes!"

Well, to begin with, the "write and run" approach is not my way of doing things. I want to respect readers by giving them the full benefit of whatever research information and current thinking is available. I didn't want to "dumb down" *The Confident Woman*. In fact, my hope was that through reading this book readers might develop some of the attitudes and actions that would help them put an end to the sound-bite life.

Before I engaged in my research, I pretty much knew about the whats and hows of confidence, but I had never quite put together the whys. In other words, I had never solved the mystery of why, and in spite of changed laws, new options, and unparalleled opportunities, women, including myself, continued to act in nonconfident, self-sacrificing, self-neglecting ways. As I sifted through all of the research materials, I began to unravel the puzzle. I saw how and why the pattern of historical and current cultural messages has taken such a toll on women's minds.

That was just the beginning. Not only did I learn about the research on optimal health, I began to practice its tenets. I saw how taking good care of herself is one of the least selfish things a woman can do. I found compelling evidence that having a strong, defined "self" is not narcissistic, but key to making a difference in other people's lives. I carefully examined the research on negative thinking including that which leads to guilt, worry, and self-criticism. I learned how easy it is to gain control over one's negative thoughts and about the power of focusing one's actions on the positive. What a relief it is to feel that you can handle life's negative challenges. How reassuring it is to know that accepting less than the positive and less than quality does no one any good.

Perhaps the most intriguing part of writing *The Confident Woman* was how I found particular books and research pieces. I believe something that writer Phil Cousineau calls "synchronicity" was at work. Following the thoughts of Carl Jung, Cousineau says that synchronicity is "a meaningful coincidence."[1] As an example, he says that every once in a while "the 'Library Angel'" brings us "the right book at the right time and the muse is invoked . . . as if on wings from heaven, the right words . . . appear and change our lives."[2]

That's exactly what happened to me: the gift of Cousineau's *Soul Moments* was one of the first examples of my Library Angel at work. Other examples included a friend calling to tell me, out of the blue, about research on what motivates people to do (and not do) what they want, a major issue in confidence. In response to an Internet request for information on optimal health, a professor from Harvard led me to a series of works that became critical for the book. After giving a talk in Seattle and deciding on a whim to spend the day on Whidbey Island, I stopped at a delightful little bookstore where I stumbled upon a book on quality environments. It too became important. And the examples go on and on. The right quote, the right person, the right concept seemed to drop into my hands just exactly when I needed it.

I don't know how you heard about *The Confident Woman*, or how the book happened to come into your hands. At the very least, I hope that you find the ideas and thoughts interesting and useful. But my real hope is that there is a bit of "synchronicity" in your finding this book, that your "Library Angel" has provided you with *The Confident Woman* at the right time to make a real difference in your life.

WHO THIS BOOK IS FOR

If you are a woman who feels utterly lacking in confidence, this is a book for you.

On the other hand, if you are a woman who has a fair amount of confidence, but could use a little more, this is a book for you too.

Even if you are raging with confidence and can't imagine needing any more, I think you will find some of the insights, information, and suggestions useful to pass along to girls and women who may not have as much confidence as you have. So this is a book for you too.

Finally, this is also a book for men. After all, there are few men who don't work, live with, and/or love some women — mothers, wives, daughters, sisters, friends, perhaps even colleagues. Over the years I have found that men who are fathers of daughters are particularly interested in knowing how to raise them to be strong and confident.

As I looked at the research and interviewed women, what I came to understand was this:

Few women have enough self-confidence.

Rarely does one have too much.
(As you will see later, those who may seem to, really don't.)

Almost everyone could use a little — if not a lot — more self-confidence.

Part I

WHAT CONFIDENCE IS ALL ABOUT

Who Am I to Be Telling You What to Do?

> A book is, after all, nothing more than a personal letter to the
> world . . . at least to those who want to read it.
>
> *Anonymous*

I can't remember when I didn't want to write this book. After a lifetime of experiencing little confidence, two separate but related incidents led me to stop thinking about it and sit down to prepare, and eventually write *The Confident Woman.*

The first incident took place when a colleague of mine, Dr. Kim Yeager, chief of the California Office of Women's Health, asked me to give a presentation for an upcoming National Roundtable on Women's Health. The other presenters were going to be people who were considered "the experts" in their respective fields, so my immediate response was to tell her that I was sure that there were many others much better qualified than I to do such a presentation. Frankly, that was the truth. Nevertheless, Kim left the invitation open.

That evening I flew up to the San Francisco Bay Area to see my kids perform in a Stanford University improv program. Before the show, I went out to dinner with another colleague, Dr. Iris Litt, director of adolescent medicine at the Stanford University School of Medicine. As we were sipping a glass of wine at a local café, I mentioned to Iris that a National Roundtable on Women's Health was going to be held in California and that she might want to get in touch with Kim Yeager about doing a piece on adolescent girls, her area of expertise. Just as an idle aside, I mentioned that Kim had asked me to give the talk on women's mental health and then casually told her of my response.

What ensued was life-changing for me. Iris, who in spite of her remarkable accomplishments is a very soft-spoken woman, took my hand in hers, looked me straight in the eye, and in an uncharacteristically strong voice said: "Marjorie, don't you *dare* not accept this invitation! Don't you know that when asked to give presentations, even the most highly educated, most qualified women — both Ph.D.'s and M.D.'s — continually take themselves out of the arena? Predictably, they say no to invitations because they don't think they know enough, are good enough, are experienced enough, are prepared enough to speak on a subject. Even when they are experts in their fields, many women don't seem to have the confidence to do the job.

"On the other hand," she went on, "when most male Ph.D.'s or M.D.'s are asked to present, they say yes readily, whether or not they know anything about the subject![1] Hey, my friend, you've been offered a wonderful opportunity! You've got to do it. What do you have to lose?"

I was stunned. Iris's words both challenged me and gave me courage to do something that I would not otherwise have done. (Now that's a good friend!) So in spite of not having the extraordinary academic credentials of my fellow roundtable presenters, I decided to participate. With the help of a colleague, I spent six months relentlessly tracking down the research on women's mental health. Eventually we managed to put together a respectable presentation. At least it was effective enough to have the sponsoring organization ask us to give it again on two other occasions. I will never forget that experience because it forced me to succeed at something about which I had little confidence.

The second incident took place just after I gave the roundtable talk. One day a colleague of mine called to ask me to lecture on The Superwoman Syndrome to women faculty members at a major medical school. My nonconfident side whispered, "Who, me? What could I possibly offer these brilliant women?" Then I thought back to the previous incident and Iris's encouragement. I realized that my colleague was asking me to speak on a topic about which I knew quite a lot. (After all, I was the author of the one and only book on the subject.) In spite of my initial trepidation, I said yes to her invitation.

Once again I relied on my trusty work orientation and decided that to feel comfortable talking before this high-powered group, I needed to know more about them and what their respective Superwoman issues were. As I agreed to do the talk, I also made arrangements to conduct interviews with about a dozen of the future audience members, all M.D.'s and/or Ph.D.'s.

As I interviewed these extraordinary women, I was astounded at how many of them seemed to lack self-confidence. They said things like (and these are their *exact* words):

I keep thinking, I hope I'm good enough.

I just don't feel up to a lot of things . . . teaching, my research, being a good mother, keeping the household going.

I know I need to take better care of myself . . . I just can't. . . . I'm worn to a frazzle; freaked out with too much to do and yet guilty and miserable when I try to take some time for me. I'm desperate for even a little bit of time alone.

I'm insecure, damn insecure, but pleazzzzzzze don't breathe a word of this to anyone.

I couldn't believe my ears! Here were some of the most accomplished women in the United States, women who enjoyed all the accoutrements of success—degrees, decrees, prestigious careers, expensive homes, children in the best schools, new Volvos in their parking spaces—yet so many of them appeared to be lacking in confidence. And they were the cream of the crop—the top of the heap—the academic dream team!

So many questions popped into my head: If these uncommonly successful academics and physicians don't have confidence, who does? Does any woman? Do people fake confidence? (Hadn't I done that myself?) If there are women of real confidence, who are they and how did they get it? Why do others not have it? Is one born with it? What can a person do to develop it? It's not as if you can traipse down to your local grocery store, open up a mail-order catalog, or even go onto the Internet to buy some. (If it were only so easy!) I also thought about young girls and what we—as mothers, grandmothers, aunts, friends, teachers, mentors—can do to insure that they grow up having true confidence.

Right then and there I decided that I had to write this book.

WHY WOULD I WRITE THIS BOOK?

Most authors write about what they need or want to know. If you have just picked up this book, you may be wondering why I should have written a book on women and confidence. There are two primary reasons.

First, I'll tell you about my personal lack-of-confidence credentials, but I am not relating these for sympathy. That serves no one's purpose. I simply want readers who have low confidence to grasp that I understand how difficult—even impossible—it feels to get yourself out of the valley of low confidence.

Second, I will briefly mention some of my professional credentials. I do this because as you read this book, I'd like you to have confidence in what I'm saying.

Let's begin.

MY LACK-OF-CONFIDENCE CREDENTIALS

I am the oldest of three daughters who grew up rather uneventfully on an isolated ranch in the Central Valley of California, far from a town or many people (let alone confident female role models). Like my very nice Danish parents, I went to a poor country school until the eighth grade, then to a high school deemed one of the worst in the Golden State. The nearest library was twenty miles away and was, therefore, virtually inaccessible. Perhaps one of my biggest regrets is that aside from schoolbooks, I didn't do much reading until I was an adult. Nevertheless, my father was a college-educated man, and my going to college was a foregone conclusion. My mother was and is a very shy housewife whose life centers solely on her family.

Because there was no preschool or even kindergarten where I lived, I began my education in the first grade, and I loved it! I remember bringing home all kinds of homework assignments, especially the daily spelling lists. Neither my teacher nor my parents (nor I) realized until the end of the year that no homework had ever been assigned. I was essentially assigning myself all of the first- and second-grade reading lists as spelling lists, as well as anything else that captured my fancy. (First and second grades were taught in the same room in my four-room school.)

The teacher and my parents decided that I should skip the second grade (which wasn't much of a jump since I had already done all of the work). Because I was always the best student in grammar school and high school, one of the earliest positive messages I got was that I was smart. But that was about it. I don't remember feeling pretty or funny (like my younger sister), or thin or clever or skilled with my hands (like my middle sister), or anything else. Certainly athletics were not a factor in my life.

At age eleven I was five foot nine, literally taller than any other person in my grammar school, including the teachers. As a result, I must have been thirty years old before I disassociated the word *tall* (and myself) from such words as *big, large,* and *big-boned* (that polite way of saying fat) and stopped extrapolating to other words such as *clumsy, graceless, unattractive,* and *gawky.* In truth I was simply tall. Although it is not an issue for me now, the image of being "big and tall" haunted me while I was growing up. I learned then that being small and dainty (shades of Tammy, Annette, and Gidget) were the essential characteristics of a desirable female.

I left my parents' ranch at age seventeen to go off to the local state college. Because I hadn't gotten into Stanford as an undergraduate, I began to question what I perceived as my one and only gift, intelligence. I knew how to do three things: work hard, get good grades, and be nice. At that stage of my life, what I didn't know was just about everything else: how to be my own person (or that there even was such a thing), how to take care of myself (or that I was supposed to), and how to handle any number of people or life situations — especially men — other than by being nice. Needless to say, like many women of my generation I was ill prepared to deal with the real world.

As a young woman, I felt unattractive and undesirable. Even though I was tall, blond, and had blue eyes, I was certain that I was not pretty enough, thin enough, "cool" enough (especially in the clothes I wore), or sexy enough to attract "cool" guys. It never crossed my mind that a lack of confidence might have played a role in my inability to attract the "right" men. Who thought about confidence then? The only way I knew to be acceptable to other people — especially members of the opposite sex — was to be nice, please them, take care of them, and be what they wanted me to be. I especially didn't know that I was supposed to set limits with men, including saying no and saying it loud and clear in difficult situations.

I grew up thinking that if I was nice and loving, I would receive kindness and love in return. I also assumed that if a man cared about me, he would treat me with tenderness and respect. It is not surprising then that over the years I found myself in a variety of situations where I had no idea of how to take care of or defend myself. I was date-raped in college (there wasn't a word to describe that when I was young — it was just "my fault"); stalked when I lived in Hawaii (this doesn't happen to nice girls — what did I do wrong?); abused in a number of relationships; sexually harassed in early jobs (I had no word for that either; in fact, I didn't realize that I had experienced it until I found myself bursting into tears while watching the Clarence Thomas Supreme Court hearings in the early 1990s).

As I enumerate these episodes, I still find the memories very painful, mostly because of how helpless and alone I felt. Like so many other women, when I was violated or abused, I couldn't believe that it was happening to me. After all, I was such a nice person! I kept trying to figure out what I had done wrong or how I could be even nicer in order to make it stop. I didn't know that these very attitudes were what were perpetuating the behavior. Moreover, I didn't ask anyone for help because I was too embarrassed to tell people what was happening for fear that I would be blamed for what I had gone through.

Today I understand that those experiences weren't my fault. I also realize that if I had had more confidence when I was younger, I probably would not have been such a sitting duck. At the very least, I wouldn't have allowed the situations to reach the extremes that they did.

The nonconfidence stories go on. For example, as a young woman I often acceded to sales pressure to buy clothes that looked just terrible on me. Add to that years of buying things only when they were on sale, and I ended up with a closet full of clothing and shoes that were in odd colors, not quite the right sizes, and of dubious fit. I was probably forty years old before I could return a purchase that was defective (God forbid that I just didn't like it) without feeling somehow that I was doing something wrong.

As I got older, married, and had children, low confidence issues still plagued me. I always put other people and their needs ahead of my own, and I ignored myself physically, emotionally, and in all other ways, especially when I was the mother of young children. On many days I would have given anything to have a doctor tell me that I needed a week of rest or some "alone time." But I needed a doctor's permission to justify my doing that. After all, taking time alone and getting sufficient rest seemed like selfish indulgences. A less-than-sympathetic statement, a questioning look, or a call for help was enough to turn me away from what I desperately needed and wanted to do. For years I dreamed of having a "room of my own."

Throughout most of my life, I have been terribly uncomfortable about asking things of others. I found it almost impossible to delegate to employees, until I wrote the Superwoman book—which gave me an opportunity to get some perspective on how I was behaving. Up to that point, it had never occurred to me to think about what I wanted or liked, or how to get it.

I lived by the "good girl" standards of trying to meet other people's expectations and trying to win their approval as a sign that I was okay. Whatever I wanted to do or have—attend an important meeting, write a book, garden, or even buy a wonderful reading chair—always felt less legitimate, less important than what my husband or children were doing or wanting. Like a secondhand rose, I expected that my needs, wants and desires would somehow get met along the way. And if they weren't, oh well.

Today I am much more confident, and do you know why? Because I was determined to find out *how* to be more confident. Because I took hold of my life and decided *not* to feel unworthy or second class anymore. Because I made it happen for myself. As you read through the various chapters of this book, you will see how you can do it as well.

MY CONFIDENCE CREDENTIALS

As for my confidence credentials, since the early 1980s I have been writing books and giving talks about women and their lives. I have also been a practicing marriage and family therapist and executive coach to women (and some men) clients.

I have been chair of the national board of Stanford University's Institute for Research on Women and Gender, as well as former chair of the California Commission on the Status of Women. I am one of the founding members of the board that advises the California Office of Women's Health and one of two public members on the California Medical Association's Foundation Board. Because of the expertise I have built, I have been asked to sit on national editorial boards for *American Health for Women* and *Healthy Woman* magazines, *At Your Best* health newsletter, and *As We Change* women's health catalog. As my books and tapes have been published, I have also appeared on most of the national television and radio shows and have been interviewed for national magazines and newspapers.

I am also an inveterate list maker, avid reader, pursuer of humor and wit, and collector of quips and quotes. I love solutions, answers, good ideas, and great recipes—whatever "works"—and as you will see, all of those things are part of this book.

ABOUT THIS BOOK

I have tried to write this book so that it is informative and personal to you, useful, and at the same time, fun. In part I of the book I define what confidence is. Through a self-test I'll help you to get a handle on how much confidence you have and in what areas. After all, you need to know where you are before you decide where you want to be.

Part II will help you to understand why so many women seem to be lacking confidence. I think you'll find this interesting because the cause of our low confidence goes back many, many generations and is manifested in multitudinous ways. In part III, through various means—thought-provoking questions, simple exercises, and assorted other activities—I give you directions for developing self-knowledge. As you will see, self-knowledge is not an end in itself; rather it serves the purpose of helping you become more whole. This is important because whole people give to others, but not out of obligation, guilt, or fear. Whole people give from their overflow.

If you truly want more self-confidence
You need to stop looking to others
And search first within yourself.

Part IV is a road map for gaining confidence—a series of ideas, directions, solutions, and even words to use both in building your confidence and in dealing with the most common confidence-busting situations. Here you will be able to use a lot of the information you gained from the earlier chapters. When you have found where your confidence is lacking and where pieces of information about yourself are missing, I'll show you how to choose the thoughts and actions that will make a real difference in your life. Finally, in the epilogue I'll leave you with some ideas about how you can be a positive influence in young women's lives.

Please approach *The Confident Woman* as an adventure, an odyssey, a search, a personal exploration, because it is all about *you*. This book is an opportunity right now to begin reinventing yourself and your world. I'd like it to be a vehicle for your finding your own authentic voice, acting on your own behalf, treating yourself as well as you treat others. I want to help you become a more confident woman.

Most of what I have written is one part "good common sense" and other parts of things told to me by women who are probably very much like you. I hope to offer you a smorgasbord of thoughts and ideas. As you will see, I'm always looking for people and resources to add quality to life. If I hear about something that seems promising, I'll try it out. It if works, I'll keep it; if it doesn't, then I'll look for something else. I hope you'll do the same. Most important, please, please, don't think that anything I suggest in *The Confident Woman* is another in a long line of *shoulds, musts,* or *have-tos.* No doubt you have plenty of those in your life already. Take all the time you need to read this book, because there is no hurry, no deadline, no schedule for you to follow.

Are you ready? To borrow words from one of my favorite books, Bill Richardson's *Bachelor Brothers' Bed and Breakfast:*

> *Now is the time for all good women to find a cozy place to sit, relax and enjoy a cup of wonderful hot tea.*

And while you're doing that, please be my guest and continue reading this book, my personal letter to you.

Let me now introduce you to the first of a continuing feature in this book: the Break. At the end of each chapter I will offer an assortment of ideas about how to enjoy yourself, take better care of yourself, or add something pleasant to your life. Since I have just invited you to have a cup of tea, it only seems appropriate to start the breaks with a suggestion for your choice of tea.

TEA BREAK

Have you ever tried one of The Republic of Tea's delicious combinations, such as Cinnamon Plum, Ginger Peach, or Mango Ceylon?

> *The tea-hour is the hour of peace. . . .*
> *Strife is lost in the hissing of the kettle—*
> *a tranquilizing sound,*
> *second only to the purring of a cat.*
>
> Agnes Repplier
> *To Think of Tea*

CHAPTER 1

How Confident Are You?

CONFIDENCE QUIZ

Take a few minutes to respond to the following twenty items in order to determine your current level of confidence. This is not a test. Think of it as a state-of-the-person confidence inventory, the purpose of which is to help you to better understand yourself.

As you read each item, determine the degree to which it describes how you think or feel or behave, then circle the appropriate number. Don't leave any item unanswered. Make sure that you circle one number for each statement. When in doubt, give it your best guess. Taking this inventory can be the first step toward becoming a more confident woman.

(Having self-knowledge)
1. I HAVE A STRONG SENSE OF MY SELF: THAT IS, I KNOW WHO I AM, WHAT I LIKE, AND WHAT I WANT OUT OF LIFE. I AM MY OWN PERSON.

1	2	3	4	5	6	7	8	9	10
Rarely or never	Not very often			Sometimes		Most of the time		Yes!! Always	

(Being self-responsible)
2. I TAKE RESPONSIBILITY FOR GETTING WHAT I NEED AND WANT RATHER THAN DEPENDING ON OTHERS TO GIVE IT TO ME, OR GET IT FOR ME, OR DO IT FOR ME.

1	2	3	4	5	6	7	8	9	10
Rarely or never	Not very often			Sometimes		Most of the time		Yes!! Always	

(Prioritizing actions)

3. I SPEND MY TIME ON WHO AND WHAT IS IMPORTANT TO ME.

1	2	3	4	5	6	7	8	9	10
Rarely or never		Not very often		Sometimes		Most of the time		Yes!! Always	

(Choosing quality people)

4. I SPEND TIME WITH POSITIVE PEOPLE ABOUT WHOM I CARE AND WHO ARE CARING, SUPPORTIVE, AND RESPECTFUL OF ME.

1	2	3	4	5	6	7	8	9	10
Rarely or never		Not very often		Sometimes		Most of the time		Yes!! Always	

(Choosing quality work)

5. I LOVE THE WORK I DO: IT'S INTERESTING, CHALLENGING, AND MEANINGFUL.

1	2	3	4	5	6	7	8	9	10
Rarely or never		Not very often		Sometimes		Most of the time		Yes!! Always	

(Choosing quality activities)

6. I ENGAGE IN ACTIVITIES, HOBBIES, SPORTS, AND EVENTS THAT I LOVE.

1	2	3	4	5	6	7	8	9	10
Rarely or never		Not very often		Sometimes		Most of the time		Yes!! Always	

(Choosing quality environments)

7. I MAKE SURE THAT THE ENVIRONMENTS IN WHICH I LIVE AND WORK ARE POSITIVE, HEALTHY, AND PLEASING TO ME.

1	2	3	4	5	6	7	8	9	10
Rarely or never		Not very often		Sometimes		Most of the time		Yes!! Always	

(Having life balance)

8. MY LIFE IS WELL BALANCED BETWEEN WORK AND PLAY.

1	2	3	4	5	6	7	8	9	10
Rarely or never		Not very often		Sometimes		Most of the time		Yes!! Always	

(Choosing a positive attitude)

9. I AM A POSITIVE PERSON; THAT IS, I AM ABLE TO FOCUS ON THE POSITIVE ASPECTS OF MY LIFE AND ELIMINATE OR EFFECTIVELY DEAL WITH THE NEGATIVE.

1	2	3	4	5	6	7	8	9	10
Rarely or never		Not very often		Sometimes		Most of the time		Yes!! Always	

(Having a solutions orientation)

10. WHEN LIFE'S PROBLEMS AND CHALLENGES ARRIVE, I ACT ON THEM RATHER THAN THINK OR WORRY ABOUT THEM.

1	2	3	4	5	6	7	8	9	10
Rarely or never		Not very often		Sometimes		Most of the time		Yes!! Always	

(Accepting of body and appearance)

11. ASIDE FROM AN OCCASIONAL "BAD HAIR DAY," I AM COMFORTABLE WITH HOW I LOOK, INCLUDING MY FACE, MY BODY, AND MY CHOICE OF CLOTHING.

1	2	3	4	5	6	7	8	9	10
Rarely or never		Not very often		Sometimes		Most of the time		Yes!! Always	

(Effectively using feelings)

12. I AM AWARE OF AND CAN IDENTIFY MY FEELINGS.

1	2	3	4	5	6	7	8	9	10
Rarely or never		Not very often		Sometimes		Most of the time		Yes!! Always	

(Having a sense of humor)

13. I SEEK OUT AND ENJOY THE HUMOROUS ASPECTS OF LIFE.

1	2	3	4	5	6	7	8	9	10
Rarely or never		Not very often		Sometimes		Most of the time		Yes!! Always	

(Choosing to have other people do it)

14. I ASK THINGS OF OTHERS, DELEGATE WHEN APPROPRIATE, BUY WHAT I NEED TO ACCOMPLISH WHAT I WANT, AND EMPLOY OTHERS AS NEEDED.

1	2	3	4	5	6	7	8	9	10
Rarely or never		Not very often		Sometimes		Most of the time		Yes!! Always	

I Take the Time to Care for Myself

15. PHYSICALLY
(Caring for my body including eating right, exercising, resting, relaxing, getting enough sleep, and seeing health care professionals when appropriate)

1	2	3	4	5	6	7	8	9	10
Rarely or never		Not very often		Sometimes		Most of the time		Yes!! Always	

16. EMOTIONALLY
(Caring for my emotional side including carving out time to renourish and reenergize myself, having fun, seeking peace and calm in my life)

1	2	3	4	5	6	7	8	9	10
Rarely or never		Not very often		Sometimes		Most of the time		Yes!! Always	

17. SOCIALLY

(Caring for myself by spending most of my time with people who are good for me, and eliminating or limiting the time with those who are not good for me)

1	2	3	4	5	6	7	8	9	10
Rarely or never		Not very often		Sometimes		Most of the time			Yes!! Always

18. INTELLECTUALLY

(Caring for my mind by making the most of my intelligence, reading, becoming as educated as I can, keeping intellectually alive)

1	2	3	4	5	6	7	8	9	10
Rarely or never		Not very often		Sometimes		Most of the time			Yes!! Always

19. FINANCIALLY

(Caring for myself by being financially aware, accountable, and responsible)

1	2	3	4	5	6	7	8	9	10
Rarely or never		Not very often		Sometimes		Most of the time			Yes!! Always

20. SPIRITUALLY

(Caring for my spiritual side by attending religious services or spending time alone to reflect, meditate, or pray, or seeking spiritual insight through reading, study, or other experiences)

1	2	3	4	5	6	7	8	9	10
Rarely or never		Not very often		Sometimes		Most of the time			Yes!! Always

Interpreting the Confidence Quiz

Now that you have completed the inventory, add up the scores you have circled for each of the twenty questions.

Your score: _____

Since the highest score you can give yourself on each question is 10, the highest possible score for the entire test would be 200. (This means that you would have circled 10 on all of the twenty questions.) Since the lowest score for each question is 1, the lowest possible score for the test would be 20. (This means that you would have circled 1 on all of the twenty questions.)

The following table will help you to evaluate your confidence level as of right now.

INTERPRETING YOUR CONFIDENCE SCORE

Total Score	Confidence Level
180–200	HIGHLY CONFIDENT
140–180	MOSTLY CONFIDENT
100–140	SOMETIMES CONFIDENT
60–100	NOT OFTEN CONFIDENT
20–60	RARELY CONFIDENT

Please do not despair if your score is not in the Highly Confident or Mostly Confident range. Most women who use this inventory actually score in the Sometimes Confident range. When you read the next few chapters, you will understand why.

Also know that if you scored lower than 7 on any item in the inventory, in no way should you think of yourself as a failure. Your score is merely an indication of where you think you are now and, therefore, an opportunity to positively change some part of your life. That is the point of and purpose of *The Confident Woman*. Every item on the above inventory represents a topic that is covered in the book. You can increase your scores by reading about the issues that are problematic for you and by following the suggestions for changing how you think and act. As you will soon see, becoming more confident really is in your hands.

Are you ready? Find yourself a comfortable spot and start reading. You're about to become a more confident woman.

QUOTE BREAK

How many cares one loses when one decides not to be something, but to be someone.

COCO CHANEL

I do not want to die . . . until I have faithfully made the most of my talent and cultivated the seed that was placed in me until the last small twig has grown.

KÄTHE KOLLWITZ

There is not as much wilderness out there as I wish there were. There is more inside than you think.

DAVID BROWER

When you affirm your own rightness in the universe, then you cooperate with others easily and automatically as part of your own nature.

You, being yourself, helps others be themselves.

Because you recognize your own uniqueness you will not need to dominate others, nor cringe before them.

JANE ROBERTS

We don't see things as they are.
We see things as *we* are.

ANAÏS NIN

Unless I am what I am and feel what I feel—as hard as I can and as honestly and truly as I can—then I am nothing. Let me feel guilty . . . don't try to educate me . . . don't protect me.

ELIZABETH JANEWAY

You'll win in the long run . . . because you'll be the prize.

JENNIFER JAMES

CHAPTER 2

Confidence Is Just Around the Corner

. . . we ask ourselves, who am I to be brilliant,
gorgeous, talented, fabulous?
Actually, who are you *not* to be?
You are a child of God. Your playing small
does not serve the World.
There is nothing enlightened about shrinking
so that other people won't feel insecure
around you.

. . . and as we let our own Light shine, we
unconsciously give other people permission
to do the same.
As we are liberated from our own fear, our
presence automatically liberates others.

> Marianne Williamson
> "Our Deepest Fear"
> Return to Love

One of the things that I worried about when I first began writing *The Confident Woman* was whether I—as a white, Danish-American heterosexual woman—could say things that would be meaningful to all women, especially those from backgrounds different from mine—women of color, lesbian women, women from different cultural and religious backgrounds. I asked a variety of people about these concerns. One in particular, Ayofemi Folayan, an African American performance artist from Los Angeles, gave me some discerning advice. Ayofemi said, "It's all about plumbing the depths of your experience, Marjorie, and telling the truth. If you tell the truth—your truth as you know it—then that's universally relevant." As you read through this book, I hope that you will sense that I have tried to make it a truthful one. Together, let's see what truths we can uncover.

SELF-CONFIDENCE COMES IN TWO FLAVORS
Global self-confidence

Self-confidence comes in two flavors: global and specific. *Global self-confidence* reflects how well you do in the world as a whole. Having a high level of global confidence means that because you truly know yourself—your needs, wants, feelings, capacities (including strengths and weaknesses), and values—you are responsible for your own choices and actions. Consequently, you control and direct your own life, as well as work to preserve a sense of yourself as an individual. Having global self-confidence also means, more often than not, that you're able to resist social pressure or criticism or manipulation (subtle and overt) by others. In other words, when other people and situations challenge you, you're able to think and act effectively, not fall back into obsequious, nonassertive, or even passive-aggressive patterns of behaviors. You don't acquiesce. You can trust yourself "to do the right thing." Finally, having global self-confidence means that while you care deeply about others, you are also faithful to and care for yourself.

Of course, it goes without saying that nobody's perfect about any of the above.

Before moving onto specific self-confidence, let me assure you that having global confidence doesn't mean that you're free of self-doubts. Not even the most confident woman is doubt-free. But having global self-confidence does mean that when self-doubts appear (as they inevitably do), you're not devastated by them. You deal with them and recover.

Specific self-confidence

Specific self-confidence relates to how well you do in particular *situations*, *contexts*, or *personal capacities*. Needless to say, there are an infinite variety of specific self-confidence possibilities. To lack confidence in one situation or even a few situations is not necessarily a serious problem. Frankly, it's human.

For example, you may enjoy a fair amount of global self-confidence but lack specific confidence when you get into conflict with your spouse (situation). Or maybe you lack specific self-confidence when you find yourself at a cocktail party and suddenly discover that you don't know a soul there (context). Or perhaps cooking a gourmet dinner for your boss or getting up to speak before a crowd is where you lack specific self-confidence (capacity). There isn't a person alive who doesn't sometimes doubt herself in some specific situation.

Far from being a handicap, self-doubt may actually serve a good purpose. First of all, it provides you with some critical information: you're getting a message from yourself that something is not quite right about a situation, context, or capacity that is important to you. This then provides you with the opportunity to figure out what's going on and make a choice about what to do or not do, say or not say. One choice you always have is to decide to do nothing. To paraphrase poet Natasha Josefowitz:

> *Everything doesn't have to be acted on;*
> *And some things aren't worth dealing with at all.*

Sometimes self-doubt ends up being a gift your mind gives to you because it causes you to hold back from making mistakes. For example, on numerous occasions good friends have asked me to join them in taking aerobics dancing classes. And in spite of my doubts, I have. Let me tell you, while I do enjoy walking and running, I'm a terrible aerobics dancer. Others feel exhilarated and love it; I feel miserable and hate it. Aerobics dancing is clearly a case where I should abide by my self-doubt. And now I do.

On the other hand, sometimes self-doubt gives you a good reason to improve on something or to learn something new or to get help when you find yourself lacking. Learning to use a computer comes to mind. In spite of enormous self-doubt and lack of self-confidence about their ability to learn, many middle-aged women today are deciding that they don't want to be left behind in the Internet dust. On their own with only . . . *For Dummies* manuals as their guides, or with the help of their kids, a spouse, or a computer tutor, slowly but surely these women are doing what they thought they'd never be able to do—e-mailing, surfing the Net, doing the household bookkeeping, and writing reports and even books. And they're loving it. As someone once said,

> *If it is to be,*
> *It's up to me.*

YOUR CONFIDENCE LEVEL AFFECTS EVERYTHING

Why are your global and specific self-confidence levels so important? Because how much confidence you have affects *every* aspect of your life, including:

- who your friends and mate are and how they treat you
- how healthy you are
- how you perform in school or at work

- what job/career choices you make and what success you experience in those choices
- what kind of parent, spouse, friend, boss, or employee you are
- how you handle money
- how balanced your life is
- how you handle life's inevitable disappointments, difficulties, and crises
- how much you are able to give freely, happily, respectfully to others and receive back the same.

Any woman can raise her confidence level once she realizes that it is in her power to do so.

The trouble is that many women are sure that most or all other women have cornered the market on self-confidence and, therefore, enjoy happier, more satisfying lives. "They" (not me) have it and know it. (It must be easy for them.) Women also hunger for confirmation that their own insecurities are shared by others. It's always nice to know that we're not alone.

As I interviewed scores of women across the country (and the world) for this book, even the best-educated, most successful, stunningly beautiful women said things like:

> *I'd like to hear about other women and how they had their confidence threatened as I have, because sometimes I wonder if I'm not too sensitive or too analytical about things. I wonder if I'm making up stuff that sets me off into a tailspin.*
>
> Twenty-something learning specialist

> *What I'd like to see is what mistakes other women have made so that I can say, "Gee, maybe I wasn't so bad after all."*
>
> Forty-something attorney

> *If only there had been somebody there for me when I was a teenager or even forty-five to say that other people shared my feelings and thoughts. I don't think I would have spent so much time feeling badly and thinking that I was different from everyone else.*
>
> Fifty-something city official

> *What I want are other women's stories—the good, the bad, and the ugly. It's so reassuring to find out "What, it isn't just me? You mean they wing it too?"*
>
> Thirty-something film executive

As these comments demonstrate, it's very human to want to know that what goes on inside your head is not crazy or selfish or completely out in left field. I can't tell you how many women have told me that they feel "different" from others of their sex, as if they're an outsider. They also speak of not feeling as attractive as other women. Think about it. How often have you heard a friend say that she holds back on doing what *she* wants. Even the most confident women I know are curious about other *really* confident women. They want to know what they do, why they're confident, and especially what their "secrets and tricks" are for having such confidence.

Every day women are bombarded with extravagant claims about what various people, products, or experiences can do for them; in other words, how they can change themselves to become more like some media-created ideal. Ads and articles proclaim our need for . . .

✓ thinner thighs!
✓ fabulous-looking, homemade (and yes, fat-free) feasts
✓ knock-'em-dead clothes
✓ sexier anything, especially the latest guy-getting gimmicks
✓ think-better, feel-better vitamins and herbs
✓ go-for-it hardware, software — Tupperware!
✓ time-saving hints
✓ power whatever

These exhortations make us feel that we are "less than," and without our realizing it, they eat away at our confidence levels. As a result, many women end up with misplaced expectations about who they *should* be, how they *should* look, what they *should* do with their time, what happiness *should* feel or look like. The marketed "ideals" even set the model for how and when we *should* feel good about ourselves. Alas, eventually what we find is that none of the magic solutions really change our personalities; improve our looks; revolutionize our sex lives; or bring us lasting peace, balance, success, or the high that each promises. And they often lead to our having less rather than more self-confidence.

It's important to know that no one can give you self-confidence; nor can you give it to someone else. You can't inherit it or hand it on to your heirs. You can't borrow or steal it; nor can anyone take it from you. Confidence is something that only you can give yourself.

If you want to grow as a person, learn more about yourself, become more effective, like yourself better, feel more centered or "whole," discover new ways of dealing with difficult people or situations, and be of help to other women, then you will benefit from increased self-confidence.

The Confident Woman has been designed for those of you who want to make positive changes in your lives. My task is to provide you with the truth as a whole variety of experts and I see it, in addition to insight, information, and practical skills. Your task is to do something with these things. I will encourage you to move ahead, act, do, and be more of who you really are!

But beware, you will find little encouragement from me if you are not motivated to do something for yourself, if you wish things (or other people) would change, if you feel like you are a victim, or if you blame others. In those cases, my words won't help you. While I understand why and how these attitudes, feelings, and behaviors occur—believe me, I've engaged in a few of them myself—the bottom line is that blame and excuses don't get us anywhere.

You are a work in progress. Therefore I'd like to help you add to your life without fundamentally changing who you are. I'd like to help you develop, enhance, and appreciate yourself as a unique and one-of-a-kind person, not a woman who tries to be like someone else. I want you to be all that you can be, not what others want you to be. And along the way I want to teach and encourage you to be more tender with yourself.

I can't offer you any quick fixes for major life problems, and my ideas and solutions are not panaceas for all. Everything in this book is mere suggestion for you to experiment with and decide if it works for you. Frankly, sometimes what I propose won't be easy. After all, a lot of what I will be describing involves action and change on your part, and as you know, change is difficult for all of us. But without hesitation I can state this: each one of us can learn, each of us has the innate need and capacity to grow, and as far as your gaining more confidence goes, it is simply a matter of deciding that this is something you want to do for yourself. Having made that decision, confidence is not just a possibility, but an inevitability. I know, because that's what I have done for myself.

> *It is never too late*
> *to be what you might*
> *have been.*
>
> George Eliot

SELF-CONFIDENCE DEFINED

Webster's Ninth New Collegiate Dictionary defines confidence as "... a consciousness of one's powers or of reliance on one's circumstances; faith or belief that one will act in a right, proper or effective way." *Webster's* adds,

"Confidence stresses faith in oneself and one's powers without any suggestion of conceit or arrogance." I especially like that last statement.

In examining mountains of research on self-esteem and confidence, as well as some of the new thinking about female development, I have come up with a new definition of confidence for women.

Self-confidence is

✓ *having a clear and distinct sense of self*
  (that is, knowing who you are, what qualities you have, what your priorities are, and what you like, need, prefer, and desire)
✓ *having the competence to deal effectively with a broad array of people and circumstances (or find resources to do so)*
  (that is, knowing how to do things and learn new things, find solutions, and create opportunities, and knowing when and how to get help when you need it)
✓ *trusting that you can, do, and will take good care of yourself*
  (that is, actively caring for yourself physically, emotionally, socially, intellectually, financially, and spiritually)

My definition supports a woman having and enjoying her own unique self—something that most health experts agree is critical. In addition, it allows that a woman can take care of herself and thrive within the context of having important relationships in her life—something to which the proponents of the new field of female or relational psychology adhere. In other words, a woman doesn't have to lose her *me* in order to be a *we*.

SELF-CONFIDENCE AND SELF-ESTEEM ARE NOT THE SAME

Many people confuse self-confidence with self-esteem, even using the words interchangeably. *They are not the same.* Most experts would define *self-esteem* as:

> A *set of amorphous feelings about how much we like, value, and approve of ourselves.*

As you are well aware, for decades now self-esteem has been a major pop culture cure-all for childrearing, education, and personal development. Pick up almost any issue of a popular women's magazine, and you can find articles about how if you raise your self-esteem, you will lose weight, stop using drugs, age gracefully, find/keep/move ahead in jobs, attract men, be a better friend, make more money, and raise great kids.

Parents and teachers have been given the message that if they have their kids chant things such as "I am special," this alone will help them to get good grades, avoid teen troubles, and become good citizens. Yes, having high self-esteem is a good thing, but what it is and how you get it is a source of much confusion. I'm going to take a couple of minutes to help you understand why focusing on self-esteem is pretty much a waste of time, while working on self-confidence can be highly productive.

At its core self-esteem is all about feelings. The word *feelings* is critical here because authorities on the subject say that feelings are spontaneous, uncensored emotional responses[1] that are elusive. As you well know, because you experience them every day, feelings come and go. You feel happy, you feel depressed, you feel excited, you feel anxious, you feel worried, you feel calm. Sometimes you experience all these feelings at the same time. What's most important to know is that feelings change only as a result of your thinking or doing something differently. By the way, just because feelings are elusive doesn't mean that they aren't important. On the contrary, the well-known author and psychiatrist Dr. Tom Rusk likes to say that "feelings are messages from our soul" and as such we need to pay very close attention to them. We'll explore this subject further — see how important feelings are and how to use them — in chapter 12.

EXPERTS SAY YOU CAN'T DO MUCH ABOUT YOUR SELF-ESTEEM

So where does self-esteem come from? Experts on the subject such as Drs. William Swann and Martin Seligman have found that self-esteem is a by-product emerging from: (1) what took place in our lives growing up in a particular family, community, and culture, (2) what we have experienced in life as adults — positive, negative, and neutral — and (3) recent thoughts and actions. With this information at hand, it becomes clear that self-esteem is derivative, not a source itself. Therefore, the implication cannot be ignored: self-esteem is something over which one has little or no direct control. And there is growing testimony to this position.

In his book *Self-Traps*, psychologist William Swann declares that in spite of a multimillion-dollar self-esteem industry involving thousands of books and just as many programs, research shows that self-esteem is astonishingly resistant to change. It seems that even wonder drugs such as Prozac cannot really elevate it.[2] This may be at least one explanation for why so many people have been ineffective in raising their own and other people's self-esteem.

On a completely different note is the work of psychologist Martin Seligman, past president of the American Psychological Association.

Seligman says that he has "scoured the self-esteem literature . . . for any evidence that high self-esteem among youngsters *causes* better grades, more popularity, [or] less teenage pregnancy."[3] Guess what? He's found none. Seligman's conclusion is that self-esteem is a symptom of how well a person is doing in the world. He likens it to "a meter that reads out the state of the system." He suggests that when children and adults do well in school or work, or do well with people they love, the meter will register high. When they do badly, the meter will register low.[4]

During the latter part of the 1990s, some researchers began to postulate that some kinds of high self-esteem might actually be bad. Brad Bushman of Iowa State University found that inflated self-esteem that comes not from actual achievement or positive behavior but from teachers' and parents' wanton, unjustified praise can actually backfire, causing a child to become hostile and aggressive. This is particularly true for children and adults who have narcissistic tendencies.[5] When we value how people feel about themselves more highly than we value what they are doing in the world, we may be barking up the wrong self-esteem tree.

BUT YOU CAN DO A LOT ABOUT YOUR SELF-CONFIDENCE

That is why I have decided to focus on confidence and how you do in the world, something which you have unlimited potential to change and control. **You see, unlike self-esteem levels, confidence levels can be changed by what you think and do.** This book is all about why you may have engaged in confidence-busting thoughts and actions in the past and how you can engage in confidence-building ones from now on.

I have read that women usually transform themselves or take a new direction only after an awakening. I would like it very much if this book would be a part of your confidence awakening. Confidence is contagious. As soon as you become more confident, your confidence will touch those around you. Wouldn't it be amazing if you could be responsible for creating a highly communicable epidemic of confidence awakenings among women you know and whose lives you touch?

Hold on . . . confidence is just around the corner.

It's Break time again. How about giving yourself a nice little Music Break? If you're at home where you have control over a music system or radio, put on what really pleases you. If you haven't thought of gathering your own supply of music, here is a list of very special CDs (and/or tapes) that assorted friends and interviewees have recommended to calm their minds and lift their spirits.

MUSIC BREAK

Joan Baez, *Classics Vol. 8, Gone from Danger; Any Day Now*

Andrea Bocelli, *Romanza; Sogno*

Sarah Brightman, *Time to Say Good-bye*

Budapest Strings, Bela Benfalvi, *Handel's Water Music*

Capella antiqua Munchen, Choralschola, *Quietude; Gregorian Chant*

Ray Charles, *Genius & Soul*

Judy Collins, *Fires of Eden*

Celine Dion, *Let's Talk about Love*

Bob Dylan, *The 30th Anniversary Concert Collection*

Ella Fitzgerald and Count Basie, *Ella & Basie*

Diana Krall, *All for You; Love Scenes*

Ottmar Liebert, *Nouveau Flamenco*

Dave Matthews, *Before These Crowded Streets*

Bette Midler, *Bette of Roses*

Itzhak Perlman and James Levine, Wolfgang Amadeus Mozart, *Violin Concertos Nos. 3 & 5*

Philip Riley and Jayne Elleson, *The Blessing Tree*

Pepe Romero, I Musici, Antonio Vivaldi, *Guitar Concertos*

Los Romeros, Academy of St. Martin-in-the-Fields, Antonio Vivaldi, *Guitar Concertos*

Diane Schuur, *Music Is My Life; Collection*

James Taylor, *Hourglass*

Turtle Island String Quartet, *By the Fireside*

Hildegard von Bingen, *11,000 Virgins: Chants for the Feast of St. Ursula*

Part II

THE MYSTERY OF
LOST CONFIDENCE

Why Women Lack Confidence

It's not bad to be good,
Lord knows, the world needs more GOOD.
But it's bad when overdoing for "them"
Negates ever being good to yourself.

There's nothing wrong with being YOUNG, PRETTY, AND THIN.
Surely these gifts can make the world go 'round.
But it's wrong when beauty is for "him" or "them,"
And you ignore the other parts of your life.

It's not foolish to be a LADY,
Being respectful of others can't be wrong,
But it is foolish when not imposing on "them"
Stops you from being respectful of "me."

It's not harmful to persist, even "go for the gold."
Hard work helps many to achieve much,
But it's harmful when you're OVERLY RESPONSIBLE for others,
And less than responsible to yourself.

Marjorie Hansen Shaevitz

D o you have a hard time taking time for yourself, especially to read, relax, or do something fun? Do you have trouble asking others to help you or actually do something for you? Do you ever feel ill at ease with certain people because of your weight, your appearance, or your choice of clothing? Do you often find yourself on a treadmill of unflagging activity, never stopping to refuel or rest? Do you feel uncomfortable about getting angry or expressing negative emotions to others?

These questions involve issues critical to having self-confidence.

We all live by and act according to rules, some written, many others unwritten. Most of the time we're not aware of the unwritten rules by which women live. These rules, however, are the source for a code of conduct that dictates not only how women think about themselves but how they live. It's virtually impossible to challenge these rules if we don't know what they are. But once we're aware of them, we have a choice either to live by them or to change them.

As I interviewed women for this book, I began to notice the existence of a Female Code of Conduct. No matter the age, marital status, or ethnic background, what I heard over and over again was:

FEMALE CODE OF CONDUCT

• The need to be unselfish and nice, please everyone but yourself: **Lady, Be Good**

• The obsession with looking good rather than treating your body and mind with respect: **Lady, Be Beautiful**

• The fear of upsetting or imposing on others or not meeting some idealized set of behaviors: **Lady, Be a "Lady"**

• The propensity for being superresponsible and trustworthy, except when it comes to yourself: **Lady, Do It All**

Women today seem to be trapped by the need to have what best-selling author Susan Howatch calls a "glittering image." Translated into everyday terms, that means women feel they must be perfectly beautiful, ever youthful, unselfish, responsible, hardworking, ladylike Superwomen of the New Millennium. All one has to do is look at women's magazines, turn on the TV, or watch a movie to confirm this. Many women think that they need to be everything to everybody, but little or nothing for themselves.

SOME INSIGHT INTO WHY WOMEN DON'T TAKE GOOD CARE OF THEMSELVES

One day in the middle of one of my interviews, I was stopped by a woman with this plaintive question: "Why? Marjorie, why, why, why do I have such a hard time taking care of myself? Why am I always acting in ways that are not good for me?"

I have wondered about that question myself. It does seem that we women engage in attitudes, thoughts, and behaviors that are unsympathetic to ourselves, if not outright antagonistic. In my therapy work with women, I have found a constant theme: whether it's changing their own behavior or dealing with someone else's, women want to understand the *why* behind something before they act to change it. In fact, most women find it difficult to take action (particularly if it's for themselves or if it feels as though it's impinging upon another's wants, needs, or desires) without having this understanding. Women want insight—which becomes their justification, perhaps even permission—to take action. Except in cases where wanting to know "why" gets in the way of doing something useful or protecting oneself from abuse, insight is often a useful step toward change.

It would be easy to explain why women fail to act on their own behalves by falling into the popular cultural habit of describing women in dysfunctional terms. How often have you heard so-called (and real!) experts declare women "self-defeating personality types," "co-dependents," "masochists," "overemotional," or "hysterical"?

The truth is that these declarations are neither legitimate nor correct; if anything, they are outright demeaning because they imply that women get pleasure from suffering or acting against their own best interests; or even worse, that women are too stupid, lazy, or foolish to change their self-defeating ways. Does it make sense that most women are pathologically bent on hurting themselves? I don't think so.

The simple fact is that women often think and act in many of the negative ways they do because of the messages they, and generations of women before them, have received from their own family upbringing and the culture itself. But what many of us don't realize is that these messages about women are often based on myths, half-truths, distorted realities, media hype, outdated or misguided scientific findings, and sometimes outright lies. As author Bram Dijkstra says in his book *Evil Sisters,* "Culture has many historical sources, most of them forgotten, and what we remember often is only a dim haze of ghostly imagery. . . . (M)uch like discarded fashions, the ghosts of heretofore long-discarded notions stay with us as incontrovertible truths."[1] Many of today's "truths" are centuries old, yet they still hold power over how women are seen and how they think about themselves.

When women put themselves at the bottom of the totem pole, they are doing what women have been taught to do for generations: follow the dictates of the Female Code of Conduct. For the most part, our thoughts and actions are on automatic pilot, which means that we're unaware of what we do because of historical cultural dictates. Women learn to

love, nurture, take care of, clean for, shop for, cook for, pick up after, organize for, plan for, transport, tutor, type for, call, write, arrange for, buy presents for, make appointments for, do errands for, complete projects, follow up on, help, attend with, sort, budget and balance, pay, gather, deposit, water, wash and dry, put away, edit or write for, check on, straighten for, change for, test, go through for, move, remove, weed, spray, and fertilize for . . .

boyfriends, spouses, significant others, children, mothers, fathers, sisters, brothers, other relatives and distant cousins, in-laws, friends, neighbors, bosses, coworkers, people we run into on subways, trains, buses, or airplanes — and anyone else we happen to meet along the way.

What women don't learn very well is how to love, nurture, and take care of themselves.

Beginning with the teenage years and then continuing on through adulthood, girls and women develop both physical and psychological symptoms — eating disorders, body image problems, depression, insecurity, workaholism, and lack of confidence to name just a few — in response to negative, biased cultural and media messages about females. What's more, it is a double whammy: the culture that produces the conditions that create these symptoms also blames and punishes girls and women for having them. Remember from chapter 1 how insecure many highly educated, professional women are?

Women and young girls also receive such messages from a myriad of other sources: parents, siblings, friends, relatives, caretakers, ministers and rabbis, teachers, and any number of other people with whom they spend time. Sadly, most of these sources unknowingly pass on many false "incontrovertible truths" about women from the past.

While many women today, especially those in their teens and twenties, feel free of historical messages, unfortunately many dictates about women have become unconscious thoughts and habits over the ages. Believe me, these messages are no less compelling in today's more liberated world. Not even well-educated, successful young women are immune to them.

Over the centuries women received a relentless number of negative messages about who they were, what they were supposed to do (and not do), and how much they were worth. As a result, women developed the debilitating Female Code of Conduct, which is with us daily as we ignore and sacrifice ourselves — our own needs, wants and desires, even our health. We know we're not free when we find ourselves doing too much, working too hard, and trying to be everything to everybody. Few women are able to take full advantage of their God-given gifts to become all that they were meant to be.

Father Darrow, a critical character in Susan Howatch's novel *Glittering Images*, says just at the perfect moment, "If we solve the mystery beyond the mystery, (the glittering image) may simply wither away."[2] It is highly likely that your own "glittering image" is based on wrong or inadequate knowledge about women and even yourself. Heeding Ashworth's call to solve, let's see if we can't uncover the mystery of why women live by such crippling codes of conduct. Like Ashworth, I think that many of us would like to have our own "glittering image" fade away. To begin the process, please join me on a ride down history lane.

Before we do that, let's take another Break.

Here is a list of very special nonfiction books that assorted friends and interviewees have highly recommended.

GREAT NONFICTION BOOK BREAK

Maya Angelou, *All God's Children Need Traveling Shoes*

Mary Catherine Bateson, *Composing a Life*

Elizabeth Berg, *Escaping Into the Open*

Joan Borysenko, *A Woman's Book of Life*

Julia Cameron, *The Artist's Way*

Susan Cheever, *A Woman's Life*

Jill Ker Conway, *The Road from Coorain; True North; When Memory Speaks*

Phil Cousineau, *Soul: An Archeology*

Annie Dillard, *The Writing Life; An American Childhood*

Isak Dinesen, *Letters from Africa 1914–1931*

Gretel Ehrlich, *Solace of Open Spaces*

Natalie Goldberg, *Writing Down the Bones*

Katharine Graham, *Personal History*

Sue Hubbell, *Broadsides from the Other Orders: A Book of Bugs*

Harriet Jacobs, *Incidents in the Life of a Slave Girl*

Tracy Kidder, *House; Among Schoolchildren*

Madeleine L'Engle, *A Circle of Quiet*

Betty Mahmoody, *Not Without My Daughter*

Kathleen Norris, *Amazing Grace*

Tillie Olsen, *Silences*

A room without books is like a body without a soul.

Cicero

CHAPTER 3

Myths, Half-truths, Distorted Realities, Bogus Scientific Findings: History's "Weaker Sex" Take on Women

> History is not truth versus falsehood, but a mixture of both, a melange of tendencies, reactions, dreams, errors, and power plays. What's important is what we make of it; its moral use. By writing history, we can widen readers' thinking and deepen their sympathies in every direction. Perhaps history should show us not how to control the world, but how to enlarge, deepen, and discipline ourselves.
>
> *Gretel Ehrlich*
> Heart Mountain

In all cultures throughout history, women have been treated as the weaker sex. What's more, women have been taught to believe that they are much less than they really are. They have been seen as not only physically weaker but also morally, spiritually, intellectually, occupationally, and emotionally weaker. It's no wonder that women have often acted in weak and self-limiting ways. Where in the world did all this negativity come from?

To try to answer this question, I read up on the new field of women's history. What I found was shocking, even for someone who has been reading about women for years. What follows is my take on some of the historical antecedents of the "women are weaker" messages. Before I go on, though, let me say this: if you think I am off on either a male-bashing or a female-victimizing toot, stop right now. I am interested in neither. What I am looking for is explanation, understanding, and cause, not blame or excuse. Enough said.

MISCONCEPTIONS ABOUT WOMEN: WHERE THEY COME FROM

Webster's defines *history* as "a chronological record of significant events often including an explanation of their causes."[1] The new proponents of women's history like to point out that history is more often "his" story than hers. Until just recently only men recorded events and wrote through their own gender-shaded lenses.

Yes, over the centuries women have had a few notable voices writing from and about the female perspective — Hildegard von Bingen, Christine de Pisan, Mary Wollstonecraft, Jane Addams, Elizabeth Cady Stanton, to name just a few. But against the huge number and volume of male voices, women's voices have seemed like a drop in a vast male ocean of words.

It's probably an understatement to say that there are untold misconceptions about what women's lives have been all about. Rich resources such as E. J. Burford and Sandra Shulman's *Of Bridles & Burnings* remind us that before people learned to write, history came in the form of ballads, chants, and storytelling.[2] We know from the few primitive peoples left today that those means are still being used to pass along information (as well as misinformation), facts (as well as myths), and tales of family traditions and triumphs (as well as secrets and lies). Because of this a great part of our heritage rests on a shadowy oral background.

Does it not follow then that we should question the validity of many assumptions, beliefs, and fears concerning women? Shouldn't we also be wary of how those assumptions might have become everyday principles and even law? After all, even if it's wrong, when something is said over and over and over again, everyone begins to believe it. Feminist historians now remind us that "since earliest times, women have wielded virtually no political or economic power" and that "all societies have gone to remarkable lengths to control and punish those it considered inferior in intellect and strength."[3] Of course, if one were female and from an ethnic minority, she was open to receiving multiple doses of control and punishment.

From history and literature we see that man has loved woman, even worshiped her at times. On the other hand, he has also feared, controlled, and punished her with apparent relish. In his capacity to make laws and declare truths, man has also dictated how women were to be thought of and therefore dealt with.

When I was doing research for this book, what most took me aback was what the most highly revered men of all time have had to say about women. Here are some examples:

Women are:

- "not to be trusted" (Homer, *Odyssey)*
- "an inferior man" (Aristotle, third century B.C.)
- "fickle, unstable thing(s)" (Virgil, first century B.C.)
- "a stupid vessel over whom men must always hold power" (Martin Luther, fifteenth century)
- "Frailty, thy name is woman!" (Shakespeare, sixteenth century)
- "God's second mistake" (Nietzsche, nineteenth century)

How devastating it was to find that Rudyard Kipling, one of the most entertaining, brilliant writers of the nineteenth century, said:

- "a woman is only a woman, but a good cigar is a smoke."

Some writers couldn't quite make up their minds. William Congreve wrote:

- "Oh thou *delicious,* damned, *dear,* destructive Woman!"

With descriptions such as these, it was inevitable that women would think and act in ways that appear to be self-defeating.

THE BIBLE

The Bible, both Old and New Testaments, is a major source for declarations that women are the "weaker sex." In the last decade or so, female scholars have been examining, challenging, and even reinterpreting this hallowed tome written almost exclusively by men about men's interests and pursuits. These scholars have discovered, among other things, that of the more than fourteen hundred people described in the Hebrew Bible, only about 115 are women. Apparently in at least five books of the Bible, there are no references to women at all.[4]

Female theologians, historians, archaeologists, and others are now beginning to identify how the Bible has been used throughout the ages to justify beliefs, laws, and actions that subjugate and subordinate women. For example, the Bible has been used to declare women as (1) God's afterthought, (2) the servant of man, (3) responsible (through Eve) for humanity's expulsion from Eden, (4) undeserving of a role in the ministry, and (5) deserving of ill treatment by men.[5]

That little is really known about women before the eighteenth century was recognized by the venerated author Virginia Woolf in 1929. She reminds us of the powerful images left by famous male writers throughout the ages. (The italics in the following passage are mine to demonstrate the contrast Woolf makes between fiction and reality.)

> *If woman had no existence save in the fiction written by men . . . one would imagine her a person of the utmost importance. . . .*
> But this is woman in fiction. In fact . . . she was locked up, beaten and flung about the room.
>
> *A very queer, composite being thus emerges. Imaginatively she is of the highest importance;*
> practically she is completely insignificant.
>
> *She pervades poetry from cover to cover;*
> she is all but absent from history.
>
> *She dominates the lives of kings and conquerors in fiction;*
> in fact she was the slave of any boy whose parents forced a ring upon her finger.
>
> *Some of the most inspired words, some of the most profound thoughts in literature, fall from her lips;*
> in real life she could hardly read, could scarcely spell, and was the property of her husband.[6]

ARE WOMEN MORALLY WEAKER?

In her best-selling book *The Weaker Vessel,* Lady Antonia Fraser explains how the notion of women as the weaker—ergo less valuable—sex came about. To begin with, woman was seen as *morally weaker* for having seduced Adam to eat that famous apple. Over the centuries man went to great lengths to keep her from falling—yet again.[7]

No area of morality has ever been of greater interest than that of sexuality. And in that realm, throughout history, man has often seemed convinced that woman was a "bottomless pit of sexual desire,"[8] a moral moron, if you will. How else can one explain the invention of the chastity belt during the Middle Ages, which—if you can believe this—was actually manufactured in France until 1910. In certain parts of the world today, societies still worry so much about girls' and women's morality that they continue to practice infibulation (the sewing together of the labia majora of the vulva) and clitoridectomy (the excision of part or all of the clitoris).

What has been said about women and their morals, particularly by distinguished men, has done more to stereotype women than anything else. Alexander Pope, for example, gave us such memorable proverbs as "To err is human, to forgive divine," and "Fools rush in where angels fear to tread," and "As the twig is bent, the tree's inclined." Unfortunately, he also had some very unflattering things to say about women, including "Most women have no characters at all" and "Men, some to business, some to pleasure take; but every woman is at heart a rake." So how do people reconcile the inspiring words of a great poet with his less-than-flattering words about women? The answer is that they tend to believe the poet's less-than-flattering words about women. And so the myths go on.

ARE WOMEN SPIRITUALLY WEAKER?

Antonia Fraser suggests that it was but a minor jump for man to equate the already acknowledged moral inferiority of women with *spiritual inferiority*, indeed, outright evil-mongering. To explain how the belief arose that woman, mother and nurturer, was also destroyer and spoiler, many historians propose that "from the beginning of time, humankind lived in terror of anything and everything that could not be understood or controlled. . . . [Since] procreation was the special power of women, with access to so much power, women became suspect of using this power for negative as well as positive ends."[9]

Testimony to this belief is the number of women throughout history who were declared witches and either hanged or burned at the stake for what most historians would agree was nothing more than superstition, prejudice, and downright lying by mischievous adolescent youth.[10] During early times ugliness, physical blemishes, and deformities — especially those associated with aging — were considered manifestations of evil or of association with the Devil.[11] But it wasn't just during the Dark Ages that women were considered evil and spiritually bereft. Bram Dijkstra notes that at the beginning of the twentieth century "biology and medicine set out to prove that nature had given *all* women a basic instinct that made them into predators, destroyers, witches — evil sisters."[12]

Even dear old Alfred Lord Tennyson, another of history's most famous poets, equated women with evil when he wrote:

She like a new disease, unknown to men,
Creeps, no precaution used, among the crowd,
Makes wicked lighting of her eyes and says
The fealty of our friends, and stirs the pulse
With devil's leaps, and poisons half the young.

                                        Alfred Lord Tennyson
                                        Guinevere

ARE WOMEN INTELLECTUALLY WEAKER?

Nineteenth-century minister John Todd preached that "as for training young ladies through a long intellectual course, as we do young men, it can never be done. They will die in the process."[13] Thank you, Reverend Todd.

Innumerable popular nineteenth-century scientists and educators further promulgated the notion that women are weaker intellectually. For example, Darwinian naturalist George Romanes, author of *Mental Differences Between Men and Women*, declared that "not only is the gray matter, or cortex, or the [woman's] brain shallower than that of the male, but it also receives less than a proportional supply of blood." From comments such as this, author Bram Dijkstra says, one could only conclude that woman was a "perpetually brain-drained creature."[14]

Here are yet other examples. Paul Mobius, an extremely influential nineteenth-century German pathologist, said that in comparison with men, women are "by their very nature feebleminded."[15] Carl Vogt, the best-known and most highly respected craniologist of the mid-1800s, offered that because the female skull is smaller than the male skull, one could surmise that "women and men belonged to two different species . . . woman's skull approaching that of the infant and in still greater degree that of the lower races."[16] Obviously, Dr. Vogt mixed his misogyny with a little racial prejudice.

Finally, prominent London pathologist Harry Campbell, author of *Differences in the Nervous Organization of Man and Woman* (written in 1891), opined that woman's passive nature made her "incapable of original thought or action . . . in fact she has a protean capacity . . . to imitate."[17] Dijkstra says that because of such views, by the mid-1800s, the idea that women were merely imitators, never originators, "had become one of the most pervasive clichés of western culture."[18]

As recently as the late 1800s, some of the most respected scientists and educators actually declared that too much education would endanger a girl's sanity and even make her infertile. As a result, throughout the nineteenth century, women were barred from most forms of education. Access to knowledge was rare; experiences outside a very constricted realm were all but nonexistent. It's not difficult to see how women came to be known as

> Not *huffy or stuffy, nor tiny or tall,*
> But *fluffy, just fluffy, with no brains at all.*
> > Sir Alan Patrick Herbert
> > (1890–1971),
> > "I Like Them Fluffy"

HAVE WOMEN BEEN OCCUPATIONALLY RESTRICTED?

Many contemporary historians now tell us that when scientists decided that women's evolution had not progressed beyond the stage of childhood, it became a foregone conclusion to link women's stunted evolution and their reproductive capacity. A woman's mind was a "useless appendage," but that didn't matter because motherhood didn't require mental skills. "Brain work required much vital energy—hence brain work was properly the realm of the male."[19] This then meant that women could hold only occupationally restricted roles in society—mothering, nursing, and teaching. Even though nursing and teaching took place outside the home, they were accepted because they were extensions of the caring and nurturing functions women provided as mothers.

Early in the 1880s and then again at the turn of the twentieth century, many women (and some men) joined together to open up greater educational opportunities for women. In spite of educators' worries about the "muscularization and masculinization" that educating women would bring about, more and more women went to school and even attended college. A few women joined the professions, although not without great difficulty. Of course, in World War II hordes of women joined the paid working force, many in nontraditional jobs. But the pendulum swung back again in the 1950s, when the ideology of motherhood was promoted once more. Certainly more women went to college to pursue a B.A., but getting an Mrs. was often paramount in their minds.

I am particularly struck by the notion of what was considered a woman's "proper place" in relation to men and society. Here's one very chilling example. We all know about the parental practice of telling children that they should be "seen but not heard." Well, believe it or not, that was also a practice used with regard to women. This eighteenth-century ballad says it all:[20]

> A wife *domestic, good and pure*
> Like *snail should keep within her door;*
> But *not like snail, in silver track*

Place all her wealth upon her back.
A woman should like echo true
Speak but when she's spoken to;
But not like echo still be heard
Contending for the final word.
Like a town clock a wife should be
Keep time and regularity;
But not like clocks harangue so clear
That all the town her voice might hear.

Certainly during these more politically correct times, fewer jokes and stories are told about women and their so-called "gift for gab." But as late as the 1960s, popular literature, TV, and movies supported the notion that women were the more garrulous sex. (Actually, social science research suggests just the opposite.[21] Especially in mixed company, men talk more, dominate conversations, and interrupt more often than do women.) While they might not say it outright, many men today still complain about their wives' nagging, especially with male companions.

Throughout history it was commonplace for men to stuff a gag into a woman's mouth should she be found to be a gossip, a scold, or a nag. During the seventeenth century this was carried a step further with the development of something called a branks. A branks (also called a scolding bridle) was a device made up of an iron frame that surrounded a woman's head. A triangular bit was attached to it to enter the woman's mouth and prevent her from speaking.[22] This was actually believed to be a more civilized way of treating scolds than the more common practice of physically beating them.

"Emotional" utterances from women—especially if accompanied by great conviction—were also considered highly inappropriate and worthy of punishment. According to Burford and Shulman, for no more than speaking their minds or preaching, Quaker women were often publicly humiliated, flogged, or imprisoned—a fate they shared with the "meanest" felons.[23]

ARE WOMEN PHYSICALLY WEAKER?

Women were also seen as physically weaker, and that at least had a reality base. Yes, women tend to be shorter, smaller in stature, and physically less strong than men. But their stature worked against them less than their unique bodily functions—menstruation and pregnancy.

Menstruation—thought to be God's "curse" against women for eating the forbidden fruit—aroused deep anxieties and fears among men. On the one hand, men saw menstruation as not only "dirty" but possibly dangerous. Early Christians thought "'menstruating women carried a poison in them that could kill infants.'"[24] On the other hand, others saw menstruation as having a purifying function. For example, in the seventeenth century it was considered unhealthy for men to have sex with menopausal women because it was thought that menstruation cleansed women of all their impurities. Not having that cleansing experience every month meant then that all kinds of unhealthy things lurked inside women's bodies. Nonmenstruating women, therefore, were considered a danger to men.[25]

The perception of physical weakness also came from the fact that most women spent a great deal of their lives being either pregnant or ill. Throughout the ages women suffered dearly during childbirth, including many who died. Even more common were the illness and death of children at birth or soon after. Mothers were the ones who usually cared for desperately ill children (which often meant that they became sick themselves). Because of this the female body—so often pregnant, and usually in ill health—became the personification of women's inferiority and need for protection. But as Louise Bernikow, author of *The American Women's Almanac*, says, "being protected, more often than not, meant being excluded from life."[26]

During late Victorian times a very strange association developed between a woman's physical weakness and her purity. The weaker, whiter, thinner, and less vigorous a woman was, the closer to God she was seen as being. A healthy, vigorous, active, energetic woman was considered vulgar, unnatural, dangerous, and masculinized. "Proper" women were weak, helpless, and frequently ill.[27]

This then led to an even more intriguing spin: if weakness was closer to godliness, it followed that physical beauty was the outward manifestation of inner beauty or goodness. Beauty and goodness, if not godliness, became synonymous.

ARE WOMEN EMOTIONALLY WEAKER?

Another arena in which women have always been thought of as weaker is that of emotions. No serious writing about female psychology was done before the twentieth century. In fact, no field called the psychology of women existed until Dr. Judith Bardwick wrote her book on the subject in the early 1970s.[28] To be sure, there has always been a lot of so-called female insanity.[29] Very often women who acted in ways that were considered disobedient, disagreeable, or aggressive toward the men in their lives—husbands, fathers, brothers, and sons—were labeled as crazy and then beaten, imprisoned, or sent off to insane asylums.

Of all the research I came across, perhaps the strangest was the belief—held during the nineteenth century, only one hundred years ago, and promulgated by the most advanced scientific authorities of the time—that:

- Women are born masochists and love nothing better than to be raped and beaten and subjected to violence.
- Normal women are naturally less sensitive to pain than normal men, so there is absolutely no reason to be squeamish about punishing them. (In fact, masochism was seen as a perversion only in men.)[30]

Even more astounding, in the literature of the late nineteenth and early twentieth centuries, an author's adherence to these "women love to be beaten" theories was a sign of extreme intellectual sophistication—an indication that one was truly well informed about matters of scientific interest.[31] What can one say, except beware of people bearing gifts of questionable scientific theory.

While the enjoyment of physical pain has never been a defining characteristic of women, personal self-sacrifice has been. The heyday of the cult of self-sacrifice occurred in the mid- to late 1800s. In painting, music, and literature as well as the popular press of the time, the ideal woman was personified as someone who sacrificed her identity and found her happiness only in the happiness of others.[32] Thus, selfless behavior became the first principle of being a good woman. No one captured this better than Virginia Woolf when she described "the Angel in the House":

> She was intensely sympathetic. She was immensely charming. She was utterly unselfish. She excelled in the difficult arts of family life. She sacrificed herself daily. If there was chicken, she took the leg; if there was a draft she sat in it—in short, she was so constituted that she never had a mind or a wish of her own, but preferred to sympathize always with the minds and wishes of theirs. Above all—I need not say it—she was pure.[33]

While Woolf wrote about her Angel at the beginning of the twentieth century and was actually describing women in the mid-1880s, the Angel continues to reside in any number of contemporary homes. Many women continue to care and nurture, sacrifice themselves, and meet the needs of those about whom they care. Some things never change.

To this day most physicians and mental health professionals still evaluate what is normal and abnormal in women based on male standards. Psychologist Carol Tavris has said that "women are constantly worrying about measuring up, doing the right thing, being the right way. It is normal for women to worry about being abnormal because male behavior . . . male psychology, and even male physiology continue to be the standard of normalcy against which women are measured and found wanting."[34]

In looking back at the history of our own country, I found it instructive to remember some basic things. To begin with, our fore*fathers* came to this continent seeking religious and other personal freedoms not available in Europe at the time. But in our foredads' minds the American dream was for white, property-owning men, not women.

WHAT IT WAS LIKE FOR THE FOUNDING MOTHERS

It is useful to become reacquainted with some of the rules of the New World. For women that meant:

- obedience to husbands
- not having the right to vote
- not having access to their own wages, if they had any
- not being allowed to sign contracts on their own
- not being allowed to own or inherit property
- being denied access to education
- having severe prohibitions against participating in public life. (For example, public spaces—stores, taverns, and courthouses—were for men only, and in church people sat by rank and gender.)[35]

It's easy to forget that the Fifteenth Amendment to the Constitution was ratified in 1870 to give all citizens the right to vote—*if they were men*. In spite of all kinds of political shenanigans to keep women from having it (including President Grover Cleveland saying that "sensible and responsible women didn't want it"), in 1920 women finally gained the right to vote, *fifty years* after the Fifteenth Amendment was passed.

For some, those dates seem like ancient history. So to have a better perspective on how recent it is that women's rights and options have become available, let's look at the more recent past. Remember:

Before the 1960s Women
- couldn't have credit in their own names
- didn't have competitive, organized sports at schools and colleges
- were often barred from being administrators of estates
- didn't have equal access to undergraduate, graduate, and professional schools

- weren't taken seriously as wage earners; it was thought that they worked for "pin money" only
- couldn't have their word be enough to bring rape charges against a man; the law required a corroborating witness
- were derogatorily called "old maids" or "spinsters" if they did not marry
- had to use the universal "he" to refer to themselves; had only two ways of being addressed: Miss or Mrs.

Before the 1970s Women
- could be demoted or fired if they became pregnant
- didn't have laws to prohibit sex discrimination
- couldn't legally have an abortion
- didn't have much of a chance of getting into law or medical school
- didn't have a field called the psychology of women
- experienced condemnation if they worked after giving birth to a child (unless, of course, they were of low income or were of an ethnic minority)
- couldn't attend Harvard, Princeton, Yale, Williams, Amherst, or Dartmouth, among other institutes of higher education, or any of the military academies
- were few in number in the military and had almost no officers
- couldn't marry someone not of her own race without great censure or even danger to her or her husband's life
- were but a minute percentage of the people sitting in Congress

Before the 1980s Women
- didn't have a large gay rights movement to support sexual rights and choices
- had never had a woman run for the U.S. vice presidency
- had never had a woman on the U.S. Supreme Court
- did not have the field of women's health or women's health centers available to them
- did not have people such as Carol Gilligan offering research and information about gender differences

Before the 1990s Women
- couldn't count on the sexual harassment laws being taken seriously. (It took the hearings of Supreme Court Justice Clarence Thomas and the testimony of Anita Hill to bring sexual harassment to real attention.)
- had never had a female attorney general or secretary of state

- couldn't count on the domestic violence laws being taken seriously. (It took the murder of Nicole Brown Simpson and the trial of O. J. Simpson to bring domestic violence to real attention.)
- couldn't be combat pilots in the military
- until Colonel Eileen Collins, never had a woman commander of a U.S. space flight

I have only skimmed the surface of what history tells us about the treatment of women. My intention is simply to acquaint you with the relentless siege of negative messages women have received over the centuries about who they were, what they were supposed to do (and not do), and how much they were worth. Before the twentieth century, the Lady Be Good, Be Beautiful, Be Well-Behaved, and Be Responsible models came as hand-me-down dictums transmitted by the spoken and sometimes the written word. Books, newspapers, and a few magazines — as well as what one person said to another — were the ways in which people learned about the world in general and women in particular. It was in those words that the seeds for the Female Code of Conduct were set, if not cast, in stone.

HOW MOVIE "GOOD GIRLS" AND "BAD GIRLS" HAVE AFFECTED US

In this century, major visual messages were added in the form of movies, which became yet another source for creating and perpetuating stereotypical notions about women. Molly Haskell, author of *From Reverence to Rape: The Treatment of Women in the Movies*, says that with the exception of an occasional Katharine Hepburn film in which she was allowed to have a mutually respectful relationship with Spencer Tracy (like *Adam's Rib* and *Pat and Mike*), movies have generally divided women into two categories: good girls (nice ladies) and bad girls (tough cookies, witches, and whores).[36] Actresses are remembered mostly for their looks and are often confused with the roles that they play.[37] Remember when you hear the old line about actresses "sleeping their way to the top" that some may have done this willingly, but many were victims of what we now know as sexual harassment.

As might be expected, "good girls" have embodied all of the positive attributes of the current Female Code of Conduct: they were (and still are) portrayed as nice, sweet, beautiful (if over forty, at least attractive), charming, sexy (but not too), well behaved, nurturing, hardworking, responsible, self-sacrificing, and virtuous.

Harriet Lerner, author of *The Dance of Anger*, says that in real life "good girls" and "nice ladies" stay silent — or become tearful, self-critical, or "hurt"; keep anger or protest to themselves in order to avoid the possibility of open conflict; and avoid making clear statements about what they think and feel when they suspect that such clarity would make another person uncomfortable.[38] We also know that "good girls" give in and go along; feel helpless and powerless; don't feel in control of their lives; allow themselves to be treated unfairly; and stay with the status quo in work and relationships. By the end of any given movie, "good girls" are usually rewarded for, well, yes, being "good" by finding or marrying the man of their dreams and living happily ever. But as most of us know, this "good girl" fairy-tale ending has little to do with real life.

"Bad girls" are another thing altogether. Movies have portrayed them as sexually promiscuous (if not predatory), self-indulgent, power-hungry, addicted, and crazy. In real life "bad girls" do get angry, if not cause a "scene"; and they complain and are aggressive in the pursuit of their interests. In movies "bad girls" inevitably get what's coming to them, which means they don't get their man (or lose him to a "good girl"), are bumped off, or are somehow punished for their "bad" behavior.

These stereotypes have been true mostly for white women in white female roles. Before the 1970s African American and Hispanic women were rarely seen on movie screens except in servant, slave, or otherwise negatively stereotyped roles. Until recently, female Native American roles were played by white women. The same is true for Asian female roles. Remember, it's only been since the 1980s that women of color have been allowed to be involved romantically with white men. Before that time it didn't happen at all in movies, or if it did, you knew for sure that eventually the African American, Asian, or Latina would lose either her man or her life. Those were the "rules."

More than anything else, what has been missing from movies is a realistic portrayal of young girls, teenage women, and women who are

- pursuing authentic, intelligent, balanced lives
- not necessarily young, beautiful, thin, or "buff" but who are happy with themselves as they are and with their lives
- successfully combining love and work without unduly sacrificing their health or personal needs, wants, and desires
- involved in relationships in which there is mutual love, respect, and sharing of household and/or parental responsibilities
- neither idealized nor worshiped, brutalized, victimized, trivialized, or devalued simply for being female

While some independent film companies and the European film industry have been moving in the direction of offering more sophisticated, balanced views of women, the increasingly bottom-line, gotta-make-asmash-hit-with-the-first-weekend mentality of the Hollywood studios certainly doesn't bode well for how American movies will treat women in the future. And this practice will surely continue to support the myths associated with the old, debilitating Female Code of Conduct.

WHAT ABOUT RADIO AND TV?

As the century progressed, other media such as radio, television, and women's magazines came to influence how the world viewed women and how we thought of ourselves. Early radio and television often had women acting like silly children. Remember Gracie Allen, Lucille Ball, Laverne and Shirley, and the women of *Rowan and Martin's Laugh-In?* (Turn on some retro-reruns tonight if you don't remember.) As funny, lovable, and adorable as they were, except for an occasional lapse, not one of them ever came through as a competent or intelligent being. And if women weren't saying and doing stupid things on radio or TV, once again they were portrayed as the proverbial "good girls" or "bad girls" through the soaps and made-for-TV movies.

On the other hand, in many ways television has also provided us with a greater variety of female images than has the movie industry. Through assorted weekly series ethnic, working-class, lesbian, even overweight women have almost become mainstream in this medium. But, almost as if someone wanted to make sure we knew our place, every few minutes we see the old Female Code of Conduct come through in television commercials. "Be beautiful . . . be thin . . . be sexy . . . be young!" the commercials call out. "Make your homes 'cleaner than clean,'" they say.

As of the 1980s a new cultural message about what it meant to be a woman emerged for women watching TV: be a Superwoman. Both in programming and especially in commercials, advertisers finally realized that many of us worked outside the home. What ensued was a deluge of messages about how the advertised products (and male advertising and television executives) could help us to be and do everything — effortlessly, I might add — while continuing to be beautiful, thin, sexy, and youthful looking. Okay, so now we should be perfect wives, mothers, housekeepers, *and* highly productive workers as well. The Code of Conduct took on even greater meaning for us. Sadly, many women attempted to live those messages.

THE POWER OF WOMEN'S BOOKS AND MAGAZINES

Another medium that we must talk about is contemporary women's books, as well as women's, girls', and teens' traditional magazines. In *When Memory Speaks,* Jill Ker Conway (best-selling author and former president of Smith College) says that novels now and in the past have often centered on a romantic heroine who has "no power to act on her own behalf. Things happen to her—adventures, lovers, reversals of fortune." Just as in the movies, "bad girls" or "anti-types," scheming women, try to create their own destiny, but they are held up as negative models of unseemly ambition.[39] Some things never change.

As far as magazines go, some are now portraying more positive images and some perpetuate the old Code of Conduct, but most fail to provide a clear message one way or the other. Clearly, the most insidious aspect of all magazines are the messages delivered in advertisements. The same old worn-out record of what women and young females should be and do according to a dominant male culture is played over and over again. Ads and articles say:

- Be tall, blond, feminine, thin, and youthful looking.
- Be popular, social, and cool.
- Wear fashionable clothes, accessories, and makeup, and make sure you have "perfect" hair.
- Be fit, buff, trim, and athletic.
- Wrinkles are almost as bad as fat.
- Shop, shop, shop until you drop.
- The most important thing in your life is love, romance, and finding Mr. Right, which means looking like, being, and doing what men want.

By implication, these ads say that if you happen to be anything different from what they portray—overweight, old, wrinkled, poor, disabled, unattractive, not cool, "out of it"—then you are what every female fears: deficient, less than, and really *bad*.

THE INTERNET

While it is still unclear how the Internet will affect women, there are hopeful signs that it will become a positive informational and communication force. With the likes of Geraldine Laybourne's oxygen.com and Candice Carpenter's iVillage, a new kind of resource seems to be opening up. Laybourne says that

> 70% of us can't stand the way America advertises . . . it's insulting and demeaning . . . women don't want to be sold, but want to buy, want information and want to be talked to as real human beings . . . expensive cars and designer clothes are not the center of our lives; but "how do I get control of my life" . . . women have 16 other jobs whether they work at home or at the office.[40]

Such comments suggest that a down-to-earth, real person who understands what women are all about is in charge of an important website. That's promising. Only time will tell.

We are at a unique time in history. At the beginning of this new millennium social, economic, and political forces are such that the possibility for women to change the rules they live by has never been greater. We can change the paradigm that has defined who we are as women, how we think about ourselves, and what we do. Now is the time for us to throw off the shackles of our own pernicious overresponsibility and overfocus on our appearance so that we can live fuller, more balanced, healthier lives. The next chapter will help you to know how to begin doing that.

I think right about now you deserve another Break.

BE GOOD TO YOURSELF BREAK

Take a hot bubble bath. • Read a favorite poem. • Listen to your favorite calming Bach CD. • Feed some birds in your garden. • Eat a perfect nectarine. • Bake some bread. • Find your down comforter, put it over you, and take a nap (in the middle of the day). • Take a slow walk (at the beach, in the park, in a field or forest). • Meditate. • Call your best friend. • Make yourself a glass of fresh orange juice. • Have a glass of wine. • Light a fire in the fireplace. • Read a classic book out loud to a child. • Leave more blank spaces in your DayTimer. • Sing in the shower. • Put on your favorite "old" CD, maybe Carole King's *Tapestry.* • Spend an hour in your favorite bookstore. • Buy some exquisite stationery. • Plant some cosmos in your garden. • Go to a stationery store and buy a "perfect" pen. • Plant a white peach tree. • Don't answer the phone for an hour. • Play with your dog. • Sit down in a comfortable chair to watch an old classic movie. • Talk to your favorite sister (brother) on the phone. • Take a quick trip to the newsstand to buy several magazines you don't usually read. • Buy a basket of fresh raspberries. • Take a Jacuzzi. • Write a poem. • Take time to just sit. • Lie on the floor on your back in a dimly lit room. • Work in your garden.

CHAPTER 4

Some New Truths for Women to Live By

Pretty women wonder where my secret lies.
I'm not cute or built to suit a fashion model's size
But when I start to tell them,
They think I'm telling lies.
I say,
It's in the reach of my arms
The span of my hips,
The stride of my step,
The curl of my lips.
I'm a woman
Phenomenally.
Phenomenal woman,
That's me.

I walk into a room
Just as cool as you please,
And to a man,
The fellows stand or
Fall down on their knees.
Then they swarm around me,
A hive of honey bees.
I say,
It's the fire in my eyes,
And the flash of my teeth,
The swing in my waist,
And the joy in my feet.
I'm a woman
Phenomenally.
Phenomenal woman,
That's me.

Men themselves have wondered
What they see in me.
They try so much
But they can't touch
My inner mystery.
When I try to show them
They say they still can't see.
I say,
It's the arch of my back,
The sun of my smile,
The ride of my breasts,
The grace of my style.
I'm a woman
Phenomenally.
Phenomenal woman,
That's me.

Now you understand
Just why my head's not bowed.
I don't shout or jump about
Or have to talk real loud.
When you see me passing
It ought to make you proud.
I say,
It's in the click of my heels,
The bend of my hair,
The palm of my hand,
The need of my care.
'Cause I'm a woman
Phenomenally.
Phenomenal woman,
That's me.

Maya Angelou
"Phenomenal Woman"
And Still I Rise

In the last few decades women have made great progress: roles and options have multiplied, laws have been changed, previously closed doors have opened. Never before have our choices been so unimpeded. As many women as men now go to medical and law schools. It is against the law for businesses to discriminate against women or to sexually harass them. Most important, the culture at large has changed in terms of what it expects of women. Literally, we can do anything!

As you may have observed, though, most of these positive changes have taken place in the more physical, structural, "outside" realm of life. What remains almost untouched is what happens in the "inside" realm, in our own beliefs about who we are and what we do with our time. Women from all ages and backgrounds are still prisoners to their own debilitating beliefs, attitudes, and everyday self-sacrificing actions. Like sleepwalking Snow Whites, we're still waiting to be awakened to the possibilities of acting on our own lives. Like hordes of "giving" automatons, we continually abandon our own choices, we ignore our own unique potentials, and we relinquish responsibility for our own health and happiness. These internal barriers must be conquered before women can truly become confident and whole. Isn't it about time to change?

Personal truth is nothing that we need to beg for from others; nor is it something that we need to prove we deserve. Seeking our own real truths is something only we can do for ourselves.

WE CAN CHANGE FOREVER WHAT IT MEANS TO BE A WOMAN

Have you ever considered that we can change forever what it means to be a woman? We can Stop

- feeling worn down and worn out
- feeling used
- wasting our energy
- losing our voices
- being so critical of ourselves

We can instead Start

- feeling full of energy and "alive"
- selectively deciding how and when we give our time
- finding things to do and people to be with who are nourishing and supportive

- having a strong voice
- being as caring of ourselves as we are of others

Yes, you can, I can, and especially if we help one another, all of us can. In the process we will emerge as more confident women. The Bible says that the truth will set us free. Obviously, we need some new truths to live by. Here are a few for you to consider.

> *I tore myself away from the safe comfort of certainties through*
> *my love for the truth; and truth rewarded me.*
>
> Simone de Beauvoir

NEW TRUTH 1
Embrace the Concept of Free Will

What does *free will* really mean? Basically it's all about having choices.

> *Having "free will" means that you feel free to have a belief sys-*
> *tem of your own and to choose and act on any decision with-*
> *out feeling coerced or restrained by outside influences.*

Besides having your own personal beliefs and feeling free to act on them, *free will* also means that what you think, feel, and want are at least as important as what other people think, feel, and want, even if you are married to, related to, or best friends with the other people. When you operate under the umbrella of free will, you say without apologies to others and/or to yourself:

I am	as well as	I am not
I believe	as well as	I do not believe
I think	as well as	I do not think
I am comfortable with	as well as	I'm not comfortable with
I feel	as well as	I do not feel
I choose	as well as	I choose not to
I want	as well as	I do not want
I prefer	as well as	I prefer not to
I like	as well as	I do not like
I need	as well as	I do not need
I know	as well as	I do not know
I will	as well as	I will not
I love	as well as	I do not love

Under the old system of false truths, women were considered too weak or too inferior to make choices, let alone good choices, even for themselves. Like children, they were told what to believe, think, say, and do. Vestiges of the too-weak, too-inferior false truths are in effect today anytime you find yourself saying:

I have to	I'll do it [even if I don't want to]
I should	I'll go [even if I don't want to]
I need to	I'll not [even if I want to]
I ought to	I'm obligated to
I've got to	I'm selfish if I
I'll feel guilty if I don't	I can't defend myself against
I'll feel ashamed if I don't	I'm not good enough to
I'll feel badly if I don't	I'm not brave enough to
I worry that	I'm scared to
I'm afraid to	I'm not competent enough to
I must	I'm too insecure to
I have to hold back	What right do I have to
I don't know	I can't say no to
I don't know how to	I'll let others down if I
I can't	How could I
I'll wait or postpone, it's not important	It's not worth a fight over

If you find yourself consistently thinking or using these phrases, let that be a signal that you are not exercising free will. In part IV of this book, we'll talk more about how you can begin making better choices and changing nonconfident ways of thinking, talking, and acting. Remember —

> It is the ability to choose
> which makes us human.
> Madeleine L'Engle

Right about now, you might be having some second thoughts about this notion of free will. I can hear some readers saying, "But, Marjorie, how can you possibly say that I have free will when I grew up in a dysfunctional family? I was abused and am still suffering from it." Someone else might say, "You can't apply this to me. No one who has been ill all of her life can possibly think of herself as having real choices." Still others might bring up issues of racial discrimination, economic deprivation, or other extraordinary personal hardships. Someone might even object on the grounds that she is suffering with cancer. To address these very legitimate questions, let us go to our next truth.

NEW TRUTH 2
Take Personal Responsibility for Your Own Life

Yes, there are a whole series of things about which you don't have much choice. Personal genetics, physiology, how one has been parented, social prescriptions, and fate do set limits on people's lives. Even if you can make a myriad of choices about how to take care of your own body, for example, you can't change your biological inheritance. As the great humanistic psychologist Abraham Maslow said,

> *What's important
> is what you do with what you have been given,
> not what you have been given.*

While it's generally agreed that free will begins at birth, you certainly had nothing to do with your own creation nor with the selection of your parents. What's more, especially in your early years, you probably had very little choice about where you lived, the people with whom you came into daily contact, or how your parents behaved toward you.

Most parents do the best job they can, but as we all know, this is one role for which society spends almost no time preparing people. So how you were parented was probably one part what your grandparents did, one part expert advice that your parents read or heard about, one part what your parents observed other parents doing, and one part your parents' wishful thinking and hoping for the best—a mixture of generally benign, some positive, and some possibly harmful behaviors.

As my husband's son, Jonathon, says with a twinkle in his eye, "Adulthood is the time you spend trying to get over all the mistakes your parents made while you were growing up." While there may be a lot of truth in this, even children who have grown up in abusive homes are not helped by focusing on how awful it was or is. According to professionals who work with these children, a good part of their mending involves getting out of the situation and then seeing where they have choices and how to get more control over their lives.

Kenneth Pelletier, a highly respected physician at the Stanford Medical School, is convinced that people can transcend their respective upbringings, including pain and adversity, even trauma, by moving from feeling helpless or hopeless to feeling in control. Not only is this shift important in dealing with crises, he says, but it's the most powerful indicator of whether you are going to be physically and emotionally healthy.[1]

So what can we learn from these observations? What's really important is not who your parents are, or even what they did to or for you, but what you now do with your life.

> We are not permitted to choose
> the frame of our destiny.
> But what we put into it is ours.
>   Dag Hammarskjöld

Fate, fortune, destiny, chance, accident, and luck

Fate, fortune, destiny, chance, accident, luck — these are all words used to describe what is unforeseen — those things that we are powerless to change and over which we have no choice. *Fate* is at work in every aspect of our lives. Sometimes we forget that fate works for, as well as against, us. You've probably heard the saying, "Life is good and then shit happens." While a little crude, this certainly gets to the heart of the matter. I think everyone experiences both blessings and bad luck.

You might be *fortunate* in the parents you were given, or you might not be. *Destiny* is the time and place you find yourself living: now in the United States you can question social prescriptions, but at another time and place you might be punished for doing so. Some of us have had life-changing *chance* meetings, and all of us have endured disastrous *accidental* encounters. "Dust unto dust" — the ultimate fate is not knowing when or why we are born or when, how, or why we die. That's a part of being alive.

Part of accepting the reality of life is acknowledging that we live with fate and its limitations. Before he died in 1970, Abraham Maslow went to great lengths to encourage people to achieve the most they could. He was particularly interested in how fate intersects with personal issues of free will, self-choice, and personal responsibility. He went so far as to say that as difficult as it may seem, those who are paraplegic, or who have cancer, or who are dying still "inhabit a realm in which [they] can accomplish either a great deal or very little."

Maslow also recounts how two of his good friends, the renowned psychiatrists Bruno Bettelheim and Viktor Frankl, both survivors of the Holocaust, vigorously affirmed the importance of free will in spite of their concentration camp experiences. Both men allowed that "even in [such a] camp, one can still do one's job well or badly . . . be dignified or undignified . . . can still be all that one is capable of being or less than one is capable of being. [And] at the edge of death, one can still be an active agent or a helpless whining pawn."[2]

Maslow's work has recently been substantiated by numerous contemporary researchers. For example, Dr. Lawrence Kohlberg has reviewed the literature on how traumatic events, especially in childhood, affect people's lives and especially their health. What he concluded is that — with the exception of schizophrenia and sociopathic behavior — the popular belief that our childhood experience determines our later adult behavior is a myth.[3] Kenneth Pelletier has also looked at the research and found that while childhood trauma (including chronic poverty and discrimination and/or having psychotic parents or going through your parents' divorce) can have a dramatic negative effect, such traumas can be transformed into positive forces in one's life.[4] It is heartening to know that people can do many constructive things if they approach their respective traumatic life events with positive strategies, skills, and attitudes.

If it's possible under the most dreadful circumstances to be an active agent, then surely those of us who are lucky enough not to have experienced such things must take up the charge to do so. As Helen Keller said in her book *Optimism*,

> *Although the world is full of suffering,*
> *it is full also of the overcoming of it.*

How we can begin to overcome

Now more than ever, women can and must take responsibility for their own lives and stop being other people's pawns. As Harvard University's Herbert Benson says, "It isn't the circumstances of life, but one's attitude toward these circumstances that seals one's fate."[5] It starts with each of us taking action. Among other things we can:

- choose to act effectively, rather than shrinking or drifting
- choose to stand tall, even if we are short
- choose to act with dignity, rather than going along with the crowd
- choose (as the popular writer Naomi Wolf says) "to leave the beleaguered foxholes of defensiveness," instead of staying hunkered down and weak
- learn to grow comfortable with our power, instead of being helpless or victimlike
- maintain our loving, giving hearts, without foolishly giving them away
- risk thinking and acting in new ways, rather than giving up or giving in
- do it ourselves, rather than always depending on others to do it for us

Most important, we need to begin thinking about what it means to become all that we are capable of being. And that leads us to the next New Truth.

NEW TRUTH 3
Be Honestly and Fully Your Own Self

Throughout history man has been counseled to "be your self" (Matthew Arnold), "be true to yourself" (Shakespeare), to "know yourself" (Delphic Oracle, Albert Camus), "trust yourself" (Ralph Waldo Emerson), and "become one's own man" (Erik Erikson). One problem: these sage exhortations for self-actualization came forth from men for men, not for women.

Becoming more of yourself

With the exception of some audacious female writers, until this century women were not trained to think and write about such things as self-actualization. Furthermore, many forces have worked against women developing a true self. They have not been brought up to have self-knowledge, to act on their own behalf, or to develop a sense of their own effectiveness. As the *Commonwealth Report on Women* said in the late 1990s, "A vast literature suggests that female gender role socialization inhibits action and reinforces helplessness, avoidance and passivity as personal styles. Women's sense that they must [always] be nurturing and caring to others may impede their ability to assert needs for themselves."[6] Everything we have been taught has been around the notion that we should live through, for, or as an adjunct to, other people and their lives.

How do I become my self?

Are you wondering what I am talking about when I use the word *self*? Here is a definition:

> Self *(also called* psyche, inner voice, soul, mind, spirit) *is one's inner world — a set of potentials, interests, and capabilities — that makes each of us who we are and who we are not.*

Stephanie Dowrick, a well-known Australian psychotherapist who has written extensively about the subject of the female self, says that self is the outcome of the interplay between a person and the world and . . . when the process works, "true self" emerges. When it doesn't, the result is a "less-true self."[7]

What does it mean for a woman to have a true self? It means to be the most authentic person you can be, which involves:

- having self-knowledge, that is, knowing and appreciating who you are — that intrinsic, one-of-a-kind person that only you can be, including your body, mind, and soul.
- having a sense of what's important (your values and priorities), knowing what you want and what you are doing and why.
- being attuned to and allowing your own positive, "healthy" thoughts to guide your everyday actions.
- being attuned to your own feelings, exploring them, and using them as information as to what's going on inside you and what's happening in your relationships with other people.
- honestly acknowledging the consequences of your own thoughts, feelings, and actions and taking responsibility for their effects on yourself and others.

I should note here that notions of self are, for the most part, Western. Many non-Western — for example, Asian and African — cultures have very different ways of viewing the concept of self for men and especially women. For example, the Japanese self is much more of a "we-self" than the Western I-self.[8] And many Native American tribes embrace a more communal self. In the more patriarchal societies, especially fundamentalist religious ones, women's inner voices are marginalized, even silenced — there is no "I" at all. But whether it is our own or another culture, whether it is self-imposed or other-imposed, denying one access to truth on a daily basis, especially about one's self, can produce a whole set of adverse emotional and even physical reactions.

Maslow was one of the first people to argue that in failing to become our real selves, we're sidestepping our own biological destinies. By not accepting who we are, he said, especially when we compare ourselves to others or want to be like them, we are evading the task for which we alone were born.

The good things that happen when we do become more of our own selves

First of all, you feel *alive* . . . you gain a zest for life the likes of which you may never have known. You see, someone who becomes more of herself develops a new source of energy.

Second, people who become their real selves are *happier and more naturally loving* — and for good reason: remember, when you are filled, you give from overflow, not from duty or deficit. Erich Fromm, the wonderful psychologist who wrote *The Art of Loving,* once said that a person who has no self-love cannot feel any real love for others.[9]

Third, people who develop themselves will suddenly *feel free.* Rather than looking to others for approval and permission, you will be the author of your own actions. Edward Deci, an expert on self-motivation, says that a person who acts in accord with herself can embrace whatever she is doing with interest and commitment. People who are self-motivated — as opposed to acceding to outside pressure or control — enjoy a special kind of creativity, thrill, and joy in all aspects of their lives.[10] As a result, they manifest many more desirable traits such as affection, friendliness, generosity, kindness, and trust.

Finally, a person who becomes more of herself *is a causer in life rather than a person being caused.*[11] This means that you are much better able to stand up for yourself when you find yourself in situations where someone acts disrespectfully toward you, or is demeaning or insulting. Also you are *less likely to be exploited, manipulated, or used.*

Why self-actualization is not narcissistic

Okay, okay, I think I know what you might be thinking: "Isn't becoming more of myself just another way of being selfish? Aren't you promoting self-absorption and self-centeredness — everything that I have been taught to hate?" My answer is very clear: absolutely not. But if you are thinking this, you are not alone. For some time now social critics such as Allan Bloom and Christopher Lasch have decried the movement toward a "culture of narcissism."

According to Edward Deci, we can't be confused by thinking that *pursuing an integrated, authentic self* is the same as being narcissistically preoccupied with the self. He says:

> *narcissism involves desperately seeking affirmation from others. It entails an outward focus — a concern with what others think — and that focus takes people away from their true self. The narcissistic preoccupation results not from people being aligned with the self but from their having lost contact with it. People adopt narcissistic values in a controlling society because they have not had the type of psychological nourishment they need to develop an integrated and healthy self. Narcissism is not the result of authenticity or self-determination, it is their antithesis.*[12]

Don't fall into the misguided notion that self-absorbed, narcissistic behavior develops from knowing yourself, taking care of yourself, or making the most of who you are. On the contrary, narcissism develops from *not* doing those things. Selfish behavior often comes from being deprived, feeling threatened, being afraid of somebody or something, or experiencing inner (or real) poverty. Healthy behavior thrives on inner riches and quality choices. Developing an honest, real self is a quiet, calm process of self-discovery and acknowledgment.

I think Oscar Wilde's take on selfishness is the best I've ever read. He said:

> *Selfishness is not living as one wishes to live;*
> *it is asking others to live as one wishes to live.*

While husbands ask their wives all the time to "live as they wish to live," rarely do wives ask the same of their husbands. Think about all the women you know who — when their husbands wanted to retire — sold their beloved home, left their friends, moved to a condo or boat, left a job they loved, held themselves back, and sacrificed their desires because they thought they needed to be and do what their husbands wanted. What physical and emotional price do women pay for living "as he wishes to live"? Women may think that they are doing their husbands a favor, but in reality very often they are doing themselves and the relationship in.

This leads to one final point: being responsible to yourself does not mean that you cannot also be responsible to others, or generous and giving with your time and energy. But these must be conscious choices, not a reckless throwing away of yourself. Moreover it is totally irresponsible to try to be everything to everybody (something the proverbial Superwoman always does). Except for very young children, you can't be everything to even one other person, nor should you, since that would rob that person of having responsibility for her or his own life.

Many mental health professionals have come to the conclusion that when you always meet other people's needs and never your own, it's like condemning yourself to an emotional death penalty. Psychopathology comes from denying, thwarting, or twisting your basic self.

Furthermore, many health professionals are convinced that sickness comes not only when you deny yourself the nutritional food that you need (remember the old adage "You are what you eat") but also when you starve yourself from healthy ways of living.

It's also destructive to allow yourself to be poisoned by a constant barrage of negative influences, such as media reports of violence, tragedy, and despair; toxic people; unhealthy environmental influences such as loud noises and pollution; or unpleasant, dreary work. These things not only damage our bodies and our psyches, they also undermine our human spirit.

Each of us needs to be honest enough, courageous enough, and healthy enough to develop as many personal capacities as we can. Remember, our own individual self is all that we really have. We must take care not to squash or squander it. As Shakespeare said in *Henry V*,

> *Self-love, my liege, is not so vile a sin*
> *As self-neglecting.*

This then leads us to the next truth.

NEW TRUTH 4
Be the Healthiest, Happiest Person You Are Capable of Being

In her 1960s book *I Never Promised You a Rose Garden*, writer Hannah Green said, "Health is not simply the absence of disease." Cutting-edge health professionals agree, while at the same time decrying so-called healthy-living measures that include endlessly going on the latest diet, fanatically exercising to become the current version of "buff," or obsessing about calories, cholesterol, caffeine, wrinkles, certain body parts, or personal inadequacies. For a great many women, working on themselves until they are exhausted or sick or both is the extent to which they take care of themselves. Many health professionals are calling these behaviors unhealthy and often worse than disease itself.

The most enlightened health professionals in our country are now expanding what it means to be a healthy person. They say that health is

- an *ongoing process* of *self-discovery* in which
- you exercise *positive choices*
- integrate your *physical, mental, social, and spiritual well-being,* and
- *live life to its fullest* so that you can
- have a *positive influence on the world.*

Physicians like Pelletier are also saying that being healthy in this way is not only *not selfish* but a *personal and societal responsibility.*[13] Now isn't that an enticing thought!

Too many of us have to be sick to take care of ourselves

Most women I know need to be sick before they feel justified in taking care of themselves. We keep waiting for someone else to give us a prescription to rest, or to encourage us to slow down or stop for a while, or to reassure us that it's okay, or best of all—fantasy of all fantasies—to make all of the arrangements for us. If we simply do it for ourselves, we are overcome with colossal guilt.

This reminds me of a conversation I had with a colleague not long ago, when we were both flying home to San Diego from the East Coast. As we sat next to each other on the plane chatting, I noticed deep furrows in her brow and asked her if she was okay. Mary said, "Gee, I really appreciate your asking," then told me that for a number of months she had been experiencing excruciating back pain. We talked about the different treatment alternatives she was considering and how in the midst of her pain she was still handling a very heavy workload and major volunteer activities.

About halfway through our conversation, she stopped and said,

> *You know, Marjorie, the pain I'm feeling is not as bad as how upset I'm feeling at my husband for not being more supportive of me — as they say — "in my time of need." For God's sake, if he had a bad back, I'd be out there calling physicians, picking him up at work, and making sure that he was eating right. You know, all that comforting stuff. But all John is doing is every once in a while asking me "How are ya doing." It's driving me crazy. I'm wondering if he really gives a ——!*

Since I know something about how differently men and women tend to deal with illness, I told Mary that men tend to deny their pain and expect others to do the same. I also talked about how men are not brought up to provide nurturing to people who are sick — something that women seem to give so easily. After a while I asked her what she was doing to take care of herself. She looked at me with a rather puzzled look on her face and said, "What do you mean?"

I said, "Well, just a few minutes ago you went into great detail telling me what you would do for John if he were ill. Have you considered doing any of that for yourself? Just because someone else is not doing good things for you, doesn't mean that you can't do them for yourself."

I'll never forget Mary's response. She looked at me and said, "Wait a minute. Don't say anything else. I'm trying to think about what you're saying. Let me allow this to sink in." She sat there for some time, and I could just see the wheels turning as she digested this notion.

Shortly after the plane landed and Mary and I went off to our separate homes, I received this e-mail message:

> *Marjorie, your suggestion that we who are caregivers to everyone else can also be caregivers to ourselves is something that really stuck with*

me. Must be one of those "forest for the trees" kinds of things. I have honestly been accepting as a standard that what we don't receive from our significant others, we do without.

Providing some of that good stuff for ourselves is such a simple thought. But it never occurred to me until you said it.

Thank you so much! Mary

Like Mary, many of us take care of others, particularly when they are not well, without really thinking about it. But we never imagine that we can care for ourselves in the same way. We tend to need permission or support from others—a physician, a spouse or partner, a good friend, or perhaps a supervisor or employer. And usually they need to convince us that we deserve the time and care!

And then there is the final truth, which may be the most important one of all.

NEW TRUTH 5
You Are More Than Your Physical Body, and Certainly Much, Much More Than the Pounds You Weigh

> As she is a woman,
> and as she is an American,
> she was dieting.
> Katharine Whitehorn
> "Meeting Mary McCarthy"
> *The Observer*

For too many women, negative perceptions of their appearance and their weight define who and what they are. Period. Even a single perceived negative physical characteristic—big hips or too-small breasts or a "jelly belly" or those "damned thighs"—are enough to send a lot of women into a psychological tailspin. I do believe that the most dreaded words in the Queendom of Womanhood are "I have gained a few pounds."

We are obsessed with our bodies!

As I interviewed women for this book, the majority—like their sisters all over the country—seemed obsessed with food and calories, dress sizes, and what their bodies looked like. At any given moment during the day or night, undoubtedly at least a million women are silently thinking to themselves, "I need to lose some weight."

African American women are much more comfortable with their bodies than other women, no matter what their size. Support for this observation comes with research from Wellesley College's Center for Research on Women, which found in a study (of young African American, Chinese American, Puerto Rican, and Caucasian women) that African Americans had the most positive self-evaluations. By comparison, Chinese Americans had the least positive, and Puerto Ricans and Caucasians had self-judgments somewhere between the two extremes.[14]

When women think badly of themselves, they also tend to say the most disparaging things about their bodies. And it starts very early. When I asked interviewees, "What would you like to change about your life to make it more positive or better?" they talked about their bodies and their appearance. One thirty-something woman blurted out, "Just about everything about my body! I still feel like I'm not tall enough, pretty enough, or thin enough." This woman was about five foot six and weighed no more than 130 pounds. She was far from overweight.

A forty-year-old remembered her teenage years when she was "tall, fat, flat, and too smart." She added that "I'm still tall, fat, flat, and too smart thirty years later!" What she wanted to change, though, had to do with her appearance, not her body. Her mother, she said, had been a "Depression kid" who never knew how to choose clothes for herself or her daughter: "you know—colors, styles, what's in and out, and especially what looks good on me." She added, "I've felt out of it most of my life."

One twenty-something confessed that when she looks in the mirror, all she sees are flaws. She described how a day—sometimes a whole week—can be ruined: "I'll look at myself and see a zit, and then declare myself a disaster. I'll go to work but hide out in my office, cancel everything on my social calendar, avoid whomever I can until I feel more comfortable with myself."

Some Asian women allowed that they wished that they didn't look so Asian. One Chinese woman described how her mother would pinch her nose, even put a clothespin on it, hoping to make it less flat, more Caucasian, and thus less Asian-looking. Another Asian woman told me how her mother forced her to have plastic surgery on her eyes to make them rounder. The mother told the daughter that if she didn't have this surgery, she would be less desirable in the dating/marriage market.

Thus, it is not surprising that *hate* is the most common verb women use to express how they feel about their bodies: I hate "my hair," "my breasts," "my floppy arms," "my double chin," "my nose," "my rear end," "my freckles," "my stomach," "my whole damned body!" At least some women have a sense of humor about it. One sprightly seventy-year-old told me, with a chuckle in her voice, that she had "feet the size of battleships."

The women I spoke with also agonized over the ways in which important people in their lives, particularly their mothers and fathers and husbands, had led them to feel uncomfortable about their looks. One thirty-year-old said that her mother was forever "critiquing what I wear. I still have to say to her, 'No, I don't want to wear my hair that way' or 'Believe me, I will survive if I go outside the house without a scarf in my pocket.'"

A seventy-two-year-old revealed that as she was growing up, the most important message she heard was "be pretty." "I remember my father saying, 'A good-looking woman can marry anyone, even the Prince of Wales.' And so I thought maybe that's what I was supposed to do, be pretty. It continues with my mother," this septuagenarian agonized. "Mother is nearly a hundred years old, I'm seventy-two, and she's still commenting on how attractive or unattractive people are—especially me. To this day she will say things like, 'What shall we do with your hair?' or 'You're too fat.' About a year ago, I finally said to her, 'Mother, if you mention my weight one more time I'm going to go home.'" Her mother begrudgingly said, "Okay," but an hour later she was heard muttering, "I wonder who in our family has such a large behind?"

The daughter recounted the ensuing scene: "I just went bonkers and yelled, 'Mom, you weren't going to say that anymore!' And she said back to me in an exasperating, exaggerated, sweet, innocent tone, 'Oh, I wasn't talking about you, I was just wondering who in our family had a large behind.' Marjorie, it hurt then, it hurts now, it always hurts—and it's hopeless."

We are so much more

Isn't it time that we began developing a new truth by which to see ourselves? As John Foreyt, coauthor of *Living Without Dieting*, declares,

> *Weight is part of one's life.*
> *It is not one's life.*

You are more than your physical body, and certainly much more than the pounds you weigh. You are also your

- intellect
- education and degrees
- work
- emotions
- personality, including some marvelous quirks, attitudes, and beliefs
- spirit

- lifestyle
- interests, activities, passions, habits, tastes, preferences, daily choices
- memory of past as well as present experiences
- abilities and talents
- capacities
- strengths and weaknesses
- values
- goals
- sexuality
- struggles and triumphs
- personal energy
- sense of humor
- relationships with family, friends, and especially the people you love

The remainder of this book is dedicated to helping you to make the most of all of these incredible parts of you.

———

Before we leave this chapter, let me say just one more thing. There is absolutely nothing wrong with being young or beautiful or thin or fit or nicely clothed or perfectly manicured. There is inherent beauty in every woman. It's healthy to choose wisely what and how to eat. Exercise can enhance the quality of life. It's a blessing to have great hair. It's wonderful to feel comfortable with one's own body. No matter who you are and what you look like, it feels good to look great! And looking great means loving your four-foot frame, your 180 pounds, your beautiful nose, your lovely breasts, your strong profile, your adorable freckles, your generous tummy that produced children. Because it's you! All of these things *can* be indications of your taking personal responsibility and good care of yourself.

> *You want to pay enough attention to your*
> *physical body and appearance,*
> *so that you can forget about yourself.*

When all is said and done, your body is an awesome, miraculous vehicle, incredibly designed for doing whatever you're supposed to do with the other parts of your life.

All of a sudden, women have the opportunity to change themselves so that they can live up to their own potential and live optimally healthy lives. To do that we must develop some new truths for ourselves, including those that we have just addressed:

* *EMBRACE THE CONCEPT OF FREE WILL* *

* *TAKE PERSONAL RESPONSIBILITY FOR YOUR OWN LIFE* *

* *BE HONESTLY AND FULLY YOUR OWN SELF* *

* *BE THE HEALTHIEST, HAPPIEST PERSON YOU ARE CAPABLE OF BEING* *

* *YOU ARE MORE THAN YOUR PHYSICAL BODY, AND CERTAINLY* *
MUCH, MUCH MORE THAN THE POUNDS YOU WEIGH

After all, as Harvard professor Carol Gilligan has said, "Having a life that is not compromised, and follow[ing] our own course rather than one that others expect of us," is what we are meant to do. It's our destiny.[15]

How about taking another few minutes to be good to yourself?

ANOTHER BE GOOD TO YOURSELF BREAK

Watch the sun set over the ocean (or lake or behind a mountain). • Watch a storm at the beach. • Take a few moments of quiet in a beautiful church. • Eat a freshly picked Hawaiian papaya. • Enjoy a plate of steamed, fresh asparagus. • Watch the very last segment on CBS's *Sunday Morning.* • Run downhill with the wind in your face. • Go to a museum store to find the most exquisite art notecards and postcards. • Eat some freshly picked blueberries from Vermont. • Bake a plate of brownies, eat one, and take the rest to a friend. • Rent the video *Singin' in the Rain.* • Go for a swim in a pool when no one else is there. • Paint your toenails. • Hold a baby. • Buy a new box of crayons, and after sniffing the wonderful aroma for a few minutes, color a picture—in or out of the lines. • Call a son or daughter who is far away from home. • Pick a home-grown tomato right before dinner. • Feel the early morning sunshine that spills across the kitchen floor. • Experience the sweet smell of night-blooming jasmine that lingers in the evening air. • Eat outdoors. • Enjoy the smell of fresh clean sheets that have dried outside on the line.

Part III

SELF-INVENTORY AND DISCOVERY

Getting to Know You, Getting to Know All About You

When one is a stranger to oneself, then
One is estranged from others too.
If one is out of touch with oneself, then
One cannot touch others.
Anne Morrow Lindbergh

The first step in becoming a more confident woman is to get to know more about yourself. Having a strong identity — that is, knowing who you are — is one of the most important, responsible, and healthy things you can do in your life.

In her book *Einstein's Wife*, Andrea Gabor says that among high-achieving women such as Justice Sandra Day O'Connor, Nobel scientist Maria Goeppert Mayer, and internationally acclaimed architect Denise Scott Brown, knowledge of self is the critical factor in their ability to create satisfying and fulfilling lives.

We must think of our "self" as a gift. It's what distinguishes us from any and all others. It is also our "magic," and it's all that we have. But many of us have abandoned this amazing fountain of potential and possibility to everyday, emergent reactions and distractions. We've fallen into the condition of acting as what my daughter Marejka calls, "human doings rather than human beings." As a result we feel fragmented, exhausted, and overwhelmed.

It's time to begin the process of defining who you are. As you begin this exciting journey, keep these two truths in mind: (1) the more you know about and are comfortable with yourself, the more you can forget about yourself; and (2) as you begin to take better care of yourself, you will have more energy to give to the people and activities you love. As Ralph Waldo Emerson once said,

What lies behind us and
what lies before us
are tiny matters,
compared to what lies within us.

YOU ARE AS A WONDROUS PICTURE PUZZLE

Let's start the search for the undeniable you by imagining that we are sitting together at a large table. Out in front of you are thousands of colorful puzzle pieces that, if we were to put them all together, would make a splendid picture of you. Unfortunately, someone has misplaced the cover of the puzzle box, so we don't know what the finished picture is.

As we look at the scattered puzzle parts, we notice that some pieces are already put together. They represent the aspects you already know about yourself. Among other things, we see some of your favorite colors, a few of your favorite friends, the music that pleases you, and that special place where you go when you want to have some time alone. This is good — because what you know now will help you in putting together the rest of your life picture.

But hundreds, maybe thousands, of other pieces are also scattered all over the table. They represent the many unidentified pieces of information about yourself that are "out there," just waiting to be discovered.

As we look at all those pieces, it's easy to feel overwhelmed by the thought of pulling them together. What's more, you don't see how the puzzle parts relate to one another or fit together. You don't have to put the whole picture together at once. All you have to do is identify one piece at a time. I think you'll find this easy and fun. Also, I remind you that this book is your guide. You are not alone.

Working on the puzzle, piece by piece, the picture of you begins to emerge. With each addition "who you are" becomes clearer. Every once in a while you say, "Wow, I didn't realize that I liked this or so enjoyed doing that. I didn't know that about me." Everyone feels what you are experiencing when she begins this journey of self-discovery.

Some parts come together quite easily and form recognizable clusters in the picture. As with most puzzles, use these as building blocks for moving on to other parts of the puzzle. Obviously, the more you add to the picture, the more complete, focused, and centered you become. The more you know about what delights you, the more avidly you'll want to pursue those interests. Or you'll add new pieces as circumstances or interests develop or change.

After a while you won't need this technique or this book to continue your journey. You'll have found your own magic. It will become automatic. You will add pieces to this picture puzzle throughout your life.

The insights you gain about yourself will make your life easier because they will become an arsenal of powerful information that will help you to better:

✓ take good care of yourself
✓ know and act on your priorities
✓ manage your everyday time
✓ make decisions about conflicting choices
✓ spend time with people who are good for you

Most important, as time goes by, you'll become more and more yourself.

To help you keep track of all of this, you need to write things down. Here are some suggestions for how to do that.

HEY! IT'S TIME TO GET SOMETHING TO WRITE IN

Right now, I want you to find something special in which to write. You may already have a notebook or journal at home that you've been saving for the "right" occasion or project. If you don't, go out and buy one, because this is an important step in your finding out how to become more of yourself.

I'd like you to choose a notebook that is a true reflection of you. Whatever suits you is just fine. There are no rules except to do what pleases or fits you.

You may prefer to use a computer, if writing in longhand is not your "thing." If that's the case, turn on that computer! If you want, you can print the computer notes and paste or tape them into a journal. Do whatever is easiest and makes sense to you.

In the midst of a crazy hectic day, sometimes I suddenly discover something that pleases me, and of course, I don't have my notebook with me. So what do I do? I take whatever is available (sometimes a paper napkin, gum wrapper, or bank deposit slip) and jot down what I want to remember. Or I tear out something that strikes my fancy from a magazine or newspaper. To save time, I tape those scribbled notes and torn pieces into my journal when I return home. Other people might prefer to rewrite them when they have time. Whatever works for you is what you should do.

Here's another thought about how you use your notebook. It is your own private possession, not to be shown to anyone unless you choose to. Therefore, don't worry about what you write. As much as you can, be spontaneous and real. Forget about writing complete sentences or even having things make sense. The last thing you want to be is self-conscious.

ANSWERING THE QUESTION "HOW DO I BECOME MORE OF MYSELF?"

To begin the self-defining "How Do I Become More of Myself" process, pay attention to what you like, what pleases you, what makes you feel good. Author Alexandra Stoddard says, "You pick up self-knowledge every day. Each selection you make, each tangible object you choose, becomes a symbol of your essence."[1] By having a written and/or a pictorial record of what appeals to you and what doesn't, you are creating a rich inventory of information to which you can refer as you make everyday choices about your time, energy, money, or other personal resources.

In the next four chapters, I will provide you with some exercises having to do with a number of aspects in your life: you, your friends and relationships, your job/career, and your home. This will serve as a springboard for helping you to choose more positive things in your life and leaving aside the negative ones.

Feel free to be selective in the choice of self-discovery chapters upon which you decide to work. Fill in only those chapters (or parts of chapters) that appeal to you. I want this to be a fun experience, not a chore. I realize that some readers may not be list-making types. If that's the case with you, follow your own personality dictates. Each of the chapters has been designed to give you just enough personal information to begin making more proactive choices and decisions, but not so much that you feel overwhelmed.

Some women who have used these exercises have told me that going through them was a "life-changing experience." What they meant was not that the exercises themselves were so extraordinary, but that the experience of discovering and/or realizing some new things about themselves was. That's what I want for you.

Again, remember that in becoming more of yourself, you're becoming more of who you're supposed to be. As Simone de Beauvoir said,

> *One is not born,*
> *but rather becomes,*
> *a Woman.*

How about a Cupcake Break?

Whenever I feel like I need a little TLC (tender loving care), I remember my Grandmother Beck and her wonderful Danish baked goods. Among my very favorite are her cupcakes. Here is her recipe. Enjoy!

GRANDMA'S CUPCAKE BREAK

1 tsp. baking powder	4 tbs. soft margarine
1½ cups flour	1 lg. egg
1 scant cup sugar	½ cup milk plus some
½ tsp. salt	1 tsp. vanilla

Put the dry ingredients into a mixer.

In a one-cup measuring cup, melt the margarine.

Break the egg into the melted margarine and fill the rest of the cup with milk. Pour the margarine/egg/milk ingredients into the dry ingredients, and add the ½ cup milk.

Add vanilla.

Mix all of the ingredients well. Pour into a well-greased cupcake pan. Bake for 20–25 minutes at 350°.

Enjoy them while they're piping hot!

P.S.: Of course, for those of you who want to be healthier, substitute reduced-fat margarine, egg substitutes, and skim milk.

CHAPTER 5

Who Are You?

To study the way
is to study the self.

To study the self
is to forget the self.

To forget the self
is to be enlightened by all things.

To be enlightened by all things
is to remove the barrier
between self and other.

Eihei Dogen, Zenji
Japanese Tendai monk,
A.D. *1200 (translated by*
Shunryu Suzuki-roshi in
Zen Mind, Beginner's Mind)

H ere are a range of exercises to complete and questions to answer that
will help you to begin the journey of finding out more about who you
are. Because many women have asked me for clues as to what to write,
I have also given examples of what women I have interviewed told me
they liked, as well as some of my own personal examples. Please use these
answers as catalysts for your own thoughts and words. And remember, nothing is "right" or "wrong."

As you will see, I have also provided you with space to note what you *don't like.* This information is just as important as what you *do like.* Defining what does not please you increases the chances for choosing what does. And in the long run you will feel better for it. Many women have told me that they didn't realize they didn't like certain things until they went through this process. They were astounded by the number of things in their everyday lives that were irritating, annoying, or unpleasant. Because they had not noticed or articulated their displeasure before, they were simply putting up with aspects of their lives that they really didn't like.

WHAT DO YOU LIKE, WHAT DO YOU PREFER, WHAT MAKES YOU FEEL GOOD?
Activities

What do you love to do? (For the moment, think of things outside your work. We'll cover the work arena in chapter 7.) In what activities do you find yourself (or remember finding yourself) losing track of time, when the minutes and hours just seem to fly by? What gives you energy or leaves you feeling refreshed? What is fun or interesting or relaxing? Do you like to collect things? Do you like to learn about something? Do you like to cook, ride horses, write poetry, climb mountains, or weave? You might note what you like to do alone and what you like to do with others.

Things I Love to Do	*Things That Turn Me Off*

Aromas

Okay, so this category may sound a little weird. But think about it — aren't some of your fondest memories connected to certain aromas and fragrances? What is your favorite cooking smell? Do you have a special candle fragrance that you like? What about perfumes or flower scents?

One reason I love Thanksgiving and Christmas is that a couple of days before and after, wonderful smells emanate from the kitchen. I also love certain flower scents because they remind me of people that I love — like my grandmother and her wonderful flower garden. One woman told me that the first thing she does every morning is cut open a lemon so that the fresh fragrance flows throughout her kitchen. Other women talked about favorite bath oils or bubble bath flavors. New research about aromas has proven them to have a positive health effect.

The Fragrances *and Aromas I Love*	*The Fragrances* *and Aromas I Dislike*

Art

What kind of art touches your soul? Forget about what is "in," or what is "good," or what other people say they like, or whether someone paid a lot of money for it. If you were to inherit some money and could spend it only on art pieces, what would you want? What makes you feel good the instant you look at it? Who are your favorite artists — painters, craftspeople, photographers, furniture makers, glassmakers, jewelry makers? What kind of architecture is pleasing to you? What kinds of museums or galleries inspire you from the moment you enter them?

Carolyn Owen-Towle, a minister with the Unitarian-Universalist Church, says that beauty and creating beautiful environments is an essential part of her life and work. She is sure that people "get things" through osmosis, and when the environment is beautiful, well kept, and respected, people feel better, stand up straighter, and want to be part of what is going on. Her church is filled with art, and the grounds with beautiful landscaping, especially big beautiful trees.

The Art and Architecture *I'm Drawn To*	*The Art and Architecture* *I Dislike*

The Artists and Architects *I Admire*	*The Artists and Architects* *That I Don't Admire*

Favorite Museums and Galleries	*Museums and Galleries I'm Not Fond Of*

Books

Do you like fiction or nonfiction? Do you like biographies or historical novels or mysteries? Again, don't worry if what you like is not considered "good" literature. If you like it, that's good enough. Who or what do you consult to find your next reading project? Who are some of your favorite authors? Where are some of your favorite places to read? Do you have a favorite bookstore?

As I interviewed women for this book, reading was by far the most favored activity. At the end of the Introductions for parts II and IV, I have listed what many have identified as their favorite nonfiction and fiction books. Interviewees told me that they sought out friends who are avid readers as sources for what to read next. Most have their fiction sources and their nonfiction sources, as well as being fans of *The New York Times Book Review*. Jing Lyman, wife of the former president of the Rockefeller Foundation and president emeritus of Stanford University (and an accomplished person in her own right!), has what she calls her soporifics: a whole bookshelf full of books that she reads over and over again. Jing says that these books are her friends, and a way of completely cutting off from all the things that nag her. She reports that her books are the key to having a good night's sleep.

Favorite Authors and Books	*Authors and Books I Don't Want to Waste Time On*

My Best Book Sources	*NOT Good Book Sources*

Favorite Bookstores	*Bookstores I Dislike*

Favorite Reading Circumstances (time, place, and other accoutrements such as a cat, hot tea, kind of music, fireplace, soft throw pillows, etc.)

Clothing

Most women don't have much time for shopping, so it helps shorten the process of buying clothes if you know what you like and what your "style" is. Do you have a favorite designer or brand name or manufacturer? Which are your favorite kinds of shoes? Do you prefer a particular kind of handbag? Is there a kind of jewelry that just seems most like "you"? What do you feel good in? Are certain stores easier for you to shop at?

In choosing clothing, certainly one goal for many women is to be comfortable. My rule of thumb is this: I want clothes that I look good enough in to not have to think about how I look. After all, when you think you look good and are not self-conscious, you're more likely to be confident and relaxed. Another rule of thumb from one of my interviewees: don't buy *anything* unless you love it! Something that is "less than wonderful" always ends up sitting in your closet for years. So buy and wear what you love.

My Style	**Not My Style at All**
(or name of person whose style you admire)	

Favorite Clothing, Shoes, Handbags, Jewelry, and Designers/Manufacturers	**Clothing, Shoes, Handbags, Jewelry, and Designers/Manufacturers I Dislike**

Favorite Stores and Catalogs	**Stores I Dislike, Catalogs I Discard**

Colors

What are your favorite colors? Which ones feel like you? Are there colors that help you to feel relaxed and at peace? Which colors are turn-offs? Think about how you can begin to make your clothing, home, and work environments more reflective of your color preferences.

A number of years back I looked around at my home and discovered that everything—including the walls, furniture, flooring, dishes, art, even the appliances—was in colors that were my husband's favorites, not mine. None of his choices were the restful, soothing ones I like. So I sat down and wrote out what my favorite colors were and slowly began the process of choosing things in colors that pleased me. Along the way I found that many of my choices pleased my husband as well. So if you were to visit my home today, my husband's favorite colors of red, orange, and yellow are confined to his study and bathroom. What has replaced them in other areas of the house are the colors that feel good to me (and to him): purple, teal, mauve, gray, black, and green.

Colors That I Love	*Colors That Turn Me Off*

Films

What are your favorite kinds of movies? Comedies? Love stories? Action adventures? Who are your favorite actors? Do you have some all-time favorites? What about theaters? Are there one or two that you feel more comfortable in than others?

Jain Malkin, one of the leading health care facility designers in the country, is an Indian movie freak (East Indian, not Native American). Since she finds few if any people who join her in this passion, she says that when an Indian movie arrives in town, she just goes off on her own and has a thoroughly marvelous time. I was really surprised at the number of women who told me that they knew they had become self-confident when they were able to go see a movie on their own. When I'm really tired and need to just "do nothing," one of my favorite things is to empty the house of people, rent a few old Charlie Chan movies, find my two cats, and spend the day under a down quilt watching Charlie solve mysteries.

Favorite Movies and Kinds of Movies	*Movies and Kinds of Movies I Can't Abide*

Favorite Actors and Actresses	*Actors and Actresses I Dislike*

Flowers

If you haven't thought about what flowers you like before, then just take a walk down the street or over to a flower shop or nursery and look. Notice among your choices what your preferred colors are. Begin writing down the names of your favorite flowers, flowering plants, and trees.

Shawn Goodman, an author of books on women's health and eating disorders, told me that having flowers in her home, even when her budget says she can't afford it, is something that makes her feel "vital." She says that she bargains with corner flower-mongers and often picks just one beautiful flower to put in her San Francisco apartment.

Favorite Flowers	*Unfavorite Flowers*

Food, wine, cooking, and restaurants

Instead of drinking any old cup of coffee, why not use your favorite (freshly ground) coffee beans? What kinds of foods do you just love? Name them, and I bet that many are also good for you. What are your favorite fruits, vegetables, meats, dishes, whatever? Do you have an ethnic specialty that pleases you? Do you have a soft drink that you prefer? What about favorite wines? Which are your "pet" cookbooks? Do you have some special recipes that are just "you"? Which are your preferred types of restaurants?

Some of the food passions I heard about include fresh steamed asparagus, chocolate, Martelli penne pasta, marzipan, chocolate, papaya, Häagen-Dazs vanilla ice cream, chocolate, freshly picked anything, and especially in the summer, Babcock peaches and white nectarines. I love my mother's homemade fruit jams, especially her apricot jam.

Favorite Coffees and Teas   *Coffees and Teas I Really Dislike*

Favorite Wines   *Wines I Really Dislike*

Favorite Soft Drinks   *Soft Drinks I Really Dislike*

Favorite Fruits   *Fruits I Really Dislike*

Favorite Vegetables   *Vegetables I Really Dislike*

Favorite Meats   *Meats I Really Dislike*

Favorite Dishes
(e.g., kung poa chicken)   *Dishes I Really Dislike*

Favorite Desserts   *Desserts I Really Dislike*

Favorite Cookbooks   *Cookbooks I Don't Like*

Favorite Restaurants   *Restaurants I Really Dislike*

Magazines

Have you ever thought about which magazines you like? Even if you just skim the pages, which are the ones you are most likely to pick up and read? What kinds of articles most interest you? Do you like light, newsy kinds of magazines? Or literary or business ones? What about fashion magazines? Think about it—if you had a stack of magazines sitting in front of you right now, which ones would you want to look at or read?

Magazines I Love	*Magazines I Don't Want to Read*

Music

This is probably one of the easiest categories to identify. Almost everyone can quickly name her favorite song or kind of music. You can tell a lot about what you like by noticing which buttons on your car radio are fixed. Do you like classical, jazz, soft contemporary, folk music, gospel, country, New Age, or rock and roll? Who are your favorite singers? Composers? Groups? Do you have some favorite songs?

My best friend, Susan Polis Schutz, is an incredible music resource. She not only writes and records her own poetry as music, but she researches a broad range of selections from classical to country western to folk. She is an aficionado of, among others, Jane Oliver, Joan Baez, and Judy Collins; she also loves Sarah Brightman and Andrea Bocelli, as well as Chopin and classical flute. Just as other people are book sources, Susan is my music source.

Favorite Kinds of Music	*Music I Can't Stand*

Favorite Songs or Pieces   *Songs or Pieces I Dislike*

Favorite Singers   *Singers I Dislike*

Favorite Groups   *Groups I Dislike*

Favorite Composers   *Composers I Dislike*

Favorite CDs or Tapes   *CDs or Tapes I Dislike*

Newspapers

Which newspapers do you like? What kinds of articles are the most interesting to you? Think about the different sections of a paper. Which do you
read first? The front page? Sports? Editorial and opinion? Current events
or arts? Travel? Do you have a favorite writer or columnist?

Favorite Newspapers	*Newspapers I Find Boring*

Favorite Newspaper Sections	*Newspaper Sections I Skip*

Favorite Journalists	*Journalists I Dislike*

Obviously, newspapers are not the only way to get information and
news. What is your favorite?

__ Newspapers
__ TV
__ Radio
__ Internet
__ Other

Play

This is an easy category for me to write about now, but very difficult when I was a full-fledged Superwoman. Too many women today don't play enough or at all. Some have even lost the capacity to do it—they haven't a clue as to what they would do with themselves if some time should accidentally creep into their lives. What about you? What is your favorite form of play or amusement?

Among the things the women I spoke with love to do is go to seminars and learn, take long walks, and visit art museums. They adore going to the theater and attending concerts. They seek out ways, times, and people with whom to laugh. Almost everyone said that she needed some time alone.

What's Fun	*What's Not Fun*

Relaxation

Renowned physicians such as Herbert Benson say that regular relaxation is of great benefit to our bodies and minds. Given the amount of stress and tension that women feel today, the expectations we have for ourselves, and the number of responsibilities we have, knowing what relaxes us is of great importance to our everyday and long-term health.

Corporate consultant Pat Zigarmi thinks that Canyon Ranch in Arizona is the best place in the world to relax. For years now social entrepreneur Jing Lyman has gone with her husband, Dick, to a remote island off the coast of Maine (where there is no phone, electricity, or mail, and the boat comes only once a day). Other women prefer going away with a girlfriend for a weekend of talk. Still others talk about meditating, getting massages, and taking a day off from "everyone and everything" to do nothing.

What's Relaxing for Me	*What's Not Relaxing for Me*

While we're on the subject of relaxation, what two or three words can you think of that are calming to you? My favorite word is *solace*.

Calming or Relaxing Words	*Inspiring or Invigorating Words*
1. _____	1. _____
2. _____	2. _____
3. _____	3. _____

Sports and exercise

What's your favorite sport—either as a participant or a spectator? Do you like to run or ski or Rollerblade? Do you have a form of exercising that you prefer? What do you like? What do you enjoy? What do you do?

I grew up in the 1950s, when girls weren't supposed to "sweat." So being physically active is not something I come to easily. I do walk and run now. The most surprising finding of my interviews was that except for a handful of women, no matter the age, virtually everyone extolled the virtues of exercise and tried to do it regularly.

Lily Balian, a retired seventy-something corporate executive, is a good example. She described how exercise has always been a priority because as a woman gets older, to compete in the workplace she needs to pay more attention to her health. At seventy-three she bounces all over the place and is a wonderful testament to taking good care of yourself.

Sports I Enjoy	*Sports I Don't Want to Have Anything to Do With*

Sports I Like to Watch	*Sports I Don't Watch*

Television

This isn't likely to be a politically correct category these days. I think we're all supposed to hate television or at least not admit that we like it. But if you truly like watching certain programs, go for it. What are they? Comedy shows? Nick-at-Nite? Old movies on AMC?

PBS, Discovery, A&E, the History Channel, the Home and Garden Channel, reruns of favorite old shows such as *Mary Tyler Moore,* and old movies seem to be what the women I spoke to like to watch. A surprisingly large number of women love watching the CBS *Sunday Morning* show, especially the last two-minute quiet segment.

TV Shows That I Like	*TV Shows That I Can Live Without*

Topics or causes

What do you really care about? When you get involved, why do you do it? What feels good?

More than any other topic, the one I heard about the most was what's happening with girls in this country. Sure, women worry about their boys, terrorism, violence, diseases such as cancer, diabetes, or AIDS, and certain social issues. But young girls and all their problems were the number-one topic of concern to a great many women I interviewed.

Topics or Causes I Really Care About	*Topics or Causes That Really Bug Me*

Travel and places to get away from the world

What fun it is to contemplate this category. Where in the world would you rather be right now? Is there a place where you yearn to go that is especially good for relaxing and getting away from it all? Which are your favorite vacation spots? Do you have a special getaway place in or near your hometown? How do you like to travel? What kind of vacations are "your kinds of vacations"? What do you like to do? Where would you like to go that you have not been? Do you like action-oriented travel or more relaxing vacations? Do you have a favorite airline or some special hotels or resorts that you prefer?

Fallen Leaf Lake near Lake Tahoe is where I would rather be than any other place in the world. I also love Palo Alto and Pacific Grove, California, Whidbey Island in Washington State, Helsinki, Finland, and the countryside of Denmark. Not that I go to these places very often, but this is where I would spend more time if I could. Iris Goodman, a wonderful photographer, loves going to remote sections of Canada to explore and canoe. A number of women I spoke to schedule time every year at a Catholic or Buddhist monastery. Some women take weekends away with their daughters in New York or Chicago. Most of the women I interviewed loved to travel — *anywhere.* Clearly, that was one of the things that they wished they could do more.

Places That I Love	*Places That I Want to Avoid*

Favorite Kinds of Vacations

NOT Favorite Kinds of Vacations

What I Like to Do While on Vacation

What I Don't Like to Do on Vacation

Favorite Vacation Places

Least Favorite Vacation Places

Favorite Airlines

Airlines I Avoid Like the Plague

Favorite Hotels (B&Bs, inns, etc.)

Hotels I Can Do Without

Other things and activities

Obviously, the above list is not complete, let alone applicable for every person. Are there other categories or specifics that you might want to add? Here is a space to do that.

```



```

I hope that you have found this exercise fun and interesting, but it's more than that. The information you are generating will be very useful to you in making positive things happen, getting what you want, and having more control over your life. In later chapters you'll see how. Now let's move on to a few more self-discovery exercises.

HOW WOULD YOU LIKE TO CHANGE YOUR LIFE?

When I was interviewing women for this book, I asked them dozens and dozens of questions. Almost every interviewee told me that her favorite questions were (1) What would you like to have more of? (2) What would you like to have less of? and (3) Is there anything in your life that you would like to totally eliminate? Because I want you to be able to answer these questions for yourself, without being influenced by others' answers, please take a few minutes to write your responses down.

I'd Like to Have More of
1.
2.
3.
4.
5.

I'd Like to Have Less of
1.
2.
3.
4.
5.

I'd Like to Have No More at All of
1.
2.
3.
4.
5.

Now, what activities, involvements, or organizations are you associated with that you might get rid of? Let's get a little clearer about this: is there anything that you now do out of a sense of obligation or guilt or just because you have always done it in the past? Is there anything you sign up to do or volunteer for but often dread or regret having to do? Do you spend time on anything that irritates you? That bores you? That doesn't feel rewarding? That is numbing? That is less than meaningful?

Some examples of meaningless activities from women I interviewed are: watching television (because their partners want them to); going to see inane movies or staying at them when it becomes apparent that they're bad; belonging to organizations that go on endlessly about stupid, senseless things; volunteering to bake or make anything "from scratch" for school fund-raisers or potlucks when you don't enjoy it and could buy a better alternative; attending a book club whose members are not simpatico with your values; accepting volunteer assignments from your kids' school that have little or nothing to do with direct involvement with your children and their needs and desires; and so on.

Activities That I Want to Eliminate from My Life

PERSONAL PURPOSE IN LIFE

My purpose in life is: to become the best teacher I can; to touch children in a way that ignites that little light inside of them that wants to learn about anything they can get their hands on.

Anna Lane
college freshman

As I said earlier, "the more you know about and are comfortable with yourself, the more you can forget about yourself," and "as you begin to know and take better care of yourself, you will have more energy to give to the people and things you love."

Dr. Kenneth Pelletier, the optimal health expert, says that healthy, contributing, successful individuals are "driven by a deep and abiding sense of purpose . . . which is like a guiding light. They feel like they have a role to fulfill in the universe. This role is their life's true work, and there is no turning back. It is not their egos that motivate them; rather, they feel a personal mission to serve a greater cause."[1]

Pelletier's happy, healthy subjects come from ordinary backgrounds just like yours and mine. They have led extraordinary lives, not because they were born to privilege and advantage, but because they have *learned* over their lifetimes to be the way they are: healthy, content, successful, flexible, creative, competent, self-confident, and increasingly unshakable in their sense of direction and purpose. Most do what they really love and spend time with the people they really care about. You, too, can learn to do this.

What is your purpose in life? In other words, why are you here on this earth, and what are you supposed to do with your own utterly distinctive time, energy, and resources? Not many people know what their purpose is. If you don't know, don't despair. Hopefully, this book will be a catalyst for you to find out.

If you do know your purpose, or some parts of it, write it down here:

My Purpose in Life Is to

_____

> *Nothing contributes so much to tranquilize the mind as a*
> *steady purpose — a point on which the soul may fix its*
> *intellectual eye.*
>
> Mary Wollstonecraft Shelley

WHAT NOW?

The following are some suggestions for how you can begin putting the information you have gathered about yourself to work right now.

Begin choosing things that please you and dumping what doesn't!

From the time you get up in the morning until you fall asleep at night, make as many choices as you can using the information you have just generated.

Do you love fresh orange juice in the morning? Did you know that it takes only one minute and twenty seconds to cut three fresh oranges, hand-juice them, and give yourself one of life's greatest food pleasures? Don't settle for bottled, reconstituted, even frozen juice if what really pleases you is fresh. You can do that.

When in your car, why listen to radio news-tales of the latest crimes and the stupid things that people say and do? Wouldn't your day be a little more pleasant if you listened to your favorite music? If you don't have tapes or CDs of your favorite artists, get on the Internet and order one or two now, often at a discounted price—they'll arrive within a couple of days. Or on your way home from work, take ten minutes—well, maybe fifteen—to stop at the local music shop and buy what pleases you. You'll have hours of listening pleasure.

Just because your phone rings, you don't have to answer it. What if you decided to let the answering machine (or voice mail or a secretary) take your calls? Then you could decide exactly which ones you wanted to return and when. Okay, so you have kids at school whose calls you don't want to miss. Consider getting a pager or a cell phone, or have a phone line installed for very special friends and family use.

And don't forget, when you want a refreshing break, take thirty seconds to send your best friend an e-mail. Take a two-minute break to call your husband just to say hi. You can do that.

What about your environment at work? Is there something you can change (in a matter of minutes) that will make it nicer, prettier, neater, simpler? Look around and evaluate everything you see on a scale from one to ten. If it's a seven or above, keep it. If it's below seven, recycle it, put it away, or dump it.

What will make your office more "you"? Take down that unattractive calendar that a colleague gave you. Just because it's a gift doesn't mean that you're obliged to keep it. Remove those annoying posters that you inherited from a previous employee. Clear out or put away those stacks of papers. Bring in one of your favorite vases to put on your desk. And while you're at it, bring in some of your colorful table mats to put on that credenza that has water stains on it.

Put that ugly metal wastebasket in the closet down the hall, and replace it with the really attractive one you saw in the museum catalog. Buy a grape ivy plant (they're easy to maintain and nearly impossible to kill, even for those of us with yellow thumbs) to put on the windowsill, or buy one long-lasting lovely flower to put on your desk. Remember what Reverend Owen-Towle said about people getting things through osmosis and how when the environment is beautiful, well-kept, and respected . . . you feel better, stand up straighter.

In any and every way you can, act on what you like. Consciously choose. You're going to make choices anyway; why not choose what and who makes you feel good? You can do that!

Confident women know who they are. They have a strong sense of what they like, what they want, what they like to do, and what makes their lives rich and full. What's more, they pursue these things with grace and vigor. Because of their vitality, other people like to be near confident women. But confident women are not reckless with their time or energy; they carefully choose with whom they spend their precious time. And that's what the next chapter is all about.

Take a Break and think about your favorite word. Here is a collection of favorite words from many of the women I interviewed.

FAVORITE WORD BREAK

Solace

Peace

Grace

Joy

Cuddle

Snuggle

Nestle

Peaceful

Soft

Cozy

Chenille

Sunshine

Rain

Giggle

Tranquil

Serene

Calm

Still

Graceful

Elegance

Solitude

Sacred

Wind

Spirit

Wise

Patience

Simplicity

CHAPTER 6

What You Want in Your Friends and Work Colleagues

I am including this "friend" chapter in your self-discovery search because I see many women spending a great deal of time — in person or on the phone — with people whom they do not really like, often at the expense of people whom they do like or having some time alone. Isn't it interesting how often we get involved with women and men who drain us rather than adding to our lives? But we don't have to do that. Remember, you have just as much of a right (and responsibility) to make wise choices in the people with whom you spend time as you do about the choice of activities and work in which you are involved. In fact, your health depends on it.

I urge you to *spend more time with people who are good for you* and *less time with those who are not.* This is a major step in becoming a more confident woman.

MY FAVORITE PEOPLE

Let's begin this process by having you identify your favorite people and why you like them.

Favorite People	Why I Like Them
1.	
2.	
3.	

4.
5.
6.
7.

Now that you have identified some reasons why you like certain people, how about letting them know how you feel? It seems as though we humans often wait until someone is very ill, or in some kind of life-threatening crisis, before we let them know how much we think of them. Why wait for that to happen? Consider saying something nice to special people right now. You could call your favorites, or drop them a note, or even send them an e-mail. You have nothing to lose (and think of the pleasure you will bring) by these simple acts of appreciation and love.

PERSONAL CHARACTERISTICS

Two ways of assessing the quality of our relationships are (1) identifying the personal characteristics we desire (and want to avoid) in people close to us and (2) evaluating how they treat you. As one woman who recently used this inventory said, "It's very helpful for me to identify who I enjoy being with rather than just accepting anybody and everybody who happens to be around. I didn't realize how much I had fallen into spending time with people because that's the way it's always been. Can you imagine, they had just become a habit."

What are some of the positive personal characteristics that you see in good friends and work colleagues or special relatives? Likewise, what are some of the negative characteristics of people about whom you don't feel good?

Here is a list of positive characteristics that will help you to identify what you like about someone. Circle the characteristics that you especially value.

Accepting	Capable	Easygoing
Adventurous	Careful	Emotional
Affectionate	Cheerful	Empathetic
Ambitious	Clever	Energetic
Artistic	Conscientious	Expressive
Assertive	Considerate	Fit
Attractive	Courageous	Flexible
Authentic	Creative	Forgiving
Calm	Dependable	Fulfilled

Gentle	Optimistic	Self-confident
Gracious	Orderly	(Has a) sense of
Helpful	Organized	humor
Honest	Patient	Sociable
Hopeful	Playful	Sophisticated
Independent	Positive	Spontaneous
Informal	Powerful	Spunky
Intelligent	Punctual	Stable
Leisurely	Quiet	Successful
Mature	Resourceful	Talented
Modest	Responsible	Uninhibited
Nurturing	Risk-taking	Unique
Open		

Sometimes it's useful to understand why we spend time with people to whom we might not otherwise be drawn. Do people you like have interests that you share, such as reading books or playing tennis? Have you experienced some common history together, such as having attended the same college or university or having children who attend the same school? Perhaps you come from the same hometown or a similar background. Do your friends like to participate in activities you enjoy? Do you work or volunteer in the same organization? Here is a space for you to identify these reasons:

HOW I LIKE TO BE TREATED BY PEOPLE

How someone actually treats you is the most telling aspect of a friendship. Here are some very important behaviors for you to consider in thinking about your friendships:

Positive Behaviors
- Is she or he caring and respectful of you?
- Is she or he helpful, supportive, or understanding when you need it?
- Is what you do and who you are appreciated?
- Is time taken to be with you?
- Is your relationship reciprocal in terms of talking and listening, giving and receiving?

- Is she or he generous and thoughtful?
- Can you rely on this person? Do you find him or her to be trustworthy?
- Can he or she keep personal confidences?
- Do you feel relaxed with this person?
- Does she or he add to your life? Do the two of you have fun together?

Here now are some negative behaviors to consider:

Negative Behaviors
- Is he or she overly self-involved?
- Is he or she needy or dependent?
- Do you experience this person as continually critical, negative, complaining, or defensive?
- Is he or she prone to irrational or angry outbursts? Are you fearful of him or her?
- Is she or he jealous of you or your relationships with others?
- Does he or she have demanding expectations about how you should behave or treat him or her?
- Is this person untrustworthy or dishonest?
- Does he or she treat you in manipulative or controlling ways?
- Do you feel drained when you're with him or her?
- Do you feel tense and on edge when you are with the person?

Again, there are many other behavioral considerations that you might want to identify. Now identify what is really important to you:

How I Want to Be Treated by Friends and Colleagues	*How I Don't Want to Be Treated by Friends and Colleagues*

In her book *Trusting Ourselves,* author and psychiatrist Dr. Karen Johnson urges women to actively seek relationships and build support networks with nurturing, caring people (including nonromantic friendships with men) who value clear and open communication.[1] She posits that we cannot pick our families, but we can and do pick our friends and our work colleagues.

If you are not spending time with people who care for you and who make you feel good about yourself, you are participating in a negative, unnecessary situation that may be contributing to your diminished confidence, even poor emotional and physical health. It is absolutely imperative that you select and maintain friendships with supportive people who will behave in loving and honest ways.

QUALITY MEN

Characteristics I want in my partner or spouse

There is no choice more important to any woman than the choice of the person with whom she will spend her life. Yet many women end up falling in love with or going into relationships with men who are not good for them. How can we avoid the "bad guys" and increase our chances of finding the "good guys"?

Karen Johnson says that to begin with, we should "first look for our mate among our good friends." Or if we already have a mate, measure our current happiness by asking ourselves the following question: "If I weren't married to him, would I choose him to be one of my best friends?"

Dr. Johnson emphatically declares that if there are specific things that you want in a partner, look for someone who already has those characteristics, because "even the power of love cannot create what is not there."

In the space provided, write out the characteristics you would like to have in a partner. If you have difficulty getting started, go back to the "Personal Characteristics" section.

Positive Personal Characteristics I Want in a Partner	*Negative Personal Characteristics I Want to Avoid in a Partner*

How I want to be treated by my partner or spouse

Certainly, you will want to be aware of all of the behaviors, positive and negative, listed in the "How I Like to Be Treated by People" section. However, there are other special behaviors that you might want to consider. (If you are currently with a man, replace the word *will* with *does*.)

Ask yourself the following questions:

- Will he support my identifying and meeting my own interests and desires as well as be aware of his?
- Will he encourage me to be "me," accepting my body and soul rather than wanting me to be some idealized version of someone else?
- Will he not confuse nurturing and loving me with sexual activity?
- Will his actions match his words when he says that he really cares about me?
- Will he take equal responsibility for our relationship?
- Will he take an active interest and responsibility for raising our children both in words and in actions?
- Will he participate willingly in the household and not expect me to pick up after him?
- Will he consult (rather than tell or inform) me about decisions that affect me (including such issues as visiting his family, inviting people to dinner, or buying a new car)?[2]

How I Want to Be Treated by My Partner	*How I Don't Want to Be Treated by My Partner (Unacceptable Behaviors)*

It goes without saying that these same questions apply if you are in a same-sex relationship.

WHAT NOW?

Now that you have generated all of this information, here are some ways that you might use it.

Spend more time with people who are good for you

How much time do you spend with the people you really care about? If your answer is "not enough," then change that situation right now. Here are some things you might do:

- Let your behavior be the barometer of your care. Don't just say it— make sure that significant time is carved out for people you love. One way of doing this is by *scheduling regular time.* (That means actually putting the

time in your calendar and not letting anybody or anything get in its way.)
Examples:
- – Send your best friend an e-mail every night.
- – Have dinner out with your husband every Friday.
- – Send your godmother a note twice a week.
- – Take a couple of hours every Sunday to have time alone with your son or daughter.
- – Meet your favorite work colleague for coffee twice a month.

• Another way of carving out time for special people is to *include them in some of your activities.* Examples:
- – Invite your significant other to join you on a business trip (especially if it's in a great place).
- – See about getting some of your best friends appointed to professional or volunteer committees or boards that you're on.
- – Ask your daughter to join you on your regular exercise walks.
- – If you have to go to another city for a meeting, invite a friend to join you for the drive. (Go to your meeting, and let her do what she likes.)
- – Ask your parents to get tickets for a concert series the same night you have them.

• Finally, *find creative ways of spending time with people you care about.* Examples:
- – Some of my friends and I have what we call e-mail Humor Breaks. When we find something amusing, we type it up (or copy it) and send it along to our favorite people. It's wonderful to get a laugh in the middle of an otherwise mundane day.
- – Take regular yearly vacations with your best friends. (Among the women I interviewed, one goes fly-fishing, another goes on a weekend health retreat.)
- – Hold a yearly slumber party (one night or even a long weekend) for your friends.
- – Take a mental health day from work, and have your daughter or son do the same from school. (Will they love that!)
- – Gather your best friends, bake cookies all day, and then take them to an old people's home.

Spend less time with people who are not good for you— even if you are related or married to them

Not-Very-Important Friends
Let's first deal with the easy ones: people you want to eliminate from your life, or spend much less time with, who are not family or old friends.

This is very simple. Stop saying yes to them when they invite you. You don't have to be rude. You can stop calling them, stop returning their calls, and eventually they will get the message. You might even garner the courage to tell someone directly that you are sorry, but you just don't want to (or don't have the time to) spend time with them right now or anymore. The most important thing is your acknowledging that you have a right to eliminate or spend less time with these not-very-important friends.

Family Members

Now let's move on to the more difficult area of spending less time with not-so-favorite or difficult family members. Obviously you don't want to cause problems by completely eliminating them from your life (although that might be appropriate if the person is purposely difficult or nasty). Again, you don't have to be rude: setting limits is often an uncomfortable but necessary action. One thing you can do is take control of how much time you spend with a family member and control the circumstances of the visit.

For example, rather than being on twenty-four-hour call to someone, set up a regularly scheduled time to call or see him or her or them. Let them know that you will be available then and for how long (and, of course, for emergencies). If they violate your "rule," then gently remind them and take measures to limit their access through the use of an answering machine and such.

Here is how one woman, a patient of mine, handled her needy mother. Sara was always complaining to me about how her mother called her every day right before she went to work, phoning her at the very moment she was about to leave the house. Irritatingly, her mother also called her at work two, three, or four times a day.

To solve this problem, I suggested Sara do the following. She should tell her mother that keeping in touch was very important to her. She should say that "to insure that they keep in touch," she was going to (1) briefly check in with her mother every morning as soon as she got to work, and also (2) set aside fifteen minutes every night around nine o'clock to call her mother. Sara liked that idea and added that going to church with her mother on Sunday mornings was something she wanted to do.

Next I suggested that Sara ask her mother not to call her at home in the morning (explaining that it made her late for work—which was the truth). She should ask her mother, with the exception of real emergencies, not to call her at work because her supervisor did not like employees to have a lot of personal calls (also the truth).

Sara told me that initially her mother was unhappy about not having the freedom to call her anytime. Eventually, however, after quite a few firm yet caring reminders, Mom adapted. Her mother even seemed to like having a schedule she could count on. Mom also liked having Sara's quality attention, which happened a lot more under the new system than it had with the free-for-all one before.

Older parents frequently call a lot because they are needy or bored or just want to feel connected to their children. Their needs are not met if they encounter distracted, busy, unresponsive people. When this happens, they often leave conversations feeling even needier, which causes them to want to call again, and the negative cycle goes on and on. Sara found that it's much better to routinize quality time with a parent.

Old Friends and/or Work Colleagues

Here are suggestions for what to do with less-than-favorite old friends and/or work colleagues who persist in wanting more of your time than you care to give.

One effective way of spending less time is to suggest that you get together at a specific time. For example, you might say to an old friend: "Since we seem to have such a hard time seeing each other, how about if we make an appointment for coffee at least a couple of times during the next few months?" or "I'd like to spend some time with you. Given our busy schedules, how about if I coordinate getting tickets for us for a couple of the summer music concerts?"

Another strategy might be to let someone know when you are available. For example, you might say to a coworker, "You know, fifteen minutes right before lunch on Mondays is the best time for me to talk. Is that good for you?" Then set a specific, limited amount of time to do the work or have the conversation you need.

Find and keep your soul mates

For some women, the issue is not about deciding which friends are most important but, rather, a lack of people with whom to spend quality time. Whether you are new to a community or have been neglectful of the friend part of your life, one of the best ways of finding soul mates is to start with your own interests and passions. What did you identify in chapter 5 that you love to do? Begin with those things, which might be hiking or reading or traveling or cooking or investing or gardening.

Often a place to find soul mates is a group composed of people who love to do what you love. Sometimes you need to try out a number of groups before you find a good fit, but don't give up. Keep looking and sorting out the good from the poor or the mediocre. Whether you are wanting female or male companionship, doing things with people is always an easier way to get to know them than engaging in the difficult chitchat route of cock-tail parties, singles dances, and the like.

Another way to find soul mates is to get reconnected with old friends. Particularly if you live near where you grew up or went to college, try get-ting in touch with people you knew well, even if it was a long time ago. What happened to that best friend from the fourth grade? What about your dear roommate from your freshman year in college? You might find that you have more in common now than when you knew one another many years ago. Of course, you might not, but you never know. Since you have already shared some history with them, old friends are a wonderful source of new friendships.

———

Some confident women have many good friends, while others choose to have just a few. But all confident women have at least one person whom they can call "my best friend." With these friends they are likely to experi-ence what Dinah Maria Mulock Craik has so aptly captured as the essence of friendship:

> *Oh, the comfort—the inexpressible comfort of feeling safe with a person—having neither to weigh thoughts nor measure words, but pouring them all right out, just as they are, chaff and grain together; certain that a faithful hand will take and sift them, keep what is worth keeping and then with the breath of kindness blow the rest away.*[3]

Special people are one of life's greatest gifts. When I asked women what they liked to do with their special friends and relatives, here is some of what they said.

THINGS TO DO WITH SPECIAL PEOPLE BREAK

Go away for a few days to do what you both (or all) like:
talk, read, shop, sunbathe, walk, watch old movies,
fly-fish, ski. • Send e-mails back and forth. •
Exchange ideas and solutions. • Send flowers for no
reason at all. • Go to a day, week, month spa. •
Attend a lecture, class, concert, whatever. • Plan a trip
together. • Have a surprise birthday, anniversary, no-
reason-at-all party. • Give an airline upgrade to first class
for a special trip. • Cook together. • Have a slumber
party. • Get together for a lingering cup of coffee or tea. •
Write a long letter. • Bring over homemade something
when he/she is sick. • Introduce her/him to other
special people. • Send her your favorite quote. • Love
and appreciate her/his children. • Put together a
scrapbook of photos, mementos, things you share. •
Take him/her for a surprise balloon ride. • Go to
a museum. • Take her/him to a park and feed the
ducks. • Go to a great play. • Do something that
neither of you has done before. • Buy him/her a
wonderful children's book. • Send her/him a list of the
ways that she/he is special. • Be there to laugh when
she/he is feeling down or blue. • Send a really silly
gift. • Rent and watch an evening's worth of great
comedy videos. • Trade childhood stories. • Nominate
him/her for an award. • Declare her/his birthday a
national holiday. • Kidnap her/him from work for a day
(having made all of the appropriate arrangements for work,
child care, etc.). • Watch old Doris Day movies on a
wintry Sunday afternoon (or Katharine Hepburn). •
Dedicate a book, a song, a poem to him/her. •
Create a new tradition.

CHAPTER 7

What You Want from Work

To love what you do and feel that it matters — how could anything be more fun?

Katharine Graham

A s a former director of adult career counseling and reentry programs for the University of California, San Diego, and for many years in private practice having helped women make satisfying career choices, I know that the first step in a proper career search is to take an inventory of yourself. People who have self-knowledge are more likely to create a work life that they like and thoroughly enjoy, if not completely love. Research also shows that people tend to be more successful in their work if they choose a job or career based on who they are rather than simply jumping at the first opportunity.

A complete career search involves (1) gathering information about one's interests, needs, wants, and preferences, as well as skills, abilities, and experience. Next (2) this information is matched with what is "out there" in terms of specific jobs and or career fields — often with the help of a career counselor, Internet resources, or even the old-fashioned way: career decision-making books. This matching usually leads a career searcher (3) to identify some tentative job or career choices, which can best be explored by talking with people who work in the field. The next step is (4) to identify how to prepare for a chosen field or find out what's needed to get a more satisfying job. Finally, the last step is (5) to develop an action plan for choosing a specific job or career and/or getting the position you want.

This chapter does not offer a complete career decision-making process. Whole books have been written about this topic. Is there anyone who hasn't heard about Richard Nelson Bolles's best-selling guide, *What Color Is Your*

Parachute? It's the Bible of career choosing. If you want to go through a complete career search, then get that book, and do everything he tells you to do. What we are going to deal with in this chapter is a continuation of your self-discovery process; that is, gathering more information about your preferences, likes, wants, and desires in terms of the work world. This, too, is an integral part of who you are.

I'd like you to know what *you* want from your work, even if you can articulate that only in disparate pieces. Knowing what you like and don't like will be useful in figuring out how to make your work more meaningful, whether you are the president of your own company or an unpaid volunteer. If the outcome of this information gathering is nothing more than getting a little closer to what you want, then it will be well worth your time. After all, if you don't know what you want in a job or career, you have little chance of getting it. And unless you're incredibly lucky, no one else is going to get it for you.

What do you want in or from your work? What do you like to do? What interests you? What content, products, or services are you drawn to? What kinds of environments and people please you? These are the kinds of questions I always ask new clients.

> *Find out what you like doing best,*
> *And get someone to pay you for doing it.*
> Katherine Whitehorn

WORK SATISFACTION

Sometimes the best way to figure out what you want from your work is to evaluate what you have now. Let's do that.

On a scale from 1 to 10 (1 being the lowest and 10 being the highest), how happy are you with your current work situation? _____

What are the positives of your job?

What are the negatives of your job?

What can you do about the negatives?

Finding a job or career that matches your interests and talents may take some work. Probably no one has a "perfect" job or career. But you can begin making choices that will get you closer and closer to it.

Most people are not able to articulate at the drop of a hat what they want in their work. So the next best thing is to identify some component parts of what you'd like to be or do. The remainder of this chapter is an opportunity for you to identify those component parts.

PEOPLE CONSIDERATIONS

There are few factors more important in your work life than the people with whom you work every day. What types of people do you like, and what types do you want to steer clear of? As I have spoken with women about this, many have said that what they want in friends is often not what they look for in work colleagues. While it might be great to spend some of your free time with a flamboyant "nutcake," she may not be the one you want to depend on to meet a project deadline. While a sweet, nurturing "pussycat" person might be a perfect weekend playmate, you may not want to have her handle a difficult client. If you have trouble coming up with words to describe different people types, go back to the list in chapter 6.

Here is an example of what I am talking about. Lisa is a free-spirited graphics designer who likes an orderly yet artistic work environment; she hates conflict, but enjoys working with folks with all kinds of ideas (so long as they are not rigid). She likes to hang out with positive, health-oriented people. Her "people likes and dislikes" lists look like this:

Types of People I Want to Work With	*Types of People I Want to Avoid*
Artistic, calm, considerate, creative, easygoing, fit, helpful, independent, orderly, playful, sense of humor, spontaneous, responsible	Critical, lazy, unimaginative, irresponsible, unhealthy (e.g., smokers), negative, messy, whiners,controllers, unreliable, deadly serious, bottom-liners, uptight workaholics, nit-pickers

Here is a place for you to identify your people preferences:

Types of People I Want to Work With	*Types of People I Definitely Don't Want to Work With*

SALARY CONSIDERATIONS

How much money you earn from doing your work is another important consideration. For some, it is a major factor; for others, it's secondary. How important is your salary to you? On a scale from 1 to 10 (1 being not important and 10 being the most important), compared to other work factors, how important is the amount of your salary: _____

What Kind of Salary Do You Want to Earn?
Now: _____
5 years from now: _____
At the end of your career: _____

FAMILY CONSIDERATIONS

If you have a partner or are married; if you have (or are planning to have) a family; if you are a single parent; or if you have elderly parents for whom you have responsibilities, there are probably some important work considerations that you want to address. Here are a few to consider.

Preferences with Regard to
Hours, Telecommuting, and Home Office Options

Amount of Vacation Time

Work Location

Amount of Travel Required

Sick Leave Options for Self, Children, and Other Family Members

Child Care on Work Site or Company Support for It

Attitude of Organization Toward Your Role as a Parent

Other Considerations

WHAT I LIKE TO DO

What kinds of work activities do you enjoy? What is interesting, fun, or stimulating? On the other hand, what activities do you know you just can't abide? Here are thirty general categories of work activities to help you articulate what you like and don't like to do. Circle any that you like, and put a check mark next to those that you really want to avoid.

Work Activities
1. Advertising, Marketing, and Public Relations
    Plan and develop
    Form relationships
    Write
    Prepare and coordinate development of materials
    Work with mass media
    Work with printers, editors, producers
    Speak
    Other:
2. Animal Care
    Breed and raise animals
    Groom animals
    Train animals
    Show animals
    Provide health care for animals
    Other:

3. Art

    Design or produce art, graphic art pieces
    Perform in theatrical, movie, or video productions
    Photograph
    Write or produce audio, film, or video pieces
    Write or perform music
    Write books or articles
    Make my environment aesthetically pleasing
    Draw
    Cartoon
    Use computer graphics skills
    Other:

4. Athletics, Agriculture, and Outdoor Activities

    Engage in physical fitness activities
    Engage in competitive sports activities
    Grow flower, fruit, citrus, or vegetable products
    Grow, harvest, or produce agricultural products
    Raise or caretake animals
    Other:

5. Building Design and Aesthetics

    Design buildings
    Design and/or decorate interiors of buildings
    Design landscapes
    Build or construct
    Other:

6. Clerical and Secretarial Work

    Serve as receptionist
    Answer phones
    Keep and file records
    Use computer for various tasks
    Organize office functions
    Other:

7. Communications

    Participate in media productions
    Speak before public
    Speak in foreign languages
    Develop written or other forms of communication
    Other:

8. Creative Work

    Work with my own ideas
    Work with others' ideas
    Other:

9. Data Involvement
   Analyze
   Compute
   Copy, store, retrieve
   Create systems for data
   Evaluate
   Organize
   Research
   Other:
10. Financial Management
   Provide accounting and bookkeeping functions
   Provide banking functions
   Budget
   Forecast
   Invest or counsel investors
   Manage money
   Plan
   Other:
11. Food Preparation and Nutrition
   Plan, prepare, and serve nutritional meals
   Plan and prepare food for people with special needs
   Plan and prepare gourmet foods
   Advise people about weight loss
   Write recipes and cookbooks
   Other:
12. Fund-raising
   Plan fund-raising activities
   Identify goals and objectives for campaigns
   Identify sources of funds
   Administer fund-raising programs
   Raise funds by selling products, staging events, calling on
     individuals
   Raise funds for public campaign
   Manage and work with volunteers
   Other:
13. Health
   Provide health care to patients
   Diagnose and treat illnesses
   Document patient progress
   Engage in preventive health care measures and education
   Recognize patient psychological needs and make referrals
   Keep medical records, make reports

    Counsel
    Other:
14. Human Relations and Personnel
    Consult
    Counsel
    Mediate and resolve conflicts
    Build teams
    Train
    Other:
15. Intellectual/Observational Work
    Learn
    Research
    Teach
    Write
    Other:
16. Investigative and Scientific Work
    Solve problems
    Conduct research
    Write articles
    Write grant proposals
    Edit
    Other:
17. Leadership
    Plan
    Communicate
    Motivate
    Make decisions
    Innovate
    Create policy
    Develop and implement strategic plans
    Evaluate
    Manage crises
    Engage in entrepreneurial activities
    Mentor
    Provide vision
    Other:
18. Legal and Civil Rights
    Identify and provide legal services
    Research legal issues
    Write legal briefs
    Represent clients in court and other venues
    Other:

19. Management
    Set goals
    Communicate
    Manage conflict
    Evaluate
    Organize
    Plan and develop
    Select staff
    Supervise
    Build teams
    Troubleshoot
    Other:
20. Mechanical and Physical Work
    Create
    Operate
    Repair
    Other:
21. Organizational Work
    Compile
    Collect data
    Manage people and information
    Manage office and projects
    Other:
22. Performance
    Act
    Perform as a musician, dancer, etc.
    Perform in radio
    Perform in television
    Produce
    Direct
    Speak
    Write
    Other:
23. Public Relations
    Conceptualize programs
    Plan and develop programs
    Identify target audiences
    Determine appropriate communications means
    Establish contacts with appropriate people
    Write, prepare, coordinate materials
    Other:

24. Public Service
     Fund-raise
     Lead groups
     Organize meetings and projects
     Run for office
     Work on political campaigns
     Work on commissions, committees
     Volunteer for nonprofit or advocacy groups
     Other:
25. Religion and Social Service
     Advise
     Minister to
     Assist
     Counsel
     Problem-solve
     Work with other people and agencies
     Write
     Speak
     Other:
26. Retail
     Sell products
     Other:
27. Sales
     Sell products or services
     Provide and maintain customer relations
     Market
     Promote
     Write reports
     Other:
28. Teaching and Training
     Counsel
     Facilitate groups
     Instruct
     Provide in-service training
     Provide feedback
     Teach
     Write instructional materials
     Other:
29. Telecommunications
     Understand and utilize computers
     Consult

Teach
Utilize Internet resources
Conduct research
Have familiarity with software and hardware
Program
Other:
30. Writing, Editing, and Publishing
Write books and other written products
Edit
Proofread
Publish
Market
Sell
Promote
Other:

Write down what you have learned.

What I Like to Do	*What I Want to Avoid*

THE CONTENT, PRODUCTS, OR SERVICES THAT INTEREST ME

Content

What topics interest you? When you read a magazine or newspaper, which stories jump out and capture your attention? When you go into a library or bookstore, are you drawn to certain subject areas? Perhaps these content areas can help you choose a job or career. Could there be anything more delightful than to have someone pay you to be involved with what you love?

The following is a very broad list of academic content areas that you can use as a first step in identifying what interests you. Circle any that appeal to you, whether or not you know anything about them or have acquired skills or knowledge in them. This time don't worry about noting what you don't like. Those areas about which you feel neutral or that you dislike will simply be the content areas that you don't circle.

Content Areas

Accounting

Agriculture

Allied health

Animal science

Anthropology

Architecture

Art

Art history

Biological sciences

Botany

Business administration (including accounting, banking and finance, economics, hotel management, human resource management, insurance, information systems, international business, investments and securities, labor and industrial relations, marketing, operations research, real estate, small business, sports management, and taxation)

Chemistry

Classics

Communications (including advertising, journalism, public relations, radio and television, motion pictures)

Computer and information technologies

Construction and trades (including carpentry, construction, electricity, masonry, plumbing)

Crafts and design (including ceramics, crafts, textiles, glass, graphic arts, metal and jewelry, printmaking, and theater design)

Criminal justice

Drama and theater

Economics

Education (including adult and continuing education, counseling, curriculum and instruction, international education, school psychology, testing/evaluation/measurement)

Engineering (including aerospace, architectural, bioengineering and biomedical, chemical, civil, computer, electrical, industrial materials, mechanical, mining, and nuclear)

English

Environmental studies (including air pollution, conservation, water and waste management)

Ethnic studies (including African American, American Indian, Asian American, Hispanic American, Islamic, and Jewish)

Film

Fine arts (including art conservation, art history and appreciation, drawing, fashion design, fine arts, painting, photography, and sculpture)

Food sciences

Geography

Geology

Health sciences (including administration, chiropractic, dental, emergency, gerontology, occupational therapy, optometry, pharmacy, physical therapy, podiatry, population and family planning, public health, speech pathology, and sports medicine)

History

Home economics

Horticulture

Hotel management

International studies

Journalism

Landscape architecture

Languages

Law

Life sciences (including anatomy, biomedical/technological science, ecology, embryology, marine biology, neurosciences, nutritional sciences)

Linguistics

Literature (including creative writing, linguistics, rhetoric, speech, and debate)

Marketing (including fashion, hospitality, insurance, personal services, retailing tourism, transportation, and travel)

Mathematics

Mechanics and repair

Military science

Music (including appreciation, composition, history, music therapy, performance, and theory)

Nursing

Nutrition

Parks and recreation

Philosophy

Physical sciences (including astronomy, astrophysics, earth sciences, oceanography, planetary science)

Physics

Political science

Psychology

Public affairs (including community services, public administration, public policy, public utilities, social work)

Radio and television studies

Religion and theology

Social sciences
Social work
Sociology
Speech and rhetoric
Statistics
Transportation
Visual and performing arts (including animation, cinematography and
   film, dance, dramatic arts, musical theater, photography, video)
Zoology

In the space provided, identify the ten content areas — broad or specific — that most interest you. If you have circled more than ten, then narrow your choices down. If you have less than ten, that's just fine.

The Ten Content Areas That Really Turn Me On
1.
2.
3.
4.
5.
6.
7.
8.
9.
10.

Products

What kinds of products interest you? What do you want to know more
about or spend time doing? What attracts you? Perhaps the following lists
will help you answer these questions. If you were walking down a city street
or a shopping mall, what kinds of stores would you go into? What kinds of
catalogs do you enjoy looking at? One way of getting exposure to a lot of
products is to simply look in the yellow pages of a telephone book. Keep
pushing yourself for specificity.

Products

Animal—birds and reptiles	Furniture
Antiques	Games
Arts and craft products	Gardening products—vegetables and fruits
Athletic and fitness equipment	Gift items
Automobiles and auto products	Greeting cards
Baby products	Health products
Beauty products	Hobby items and equipment
Books and other writing products	Holiday and celebration products
Business products	Household furnishings
Camping and outdoor items	Interior design products
Children's items	Internet products
Clothing—apparel and shoes	Jewelry
Adult	Kitchen and garden tools
Children's	Magazines and newspapers
Computers and computer products	Marine, fishing, boating products
Cosmetics and perfume products	Medical products (including pharmaceuticals)
Educational products and materials	Military products
Electronic devices and equipment	Money
Entertainment items and products	Motion picture and film products
Exercise products	Multimedia products
Financial products	Musical instruments
Fine arts—gifts and gallery products	Personal care items
Flowers, plants, and trees	Pets and pet products
Food—bakery, beverage products, and gourmet cooking equipment	Pharmaceuticals
	Sports products
	Stationery
	Toys
	Travel products
	Other:

From the above list and your push for specificity, identify the "things" that you are naturally interested in and those in which you have no interest:

Products That Really Interest Me	*Products I Want to Avoid Like the Plague*

Services

Generally there are two kinds of services: those that deal with products and those that assist people and other living things. If you are interested in the former, go back to the product list and see if you can come up with some services associated with the products that interest you. If you are interested in people and other living things, take a look at the following, and circle any that interest you. Put a check mark next to those that you absolutely want to avoid.

Services

Animal
Architectural and interior
  design
Beauty and personal care
Building
Business
Buying and selling
Communications
Community
Computer and Internet
Consulting
Educational
Emergency
Entertainment and leisure
Exercise and fitness
Family
Financial and banking
Food, catering, and cooking
Government
Home and garden
Information

Investment and banking
Legal
Maintenance and repair
Medical, dental, and health
Multimedia
Personal care and beauty
Psychological
Real estate
Recreational
Religious
Retail
Sales
Shopping
Social services
Teaching, coaching, tutoring
Travel and transportation
Vacation
Writing and editing
Women's
Other:

Take a minute to summarize what you have noted.

Services That Interest Me	*Services That Leave Me Cold*

WORK ENVIRONMENT CONSIDERATIONS

What kind of environments do you like to work in? Here are some factors to help you define what you like and want in a work environment. Once again, circle those that you desire and put a check mark by those that you don't desire.

I want to work

- Indoors, outdoors, or some combination
- Alone, with a few people, with small groups, with large groups, or some combination
- In an old or a new building or at home
- In an environment in which no one knows you, some people know you, many know you, everyone knows you
- In your own office, in your own cubicle, in a large room with many other people around
- In an environment that is neat and tidy, chaotic and messy, organized or disorganized, little activity or constant activity
- In a room or building with or without windows
- In a formal, informal, or mixed atmosphere

People

What kinds of people would you like to work with? Here are some considerations:

Numbers

Individuals
Small groups (1–25 people)
Medium-size groups (25–75 people)
Large groups (over 75 people)
Other:

Ages
  Babies
  School-age children
  Teenagers
  College students
  Twenty-somethings
  Thirty- or forty-somethings
  The middle aged
  The elderly
  People of all ages
  Other:

Gender and Sexual Orientation
  Men
  Women
  Both sexes
  Heterosexuals
  Homosexuals
  All people
  Other:

Class
  Blue collar
  White collar
  Professional
  Executive
  Volunteer
  Homeless or welfare recipient
  Retired
  Unemployed
  Other:

Health Status
  Healthy people
  People with short-term, curable illnesses
  People with long-term, chronic illnesses
  The disabled or handicapped
  People with psychological problems
  People with addictions
  Smokers
  Health and fitness enthusiasts
  Other:

People of a Certain Background
> Cultural
> Socio-economic
> Educational
> Religious
> Political
> Family orientations
> Other:

Take another minute to summarize what you have noted.

People and Environmental Considerations That I Want	*People and Environmental Considerations That I Want to Avoid*

WHAT I KNOW AND CAN DO

Another way of looking at yourself is to identify what you know (that is, your knowledge and expertise in certain content areas, topics, and subject matters) and what you can do (your competencies, talents, skills, and abilities).

Cheryl, a thirty-something married woman, wants to go to law school. Because of her volunteer experience with a local women's group over the past five years, she is an expert on the mental health services available in San Diego. She has also been the group's treasurer and is totally responsible for her family's personal finances. Among the things Cheryl knows about are: public policy relevant to mental health issues, constituencies concerned with mental health, federal and California laws relating to issues of mental health, financial planning, bookkeeping and accounting principles, fundamentals of investing.

These are some of the things that Cheryl says she can do: build relationships with a variety of people and organizations, plan and organize coalitions, obtain financial support for causes and programs, draft legislation, lobby various constituencies, present arguments and evidence to support a position, plan and prepare budgets, maintain financial records, use the computer and computer software including Internet resources.

Here are spaces for you to identify what you know and can do:

What I Know
_____

What I Can Do
_____

MAKING MY LIFE BETTER BALANCED

Outside the job itself, what would make your life easier and better balanced? A husband's (or partner's) greater participation in household maintenance? A husband's (or partner's) greater participation in childrearing? Better or more child care? More outside household or personal assistant help? Exactly what and how much?

What Could I Really Use? Identify Who, What, Where, When, How, and Why
_____

AN IDEAL JOB

Now that you have been gathering information about yourself and thinking about it for a while, let's put it all together. One of the most interesting and useful exercises in gaining self-knowledge about one's work is to answer this question: If I could be (or do) exactly what I wanted to be (or do), what would that be?

For the moment, think of me as your fairy godmother, and I can make anything happen for you. And so I say to you: close your eyes and create a mental picture of your ideal job. Don't worry if it's not complete or perfect. In your mind, paint a picture of what your workplace looks like, including the city, the area, the building, the room, the furniture, and the objects around you. Also paint what you would be doing with your body, hands, and mind and, of course, how much time you would be doing it. Dab in what you would be working on—the content or products or services that have personal meaning to you. Color in who you talk to and work with. You might even add a little section about what you would do when you're not working—leisure or play time to be with family, friends, or alone. Be courageous in your picture. Don't be afraid to dream or desire.

Now write down the details of your dream.

If I Could Do (or Be) Exactly What I Want to Do (or Be), I Would

If you have trouble coming up with a mental picture of an ideal job, sometimes it's useful to go back to what you dreamed of doing when you were a child.

Susan Polis Schutz says that from the time she was five years old until the age of thirteen, she wanted to be "a famous actress." After spending a summer as an apprentice in a summer stock theater in New York when she was thirteen, she realized that she loved the theater but didn't love acting. Another strong interest throughout her childhood was writing. She was always busy putting together stories, essays, articles, and poems. In her teenage years, she decided that she wanted to be a writer. As you probably are aware, she became not only a writer but one of the best-selling poets and authors in the country.

Do you remember your childhood dreams of fame and glory?

What Did I Want to Be "When I Grew Up"?

If you're still having trouble coming up with an ideal job description, I have one more trick left in my career choice bag. Many years ago, as I began thinking about all the things I'm writing in this book, I came upon a question that hit me right in my gut. It was so striking that I wrote it down on a three-by-five card and taped it to the front of my computer. It sits before me even as I write this sentence. This simple question is a piquant reminder of how to stay on track as a confident woman. I hope it helps you to describe or keep on track as to what you want to do with your work life.

If I Knew I Couldn't Fail, or If I Weren't Afraid, What Would I Do?

WHAT NOW?

Hopefully this chapter has served as a catalyst for gaining real insight into what you want from your work. It may have opened up some ideas about developing a new or renewed work direction. Sometimes articulating elements of what you like and want is enough for a person to know what her next career step is going to be. Some people, however, need to get help in taking this information to the next level. In the appendix you will find a bibliography of books and resources to which you can turn for coaching or help.

Knowing who you are helps you to separate yourself from what is false, inauthentic, phony, or trendy. Don't forget this: you are the world's greatest authority on you. Nobody knows better than you what's good for you, what's bad for you, what's healthy for you, and what's not healthy for you. And please don't let anyone persuade or seduce you into doing what you know in your heart is not the right thing for you.

Hey, I think it's time for another Break!

PERSONAL REMINDER BREAK

Not everything needs to be done perfectly; some things shouldn't be done at all.—Natasha Josefowitz

Your time is valuable.

Discipline is remembering what you really want.

Asking for help is a sign of strength.

Housework, if done properly, will surely kill you!—Kathleen Brown

Work smarter, not harder.

Delegate it, buy it, ask for help, or don't do it at all.

Just say no.—Nancy Reagan

Real men pick up after themselves.

An ounce of prevention is worth a pound of cure.

Conflict is inevitable; fighting is a choice.—Ann Wilson Schaef

Superwoman doesn't live here anymore.

CHAPTER 8

What You Want in a Home

In my mind the word *home* can be applied to anything from a dorm room to an apartment to a large residence in the suburbs. Most women are "nesters" who need to create warm, friendly environments for themselves and the people about whom they care — no matter where they find themselves.

Home is where you live right now. In order for you to experience your current living space as a source of comfort and solace, it should reflect who you are, what you like, and your particular "style" (which could be anything from hand-me-down chic to *très* chic).

Your home is one of the few places where you can create pleasure and beauty by simply paying attention to the choices you make. Since, no doubt, you will be buying things for your home from time to time, why not select that which pleases you, or better yet, that which *is* "you"? Surround yourself with the colors, textures, objects, furniture, furnishings, art, books, music, flowers, fragrances, foods, and personal treasures that make *you* feel good. This does not necessarily mean spending a lot of money. I have seen wonderful, loving homes made from the simplest circumstances. It's neither the structure nor the expense of the objects in it that makes a living space a home. Usually your own personal care and touch are what make a home what it is. As Helen Rowland said in *Reflections of a Bachelor Girl*,

"Home" is any four walls that enclose the right person.

If you are sharing your home with someone, needless to say his or her needs and wants can and should be reflected as well. But acknowledging their preferences should not come at the expense of sacrificing your taste or needs. By identifying what you like, you are more likely to choose what pleases you when the time comes for buying new furniture and other things or even a new home itself.

Here are some things to think about as you articulate what you want in a home. Remember, you want to identify what you like and prefer and also what you don't. While you may not be able to act on some things right away—such as changing the locale of where you live—at least you'll have the idea in your head. As I've said before, unless you know what you want, there is little chance of your ever getting it. And if what you want is really important, then you can begin the process of making your dream come true sooner rather than later.

Home Environment

On a scale from 1 to 10, rate how pleasing, nurturing, and self-enhancing your home is: _____
Do you have a room or private space of your own in your home? Yes _____ No _____

If your answer is yes, then you might want to figure out what you can do to make your home or space even more pleasing. If the answer is no, consider how you can create such a space, even if it's only part of a room.

GEOGRAPHIC LOCATION: WHERE IN THE WORLD I WANT TO LIVE

If you could live anyplace in the world, where would that be? In a city or in a suburb? Maybe you want to get away from it all in a small town or even a rural or mountainous area? What do you want to avoid? Don't think about what's realistic or possible right now. *Think about ideal.*

Many people who live in San Diego have come from cold weather places. Yet any number of others have left California because it's "just too crowded." My own sister, Barbara, and her husband are looking for a mountain location to move to permanently. Every chance they have, they take an exploratory trip to see if some newfound location is going to be "it." Some years ago Dr. Iris Litt decided that Carmel was her soul-home. Even though she works at Stanford University in Palo Alto, slowly but surely she's finding ways of spending more and more time in Carmel. Some very fortunate people are able to have it all by living in one place and then having a second getaway home at some other wonderful location. Oh, would that were the case for us all!

Where I Want to Live	*Where I Don't Want to Live*

WEATHER

Do you like one kind of weather, such as that found in Southern California? Or do you prefer living through the variety of seasons that you'll encounter on the East Coast or in the Midwest? Do you like rain? What about snow? Do you yearn for the sun? How do you feel about humidity? What kind of weather pleases you?

Personally I love rain. Maybe it's my Danish genes, but that's not the case for many others. Carol Dressler, president of Dressler Associates, loves the sun. She can't get enough of it. Every extra moment is spent in the desert or in Hawaii. Still, many other women love snow and can't imagine living in a place where there aren't distinct seasons to celebrate.

Weather Conditions *That Please Me*	*Weather Conditions* *That Bother Me*

ARCHITECTURE: HOW I WANT MY HOME TO LOOK

What kind of architecture is pleasing to you? You know, you don't have to own a home to have preferences. Renters have choices too. Have you ever had a dream house in mind? What kinds of design styles are pleasing to you? Obviously different rooms in your home can reflect one or more styles. Are you a modern or postmodern kind of person? Do you prefer a country or a Mediterranean look? Is your dream house made of adobe, wood, glass, concrete, or brick? What about furnishings? Are you attracted to the more traditional? Do you prefer a mixture of things? Is there one style or even two that feels like you? Many of the things you have identified in chapter 5 can be applied here.

Architecture I Like	*Architecture That Annoys Me*

COLORS

How can you begin making your home more reflective of the colors you like?

Colors That I Love	*Colors That Irritate Me*

FLOWERS, BUSHES, SHRUBS, AND TREES

Whether you have a veranda attached to an apartment, or a small side yard by a rented house, or five acres of land, you can still pay attention to and enjoy the "green" parts of your home.

Even when I was a poor struggling student, I always had plants in my room. I can't tell you how many of the women I interviewed told me that having a garden is one of their greatest joys.

Favorite Flowers, Bushes, Shrubs, and Trees	*Not My Favorite Flowers, Bushes, Shrubs, and Trees*

Favorite Landscape Ideas	*What I Don't Want in My Landscaping*

MY FAVORITE THINGS

What things in your home do you love? Do you have a favorite chair or table? Is there a special room that is a true expression of your taste? Do you have objects or art pieces that you especially like? If you don't have what you like, what would you add to meet your heart's desire?

For years I yearned for a big, overstuffed reading chair with fabric as soft as a down quilt. I didn't get it because I thought it was too expensive and not necessary, an extravagance that I didn't deserve. You know the rap. I finally gave myself permission to buy this long-lost reading chair. It fit me perfectly. I selected the softest, most beautiful purple chenille fabric to cover it. It's wonderful. I can't tell you what pleasure it gives me to sit and read in it, even to look at it. It may well be my favorite thing in our house. As I spoke with women about their respective favorite things, I heard about furniture handed down from parents and grandparents, collections ranging from teacups to figurines, a cherished piano, artwork collected on special vacations, and gifts from friends and loved ones.

Favorite Things	*Not My Favorite Things*

THE MOST IMPORTANT ACTIVITIES IN MY HOME

Do you want your home to be a gathering place for your friends or your children's friends and your family? Perhaps you want it to be a serene retreat from the hectic pace of your work world. Do you want it to be your workplace? What purposes do you want it to serve?

I love working at home, but I also adore having people come to the house, particularly my children, their friends, and my special family and friends. It gives me great pleasure to do "little" things to help guests experience the warmth I feel for them. I like having wonderful music playing throughout the house. I always have flowers from my garden placed around. Sometimes it's just one beautiful rose; other times it's a mass of cosmos. Whatever looks good but doesn't take a lot of time is what I do. If there is a slight nip in the air (which in California is probably below 65 degrees), I light a small fire in the fireplace. Grandma's cupcakes (which take five minutes to mix and twenty-five minutes to bake) are a constant fixture, along with the smell of fresh coffee or hot cider. That's what's important to me.

Important Home Activities	*Activities I Want to Avoid at Home*

I know I've said this before, but it particularly applies to what you want in your home. It's much easier to express what you like with photographs clipped (or torn) from magazines, newspapers, or catalogs. Some women I know have a special loose-leaf binder in which they keep clippings. Others have manila folders or files into which they put their finds. If you would like to create one of these filing systems, here are categories to use:

HOUSE IDEAS

ROOMS	FURNITURE	GARDEN AND PATIO IDEAS
Bathrooms	Accessories	Patios
Bedrooms	Appliances	Pools
Children's rooms	Beds	Flowers
Dining room	Chairs	Plants
Family room	Miscellaneous	Trees
Kitchen	Sofas	Vegetable gardens
Living room	Tables	
Storage		
Study/office		
Floor plans		

Again, the purpose of creating this system is to keep reminding yourself of what pleases you and what you like. What's more, it saves time in the long run, because when you do need to make some household choices, it's nice to be able to refer to what you like in your notes and clippings.

> *There are homes you run from, and homes you run to.*
> Laura Cunningham
> *Sleeping Arrangements*

WHAT NOW?

Here are some ideas about how you can follow through with the ideas and information generated in this chapter.

Dump the excess, the negative, the junk

I usually prefer to start with the positive, but when it comes to a home, very often there is so much negative clutter around that there is little or no room to add some positive. So let's start by getting rid of the junk.

Consider giving away or recycling whatever is extraneous, unnecessary, irreparably broken, irritating, ugly, or negative.

Not long ago I was doing some executive coaching with Fran, an accountant, who was looking to make her life "simpler, easier, nicer, better." At the time she was thinking about selling her home because it was "such a bother." Before she did so, she wanted to talk about some of the reasons why she might sell. In discussing what exactly bothered her, we discovered that her house was still dominated by an ex-husband's influence, including his colors, taste, furniture, and organizational style. She had even held on to appliances that he had been reluctant to fix. Also nearly every room was filled with family "heir-junk" that Fran felt duty bound to keep.

In the course of our discussion, we also discovered that Fran was living by some old family rules, including (1) "You should keep and read every section and every story of every newspaper and magazine you get." Holy cow! Can you imagine! (2) "You never throw anything away because someday you might need it. To get rid of things is to be wasteful and foolish and you should feel guilty." Oh my gosh!

I offered Fran the following ideas and suggestions:

As an Adult, One Does Not Necessarily Have to Live by a Parent's Rules.

As strange as it may seem, Fran wasn't aware that she was living by her parents' rules until we had our discussion. She was thrilled by the prospect of giving them up, but she needed help in doing it.

I asked Fran if she thought her parents' Rule 1 made any sense. Would she recommend it to her best friend? Her answer to both questions was "No, no, no, no." So I suggested that Fran immediately start reading only those parts of newspapers and magazines that interested her. If she began to feel guilty, she should say to herself, "Stop! Reading what I want is healthy and a good thing!" We also talked about the merits of throwing away, better yet, recycling, old newspapers and magazines. Guilt in this situation, I pointed out, was nonproductive and unhealthy.

Of Your Possessions, Keep What You Want and Like and Get Rid of What You Don't. Evaluate Your Possessions on a Scoring System from 1 to 10.

Because she did not have a lot of extra time to deal with her parents' rule 2, I suggested that Fran begin assessing her home (the location of which and structure she loved). She should take a couple of hours every weekend to go through the house room by room and decide what she wanted to keep or get fixed and what she wanted to give away, throw away, or recycle.

Because Fran said that she anticipated having a hard time doing this, I gave her my old formula of evaluating things on a score from 1 to 10 (1 being "I hate it," and 10 being "I love it"). Keep anything that is 8 or above, and get rid of anything that is below 8. We then mentally went through one room in her house. I'm happy to report the process was such a success, Fran could hardly wait to get home and do it for real.

You may be interested to know that once Fran went through her house room by room, she decided to keep the house.

From now on, buy or keep only what is at least an 8

You can use the formula that Fran used in order to evaluate what to add to your home, whether it's a coffee cup or some new sheets or a new sofa. Refer to the lists in chapter 5 for your 8s, 9s, and 10s.

You might also want to apply this formula to gifts that people give you. You can be wonderfully gracious about receiving a gift, but you don't have to keep or use it if you don't like it. That's a choice. Of course, there are exceptions to the rule. For example, I would never give away or throw away anything that my little boy or girl gave me.

List what would make your living space more pleasant or more "you"

In the next week make a list of the two or three things that you want to add, replace, or move. It can be an object, a piece of furniture, a sculpture, a book, some music, a flower, a fragrance, or some personal treasure — something that will make *you* feel good. Just do it, and then when you're finished with the list, create another one and do it some more. That's what confident women do.

You've engaged in some pretty hard work in this chapter. I think you deserve another Break.

In the following Aesthetic Break, Dieter Rams identifies how you might approach the design of just about anything in your home, maybe even in your life.

AESTHETIC BREAK

To me, good design means as little design as possible.

Simple is better than complicated.

Quiet is better than confusion.

Quiet is better than loud.

Unobtrusive is better than exciting.

Small is better than large.

Light is better than heavy.

Plain is better than colored.

Harmony is better than divergency.

Well balanced is better than exalted.

Continuity is better than change.

Sparse is better than profuse.

Neutral is better than aggressive.

The obvious is better than that which must be sought.

Few elements are better than many.

A system is better than single elements.

DIETER RAMS
THE SIXTEEN COMMANDMENTS

CHAPTER 9

What Do You Want to Be? To Do? To Have?

As I queried women about what they wanted *more* of in their lives, most really didn't know. If they did know, usually it took the form of "what I need less of," especially *less* worry, *less* stress, and *less* work. Fewer women could answer the "what do I want to do" question, with the exception, again, of wanting to "do less." Even fewer women knew what they wanted to be. Frankly, most women told me that they had never seriously considered any of these questions—they didn't have the time or energy.

Just so you know what others are thinking, here are a few of the most frequent responses:

What I Want to Be	What I Want to Do	What I Want to Have
• A success	• Travel	• More money
• Well-known, famous	• Exercise more	• Financial security
• A writer	• Play more	• A new house
• A mother	• Learn to play the piano, cello, harp	• More time
• A filmmaker	• Work less	• More relaxation
	• Live near the ocean	• An advanced degree
	• Write fiction	• A man in my life
	• Do work that makes a difference	• My own business
	• Worry less	• A new car
		• A vacation home
		• Solitude
		• More of myself

Articulating what we want to be, do, or have is a useful exercise because it helps us set goals and make plans. It also gives us direction and a sense of how to better use our time. It is what confident women do.

From personal experience, I know that fate, other people, and the status quo always prevail unless I say differently. I'm sure you've heard the old adage "If you do what you've always done, you'll be what you've always been." My husband, a clinical psychologist, says it slightly differently: "Insanity is doing the same thing over and over again and expecting a different outcome."

You have already generated much information about your likes, dislikes, wants, and desires. To begin putting some of this information to work, here is a wonderful technique to bring focus to your life. I came upon this when I read Peter McWilliams's *You Can't Afford the Luxury of a Negative Thought.*[1] When I first approached his "10 Steps to Get Anything You Want," I found them not only easy to follow but also eliciting results that really made sense. One by one I followed his directions, and suddenly what I wanted to do and how I wanted to focus my time became crystal clear.

What confidence this gave me! How energized I felt! Immediately I began working on the two or three things that emerged as my major *wants, dos,* and *bes.* I'd like you to feel that same confidence, energy, and power, so the following is my adaptation of McWilliams's formula for finding focus.

WHAT DO YOU WANT TO BE? TO DO? TO HAVE?

Step 1. Gather three-by-five cards

The first thing you need to do is gather a bunch of three-by-five index cards, as many as fifty of them.

Step 2. Get away and brainstorm

Find a quiet, secluded place (such as a library, a room in your house, a table at a favorite café, a bench at a park, or a seat on a plane), and for at least half an hour of uninterrupted time, brainstorm with yourself about all the things that you want to be, do, or have. Do this just for you, not for anybody else. Write down each thought on a separate card, and identify it as a *be* or a *do* or a *have.*

Really important: Don't evaluate what you write down. Don't worry about whether it is realistic or if you can make it happen or how much money it will cost or whom it might affect. Let yourself go. Imagine that you *can* have anything and everything in the world. Exhaust yourself of all wants, needs, desires, goals, even seemingly impossible fantasies. For the first time in your life, be utterly, totally, completely, thoroughly, outrageously selfish. Whatever you do, don't feel guilty. After all, you're just writing things down. You haven't acted on anything yet. Remember, this is just an exercise. Nobody is looking over your shoulder. *You have nothing to lose.*

Step 3. Assign a value

Now go through your cards and assign each one of them a number between 1 and 10 (1 = "I don't really want this at all," 10 = "I want this the most").

For example, I want to write useful books for women (9+), and I want financial security (9). (These first two are obviously biggies.) I want more time for reading and relaxing (6), I want to have a lush, tropical garden (5–6), and I want to have bookcases built in every room of the house (5). (The last two are of medium importance.) I want to have a getaway home (3), and I want to learn how to develop a handwriting style like architects have (1). (These last wants are not strong at all.)

Don't be surprised if some cards have low numbers. After all, if you really wrote everything down without thinking too deeply about the implications, undoubtedly there will be some things that you don't really want at all. Look at the last statement in the above paragraph: "I want to learn how to develop a handwriting style like architects have." While I would love to be able to do that, do I really want to take the time to learn? No. Ergo, I give this want a 1.

Step 4. Select the ten most important cards

Now go back to your cards and pull out all of the 10s, whether they are *bes, dos,* or *haves.* If you have less than ten 10s, then add in 9s. If you don't have ten 9s and 10s, then go down to your 8s and 7s, until you have a total of ten cards before you.

Step 5. Rank the cards

Once you have your ten cards, order them by how important they are to you. The top card should be your most important; the next card the next most important, and so on. Continue doing this until the cards are ordered from most important to least important. Write down what your cards say in the following form.

Wants	Be	Do	Have
1.			
2.			
3.			
4.			
5.			
6.			
7.			
8.			
9.			
10.			

Note how many *bes*, *dos*, and *haves* there are. You might find the result quite interesting.

You now have before you what you really want to be, do, or have. The next step is to take the top one, two, or three and begin to make them a reality. I'll show you how to do that later in this chapter.

Don't worry about whether this list will endure—it is not meant to be cast in stone. No doubt it will change with time and life circumstances. You can repeat the process anytime and as frequently as makes sense. You can even do it again right now if you want. Also, as your wants come true, cross them off with great pleasure and add other more up-to-date ones.

Step 6. Do a double-check

Before you act on your top wants, you might like to see how two women dealt with their list. Let's take the real-life desires of two women, Ellen and Susan, as examples. Ellen is a forty-two-year-old management consultant from Seattle who is married and has two young children. In going through the above exercise, Ellen's top card (a 9++) says that what she wants most in life is to write. Susan is a single twenty-seven-year-old Chinese American who currently works as a research associate for a biotech firm in the Bay Area. Susan's top card (8–9) says she wants to go back to school to get a Ph.D.

First Check—Truth

Do I *really* want this, or is it a *should, must,* or *have-to* of mine or someone else's? Is anyone pressuring me to do it?

ELLEN
*When Ellen asked herself, "Do I really want to write?" she wasn't sur-
prised by her answer—a resounding "YES! That's what I want to do*

more than anything else in the world." When she asked herself the second question, "Is this a should of my own or someone else's?" there wasn't a smidgen of should, must, or have-to in her response. On the contrary, many of her family and friends had not been all that supportive of her writing aspirations, so the desire was completely self-motivated.

Susan

When Susan asked herself, "Do I really want to go back to school? Is this something I want to do or is it something I think I should do?" she really thought about it. Going back to school had become a foregone conclusion, something she was always going to do. She realized that at some level, getting a Ph.D. was a should.

So she moved on to the next question: "Is this mine or someone else's idea?" She answered the question by acknowledging that "part of me wanted to get a Ph.D., but another part felt hesitant." So she pushed herself to assess where the idea of getting a Ph.D. had come from. As she thought about it, she realized that ever since she could remember, her parents had talked about her getting a Ph.D. "someday." She recalled comments stretching all the way back to her grammar school days. Susan concluded that even though she had thought going back to school was a high priority, on second look, she wasn't sure.

Second Check—Feasibility
Is what I want realistically available to me? Can I make it happen?

Ellen

As Ellen asked herself, "Is writing something that is realistically available to me?" once again she answered the question with a resounding "Yes!" Although not at a professional level, Ellen has spent much of her life writing and editing. She is also an avid reader, which is often a prerequisite for being a good writer. To the question "Can I make it happen?" again the answer was yes. While some people who want to write only talk about it, Ellen actually does it, almost every day. She then asked herself another critical question: "Can I make this happen for real? Can I get published?" While she was less sure, she knew that she would do everything she could to make it a yes.

Susan

Susan asked herself, "Is going back to school something that is realistically available to me?" Since science had been her major in col-

*lege and getting a Ph.D. in biology her goal, she was pretty sure that
she could answer yes. Susan then asked herself the second question,
"Can I make it happen?" Since she was unsure of her motivation,
Susan decided that she couldn't realistically give an unequivocal yes.*

Third Check—Commitment

Am I willing to find out what is needed to make this happen? Am I willing
to do what is required?

Wanting something can be different from being willing to go through
the steps to actually achieve it. The first step to making something happen
is to be very specific about what you want.

The second step is to do enough research—on your own and with the
help of others—to determine all the steps necessary to get from the statement of your goal to its actual accomplishment.

The third and final step in making something happen is to figure out
whether you're willing to do the necessary work to accomplish what you
want.

ELLEN

*Because writing a book is Ellen's passion, she could easily say yes to
the question "Am I willing to find out what is needed to make this
happen?" While initially she didn't know about everything involved
in writing a novel, let alone getting it published, she decided that
she would leave no stone unturned in finding out. Second, she knew
that she was willing to do whatever was required to make her dream
happen. Statistically, she understood that the chances of actually
getting published were not great, but the negative numbers didn't
deter her. One way or another she was determined to make it happen. Her double-checking left her even more determined to carry on
with the desire to write.*

SUSAN

*Because Susan was not sure about her motivation, she decided that
finding out what was involved in getting into a Ph.D. program was
a useful step in determining whether she wanted to do it. In researching the various programs, she found out that she would have to take
more undergraduate science courses in order to be a serious candi-
date for the best ones. Because it had been almost ten years since she
had taken the SAT, and six years since she had graduated from college, she realized that she would probably need to take a Graduate
Record Exam preparation course in order to score well on the GRE.*

Finally, she confronted some sticky practical issues in going back to school: (1) giving up a job in a company that she really liked, and (2) possibly having to leave the San Francisco Bay Area, a place that she loved and where her current serious boyfriend was firmly settled. After some serious thought, she decided that all of the above factors were enough for her to say no to the second question, "Am I willing to do what is required to go back to school?" The job of double-checking her top goal was done. She decided not to go back to school. After going through the "What Do You Want . . ." exercise again, her top goal became to take the next year to find a career goal that really met all of her needs, wants, and desires.

We'll leave Susan now and go back to Ellen. Given that Ellen is very clear about what she wants, let's see what steps she can take that will make her desire to become a successful fiction writer a reality.

SEVEN STEPS TO GET WHAT YOU REALLY WANT: AN ACTION PLAN

Step 1. Be very specific

The first step to getting what you want is to describe it in terms of what, who, when, where, and how (or how much).

This is how Ellen described what she wanted:

I (who) *want to spend at least two hours every day* (when) *in a room of my own* (where) *writing a book on the order of a Jane Smiley, Alice Walker, or Rebecca Wells* (what) *novel that touches women readers with slices of life that have real meaning to them* (how).

I *also want to find a first-rate agent who will sell my book to a publishing house that really loves it.*

Step 2. Visualize

The second step in getting what you want is to be able to (literally and figuratively) see, hear, feel, taste, and touch what it's all about. It's especially important to have a clear visual image of what you want to be, do, or have. To gain one, you might collect examples of what you want (in Ellen's case, favorite books), or draw pictures of what you want (before she put it together, Ellen drew up a number of sketches of her writing room), or cut out pictures of it (magazines, newspapers, and even catalogs are good resources). If you're not exactly sure of what you want, identify component parts or pieces.

To visualize what she wanted, Ellen wrote:

In our house, I want to create a room of my own that is filled with all of my favorite books and other resources I need to write the book. In that room I want to have a CD player so that I can play wonderful soothing music as I write. I also want a comfortable reading chair, a really good computer, a printer, and plenty of book and table space to spread my things about.

Once the book is published, I see myself going to universities and bookstores on a speaking tour so that I can talk with readers, especially young women.

While Ellen's picture is not complete, it's a beginning. From this image she can begin making time, space, and other circumstances more and more of a reality.

Step 3. Become totally focused

The third step in getting what you want is to make this goal your major, overriding activity and don't let anything or anyone get in your way. Become obsessed with getting or achieving what you want. Too often women let everyday chores and errands, other people's desires and needs, ongoing commitments, and just plain Life get in the way of their doing what they want. *Don't let this happen.* If you want something enough, then you have to make it happen. "Being possessed" doesn't have to last forever, just until you get it. That's what it takes.

This is what Ellen did:

Ellen took her date book and literally crossed out two hours every day (except for Sundays) for six months and promised herself that with the exception of real emergencies (which did not include phone calls, requests for help, drop-in visitors, or others' pleas for time or energy), she would not let anything or anyone get in the way of her writing. She promised herself to say no to virtually all invitations to do anything, even good things. She postponed all volunteer commitments for those six months. She also let her friends and family know what she was doing.

Step 4. Be positive

The fourth step in getting what you want is to be positive and enjoy what you do. Think about all the satisfactions of doing it, not the difficulties (although there will be those too). Be convinced of your future success. Give up all activities and all attitudes that will impede your progress.

Ellen's positive focus included the following:

During previous attempts to write, Ellen discovered that finding time to write was an impossibility. She let everything get in her way. She would mull around in her head all the other aspects of her life that she needed to get settled first — money saved, children more advanced in school, the house finished, the closets and garage cleaned out, et cetera — before she started to pursue what she wanted. She often put herself down and felt discouraged. Her new positive approach was to be very active and enthusiastic. For example, the first thing she did in the morning was talk to herself about how excited she was about doing her writing that day.

In the "old days," whenever Ellen hit a roadblock, she would just give up. Now she would find ways to overcome the problem, often seeking out ideas from others about how to effectively deal with whatever threatened or impeded her. On down days she would say to herself, "Even if I'm not accomplishing a lot today, I'm still doing something. Everybody hits a wall sometime. It won't last forever. Tomorrow will be better."

Step 5. Develop a plan of action with due dates

The fifth step in getting what you want is to develop an action plan, which is really nothing more than a series of "to do" lists with due dates attached to the items.

Ellen's job was neither simple nor easy. Her action plan went something like this:

She first determined there were three big "to do's": (1) write the book, (2) find a literary agent who would be successful in getting her a publisher, and (3) get all the other parts of her life organized so that she could do 1 and 2.

To deal with her first "to do," "write the book," Ellen wrote out the following list:

1. *Put together writing room.*
   a. *Clear out extra bedroom.*
   b. *Buy writing table. Bring in good chair from family room.*
   c. *Bring in bookcases from garage and office.*
   d. *Bring extra computer home from office.*
   e. *Buy printer.*
   f. *Get CD player.*
2. *Find out what the best books on fiction writing are, and read them.*
   a. *Call or visit local bookstores.*
   b. *Look up books and reviews on amazon.com.*

3. *Find out what the best fiction-writing classes are in town, and enroll in one.*
   a. *Call or visit local bookstores.*
   b. *Call writer friends.*
   c. *Look in newspapers.*
   d. *Call universities and university extensions to see what they offer and recommend.*
4. *Check out resources at local library and the university library, especially* Publisher's Weekly.
   a. *Look for weekend writers' workshops in other cities.*

By the way, Ellen used the rule of thumb "Every time you talk with someone new, make sure you leave with the names of two other people to talk to."

5. *Begin writing.*
   a. *Write down ideas.*
   b. *Develop an outline.*
   c. *Write something every day.*
6. *When three chapters are finished, get feedback.*

After completing her list, Ellen selected dates for accomplishing each of the items and noted them on her calendar. She was realistic about time. She knew that the fall, particularly from Halloween through Christmas, would be very busy, so she decided to carve out the six months from January until June as her writing time.

Step 6. Persist

In his book Peter McWilliams asks, "How do you know how much work is required?" His answer: "When you have what you want. That's when it's enough. Until you've got it, it's not enough."

> *All I can say is that Ellen is in the final stages of writing her book. She is in contact with a number of literary agents. I can't wait for the day when she calls to say that her book is not only finished but is being published. I know that will happen.*

Step 7. Be grateful

Most of us are already blessed with more than we need in material things, loving family members, and wonderful friends. It's healthy to be responsible and seek out what we want, but it's also important to be thankful for what we already have. Every day stop for a moment to appreciate something beautiful, something delightful, something touching, or someone wonderful.

––––––

It's time for another Break.

THINGS ABOUT WHICH TO BE GRATEFUL BREAK

Children • Someone you love • Health • Your best
friend • Flowers • Mozart • Fresh, crisp, sweet
apples • Sunshine on a chilly day • Beach balls •
Sunday mornings • The first snow • Surprise parties •
A cat in your lap • Your dog • Brie • Homemade
vanilla ice cream • Lena Horne • The Pacific Ocean •
Glycerin soap • Down quilts • Mothers • Fathers •
Sisters • Brothers • Handwritten letters •
Ahava lotion • A Le Corbusier building • A simple
park bench • A pond • The smell of pine trees •
Natural light • San Francisco • Wood crackling in a
fireplace • A wonderful book • A perfect coffee cup •
Fresh-squeezed orange juice • Black and white
photography • Carrara marble • A Shaker chest •
Soft pajamas • Simon and Garfunkel • Rain •
Dreams • A brook • Balloons • Oboes • Feather
beds • Lilies • The color purple • Finnish design •
Crashing waves • Moonlight • A green field • A choir
singing in a European cathedral • A slight breeze •
Fountains where you don't expect them • Newly cut
hay • Fall • Thanksgiving dinners • Good neighbors •
Competence • Children's bookstores • Simplicity

Part IV

DEVELOPING YOUR
CONFIDENCE

Let's Get Practical

Time is God's way of keeping everything from happening at once. Death is nature's way of telling us to slow down.

Anonymous

In part I you learned something about what confidence is and why women tend to be lacking in it. In part II you were introduced to some new "truths" by which to live. My purpose in writing those chapters was (1) to give you information and a new perspective on how and why the culture — and especially women themselves — have perpetuated inaccurate and limiting ideas about being female; and (2) to give you permission (if you need it) to begin thinking and doing things differently with your life.

In part III you were shown how to learn more about yourself. The more you know about you, the better you'll be able to make wise choices about what you do with your time, body, energy, talents, and resources. You were also given the opportunity to define the qualities of the kind of people who seem to be "good" for you, those with whom you might choose to spend more time. Hopefully, this exercise also helped you to figure out who is *not* "good" for you. And if you're wise, you'll spend a lot less time, if any, with these people. You were also offered a chance to articulate what you want from your work, whether it be a job, a career, or even a major volunteer commitment.

In part III I also urged you to think about how you might enhance your home and work environments to be more reflective of your unique tastes and preferences. I urged you to give yourself permission to make quality choices. Each positive choice you make sends biochemical messages to your brain that help you to be healthy. Furthermore, as you will soon see, every choice you make has the potential for making your life more meaningful, self-enhancing, and healthy.

In part IV you're going to be able to use what you have learned about the female world and about yourself from the previous chapters. These coming chapters will show you how to think and act more confidently, through some new powerful ways of mobilizing your thoughts, feelings, and behaviors.

When push comes to shove, there are really only three steps you need to take to become healthier and more confident. They are:

1. *Thoughts:* Stop thinking negatively; instead, focus your energy on making positive choices.
2. *Feelings:* Learn to listen to your feelings.
3. *Actions:* Act in healthier, more effective ways.

Becoming a more positive person is not difficult at all. It's just a matter of deciding that you're going to act and then, as the Nike ad says, "Just do it." But doing it doesn't mean that an entire lifetime of familiar patterns must be changed. To become fit, you don't have to run a marathon or even a mile. You can begin by walking ten or fifteen minutes a day, every day. You don't have to organize your life completely. You can plan the next half hour. You don't have to get a Ph.D. in business by the time you're forty (or fifty or sixty). You can get on the phone, request a catalog from your local university, and then sign up for a couple of business classes. Find little pieces of time. One step at a time. That's "just doing it."

To act on these three steps, there are things that you can do right now. If you're at a loss for what, you might refer to the Be Good to Yourself Breaks at the end of chapters 3 and 4, as well as to some of the things you wrote in chapter 5. Even seemingly minor actions can help you to feel better immediately.

As you read the next chapters and engage in new behaviors, remain persistent and stay with it; don't get upset if you don't set the world on fire within a week or two. If you have a propensity to be overly demanding, perfectionistic, or critical of yourself (all of which we'll deal with later), keep in mind that butterflies take from ten days to several months to transform themselves from their caterpillar stage—and they have brains the size of a dot. If a butterfly is patient about change, why shouldn't you be?

Remember, when a person is feeling less than confident (depressed, ill, in crisis, overwhelmed, or overloaded), she will often engage in behavior that is just the opposite of what is good for her. Instead of working harder, taking less time, and pushing yourself even more, you need to take some time alone, rest, and do healthy things for yourself.

So before you begin reading part IV—which is filled with opportunities for action and change—let me anticipate two possible reactions you might have to reading, let alone acting on, the material. And let me assure you, these are barriers that you can overcome.

BARRIER 1: TIME
"I Can't Do That. I Don't Have the Time."

> *Our perception that we have "no time" is one of the distinctive marks of modern Western culture.*
>
> Margaret Visser
> *The Rituals of Dinner*

The number-one complaint I hear from women is that they don't have enough time to do what they must, especially for themselves. Here is what some women have said to me about their time problems:

There is never, ever enough time.

My life is a merry-go-round of endless activities, chores, errands, and things to do.

Every day is just one big checklist. In fact, the only pleasure I have right now is checking things off my list.

I feel like relaxing and playing are a waste of precious time, almost like a sin.

I was brought up to believe that busyness, not cleanliness, is next to Godliness.

Somehow we place great value on the business of doing. Obviously we have great fears about wasting or squandering time. What's more, some of us think that whatever gives us pleasure is probably a time-waster or time-squanderer. Yet we often allow others to control or waste our time *on their behalf.* If you find yourself saying any of the above or embracing one of the aforementioned beliefs, please take a look at a few relevant time facts:

Time facts
1. We all have twenty-four hours a day (actually sixteen to nineteen hours of actual usable waking time, depending on how much you sleep), or 168 hours a week.
2. There isn't enough time in one lifetime to do everything.

3. One of the century's most important medical insights is that a person's sense of time is translated by the body. Our time sense "affects the entire body as profoundly as blood and oxygen do—and it can kill or preserve us, serve us or slay us."[1]
4. "Time for yourself" rarely appears on women's calendars or "to do" lists.
5. To stay healthy and productive, the body and the mind need time for renewal and nourishment in the form of:
   - sleep
   - relaxation
   - having fun and play
   - smiles
   - laughter and humor—yours and others'
   - having fallow time
   - vacations and sabbaticals—mini and real
   - feeling free from doing
   - doing more of what we want to do
   - doing nothing in particular.

> *A neglected key to good time management that is usually not seen as a vital enhancer of productivity and quality . . . is play.*
>
> Ann McGee-Cooper[2]

Here are some ways for you to *create time* to continue reading this book and to act on its ideas and suggestions.

Time solution: Get out your calendar and carve out time for yourself

Is there a woman alive who doesn't have a "day/week/or month-at-a-glance" calendar? Some of us have minicomputers such as the Palm Pilot that keep our time organized for us.

Whatever you use, get out your pen (or open up your computer) and schedule in (literally mark off like an appointment) time for yourself each day, each week, and each month.

> *Quick Tip: If at first you are uncomfortable putting your name on the blocked-out time, try using just one letter to denote your time. And have a little fun while you're doing it. For example, write M for "me," or E for "exercise," or A for the name of the author, Allende, that you're currently reading. Some women I know create a fictitious person to fill in their time spots: you can use an old "pet name" from childhood, a name you wish your parents had given you, or maybe even a name you're going to give some future child—whatever you like.*

Daily Personal (or Alone) Time

On a daily basis — it may be as little as fifteen minutes — take a quiet tea break or a short walk or a sit in a quiet garden. Or use a half hour before you go to bed to read. Many women carve out the first hour of the day to do some kind of exercise. You may choose one short break or several. (And time for yourself does *not* include doing the next thing on your "to do" list!)

You know you're not going to do it unless you carve out the time. That time will *not* just appear, develop, or come to you. *You* have to make it happen. And unless it's an emergency or really important, don't let anything or anyone push that time out of your schedule. I know, it's not going to be easy. But once you begin (and say to yourself, "This is my time — I have to remember that it's good for me; I really need it to be healthy"), you'll see that it will get easier to continue.

Now the other side of creating the time is determining what you are *not* going to do during that time.

Do Not, I Repeat Do Not

- Answer the phone.
- Allow other people to physically interrupt you (To adults, nicely yet firmly say, "I'm busy right now; I'll get back to you in _____." To children: "Hey sweetie, I can't do _____ right now. Why don't you _____ for the next __ minutes and then we'll _____.")
- Get distracted by some chore, errand, or "need to do" in the middle of your time.
- Feel guilty about taking the time, or think about all of the things that you should be doing with your time. (We'll deal with guilt in the next chapter.)

Since it's very easy to mark off one week and then forget about the next, take a little time to carve out daily time for yourself for the next month. And at the end of that month, make a note to carve out time for the next.

Weekly Personal (or Alone) Time

Fifteen minutes here and there is an easy enough block to schedule, but what about more time — like a couple of hours for a manicure or a massage or to putter in the garden or to wander in a library or bookstore. Most women have great difficulty taking this kind of time, yet it's very important for their health. Once again, let me remind you that it's not going to happen unless you carve out the time and put it in your calendar. Here are some actions to consider that might help you create those couple of hours for you:

- Hire a high school or college student (or one of your kids) to do errands for you (go to the cleaners, shop at the grocery store, return videos to the video store, go to the bank, buy stamps at the post office). Better yet, give yourself the gift of a personal assistant on a particular day, such as Friday afternoon or Saturday, and use that regular time for yourself.

• Hire a baby-sitter to come at a regular time on a weekly basis. If you can't take all of the time for yourself, then use part of it to complete whatever you must, and leave the last hour just for you.

• Exchange baby-sitting time with a friend. You take your and her/his kids on Tuesday nights, and she/he takes care of them on Thursday nights.

• Decide to eliminate something—an activity, organization, or involvement—or someone from your life.

• Declare a moratorium on doing anything (or anything new).

• Say no for a few minutes, an hour, a half day, a whole day, a week, or a month. For how to do that graciously and effectively, I refer you to chapter 13.

Monthly or Yearly Personal (or Alone) Time

The more confident women I interviewed shared one important characteristic. On a regular basis ranging from every month to once or twice a year, they take time to get away from it all.

Sometimes they go off on their own; sometimes they go away with a couple of girlfriends; a few go away with one person who fits the category of the-easiest-person-in-the-world-to-be-with: the most nurturing, sensitive, flexible, nondemanding, you-like-to-do-what-I-like-to-do-even-if-it's-nothing, you-won't-be-upset-if-I-spend-some-time-alone person. Note that this monthly or yearly personal time is separate and different from time alone with a husband or partner (unless he/she happens to fit the easiest-person-in-the-world-to-be-with category); and certainly this time is not family vacation time.

Just in case you're wondering where people go, here are some suggestions. Remember to go to a *favorite*, not just an ordinary, place:

• a health spa
• a friend's cabin in the mountains
• a church sanctuary
• a meditation sanctuary
• a beautiful, luxurious seaside resort
• a women's health retreat such as Stanford University offers at Fallen Leaf Lake, California
• a B&B in a quaint little village
• a stay in someone's wonderful home, loft, apartment when they have gone away for a day, a weekend, or a week. (Sometimes you end up feeding the cats, but that's okay.)
• any combination of the above

If you create time to do something, then everything else should fall into place.

> *To be quite oneself one must first waste a little time.*
> Elizabeth Bowen
> *The House in Paris*

BARRIER 2: EVERYTHING ELSE HAS GOT TO GET FINISHED FIRST
"I Can't Relax or Do Something for Myself or Finish Reading This Book Until . . ."

- after I lose some weight
- after the sea of stuff on my desk (in my office, on my bedroom floor) is gone through and cleared
- after the kids go to college
- after Christmas, the holidays (whatever they are), the birthday, the anniversary is over
- after the visitors (or the family) have gone home
- after the kids get back into school
- after the book is finished
- after the house is done
- after the garden is planted
- after I finish my degree
- after my husband, boyfriend, significant other, gets a degree
- after I get my promotion
- after I retire
- after I finish all those unnamed things I should do, including
  - cleaning and organizing my drawers and closets
  - organizing the finances
  - cleaning out the garage or storage unit
  - refinishing the floors
  - answering all the letters that have been sitting on my desk for years
  - entertaining everybody I (we) owe dinners to
  - sending thank-you notes
  - going through and reading all the magazines and catalogs that have been stacked up for weeks (months, years)
  - collecting and having all the household rummage delivered to the appropriate charity organization

Because you are so overwhelmed by what you think you have to do already, you feel like you can't add one more thing to your "to do" list even (and especially) if that one more thing is taking better care of yourself. In fact, you might even be thinking right now that the best thing you could do is to shut the covers of this book and get on with what you need to do before more "stuff" gets added to your list.

The facts

1. Where does it say that all of this stuff has to be done?
2. It's never going to be all done.
3. If you don't enjoy it, why are you doing it?
4. So much of what we do is insignificant, rarely makes a real difference in the world, and is often unappreciated by others.
5. Choosing to do nothing is sometimes exactly what you need to do. As the great Chinese sage Lin Yutang wrote:

> *If you can spend a perfectly useless afternoon in a*
> *perfectly useless manner, you have learned how to live.*

Whether you get things done, or meet your real or so-called obligations, should have nothing to do with whether you take some time for yourself. Relax and take good care of yourself.

The solution

If "The Facts" haven't done their job for you, as you become overwhelmed by all that you think you have to do, you might try using the following formula:

Eliminate it.
(Ask yourself: *Is this really necessary? What's going to happen if it doesn't get done?*)

Delay it.
(Ask yourself: *Does this really have to get done right now?*)

Simplify it.
(Ask yourself: *Am I being compulsive, preoccupied, driven or perfectionistic about this? What's an easier way to do it?*)

Delegate it.
(Ask yourself: *Who else can do this? Then, either ask, delegate, or pay someone else to do the task for you.*)

And always remember this: **When in doubt, dump it.**

I think it's time for another break. Here is a list of fiction books that friends and interviewees have raved about.

GREAT FICTION BOOK BREAK

Isabel Allende, *Paula*

Maya Angelou, *The Heart of a Woman; I Know Why the Caged Bird Sings*

Jane Austen, *Pride and Prejudice*

Elizabeth Berg, *Talk Before Sleep*

Chris Bohjalian, *The Law of Similars*

T. Coraghessan Boyle, *Tortilla Curtain*

Pat Conroy, *The Prince of Tides*

Joan Didion, *Slouching Toward Bethlehem*

Annie Dillard, *The Living*

Harriet Doerr, *Consider This, Señora; Stones for Ibarra*

Elizabeth George mysteries

Kaye Gibbons, *Charms for the Easy Life*

Arthur Golden, *Memoirs of a Geisha*

William Goldman, *The Princess Bride*

David Guterson, *Snow Falling on Cedars*

Keri Hulme, *The Bone People*

John Irving, *The World According to Garp*

Barbara Kingsolver, *Animal Dreams; The Poisonwood Bible*

Wally Lamb, *She's Come Undone*

Doris Lessing, *The Children of God* series

E. Annie Proulx, *The Shipping News*

Ayn Rand, *The Fountainhead; Atlas Shrugged*

Bill Richardson, *Bachelor Brothers' Bed and Breakfast*

Conrad Richter, *The Trees; The Fields; The Town*

Tom Robbins, *Jitterbug Perfume*

Jane Smiley, *The Greenlanders; A Thousand Acres*

Wallace Stegner, *Angle of Repose; Crossing to Safety*

Laurens van der Post, *A Far-Off Place; A Story Like the Wind*

Mildred Walker, *Winter Wheat*

Rebecca Wells, *Divine Secrets of the Ya-Ya Sisterhood*

CHAPTER 10

Accentuating the Positive . . .

THE MANTRA OF AN AMERICAN LADY-IN-WAITING

I'M NOT *thin enough, young (or old) enough, pretty enough,*
  sexy enough, cool enough, smart enough, good enough to . . .

I CAN'T *do what I want, stop working so hard, stop doing it all,*
  take good care of myself, stop trying to be perfect, say no,
  stand up for myself, set limits,
  stop taking things so personally, stop being defensive,
  do well on tests, say what I really think . . . OR

disappoint others, upset others, impose on others, be angry
  with others, get help from others, stop being resentful
  of others, stop comparing myself to others . . .

I'LL NEVER *find a good man, have a job I love* . . .

I DON'T HAVE TIME *to read, have fun, be alone, exercise,*
  have peace of mind, enjoy a day with no responsibilities

I WORRY ABOUT *money, my children, everything* . . .

I'M AFRAID . . .

IT'S TOO LATE *to do something or be somebody* . . .

I SHOULD (OR SHOULDN'T), HAVE TO, OUGHT TO, NEED TO, MUST,
  BE OBLIGATED TO DO THINGS *because that's what "nice,*
  responsible, attractive, ladylike women do," others expect
  me to, I'd feel guilty if I didn't, I'd be letting others down
  if I didn't

I'LL DO . . . *even though I don't want to.*

I'LL GO . . . *even though I don't want to.*

I'LL WAIT OR POSTPONE *what I want until . . .*

I'LL HOLD BACK *on what I want; it's really not important.*

A s I have pondered this mantra—things said to me over the years by a large assortment of women—I have come to the conclusion that American women are a new breed of "ladies-in-waiting." Rather than waiting *on* other noble women, as was done in medieval times, today we are forever waiting *to* act on our own lives. Without realizing it, women are letting their lives slip by as they postpone and put off their desires and dreams, usually at the behest of what they tell themselves are the needs of others, *but in reality their own negative thoughts, beliefs, and attitudes are what's holding them back.* The tragedy is that these negative mindsets are usually based on exaggerations, myths, and even outright lies we tell ourselves.

A modern lady-in-waiting

Jan is a typical modern lady-in-waiting. She is one of an assortment of friends and colleagues to whom I gave different sections of this book for feedback. After giving Jan part III, "Self-inventory and Discovery," she e-mailed this message:

> *Marjorie, I love the self-discovery section. It's a keeper! Even though Vicky [her daughter, a senior in high school] is in the middle of finals, I took the material right over to her and said, "You've got to read this." Oh, how I can see her becoming more and more of herself, especially as she goes off to college. As for me, well, I think it's a little late. I didn't start early enough. Besides work, I just have too much to do for my husband and my parents and the kids. I'm not free. It's not my time, Marjorie; it's Vicky's.*

Jan is only forty-five years old! She has no clue that her statements "it's too late" and "it's not my time" are classic examples of negative thinking. On the contrary, she sees herself as a very positive, upbeat person. Jan doesn't comprehend that her beliefs are what keep her from doing what she might; it's not others who hold her back.

I still see women suffering from the Superwoman Syndrome (a term I coined almost fifteen years ago) who think that getting control of their frantic, overwhelming lives is impossible. They join millions of other women who are waiting for every last thing to be finished, fixed, get better, taken care of, settled, cleaned up (or out), filed, paid for, turned in or grown-up before they do what they really want. And, of course, there are always the distinctive stresses of the workplace: conflicts between what you and other people think and want, demands that are never-ending, and untotaled worries that occupy your mind and infringe upon your time and life. Sacrificing themselves and settling for less is the order of the day for many women. Because of years of female socialization, some women don't think they have the right to do what they want. I am here to say that they do and so do you.

Ladies-in-waiting are getting younger and younger

Unfortunately this waiting game is true not just for the typical thirty-something working mom or even the middle-aged woman. A 1998 survey of freshman college students conducted by UCLA's Higher Education Research Institute found that while "college men are spending more time doing things that inherently can be fun — exercising, partying, watching TV and playing video games — college women are juggling more household and child care chores, studying more and doing more volunteer work." Survey founder Alexander Astin says that "young women are taking on more and more responsibilities and feel stressed by all they have to do . . . [thus] experiencing an early version of the stress that 'supermoms' feel later in life."[1]

Whether she is a young college student, a thirty-something executive, a middle-aged mother, or a woman in her seventies or eighties, ladies-in-waiting are not confident women.

How men relate to women's self-sacrificing ways

Unlike women, men are not brought up to deny their own desires; in fact, from early on they're taught to "go for it." Therefore there is a profound disconnection for men when they hear that "women aren't doing what they want." As Simone de Beauvoir wrote in *The Second Sex,*

> The most sympathetic of men
> never fully comprehend woman's concrete situation.

I can't tell you how often in couples' therapy I have heard men say things such as "What do you mean she's not doing what she wants? She said going on hiking trips was okay. If she didn't want to do that, why didn't she just say so? Was she lying? I don't believe it!"

No matter what their age, many men cannot conceive of why women think and act in self-sacrificing ways. They might understand doing something you don't want to do once in a while—but most of the time? No way! This lack of empathy is often a real source of pain and/or resentment for women and a major point of conflict for couples. In describing this dilemma, my aim is not to blame men for lacking empathy, but to describe and explain their attitudes and behavior in order to help women.

Before I spent time researching the subject of negative and positive thinking, I never thought of myself as a negative person. Like Jan, I am a very positive person. I'm not critical, nor do I complain or try to find fault. In fact, I make a real point of encouraging and complimenting people. I like being that way. It feels good. It's a part of who I am.

So the notion that I was negative seemed ridiculous. Who me, negative? Never! No way! Not on your life!

But as you may have guessed (because you do it yourself), all of my positive words, thoughts, and actions were on behalf of others, and rarely for myself. I thought that was the way it was supposed to be. I didn't know that it could be different. I was both naive and wrong.

YOU CAN'T BE NEGATIVE AND CONFIDENT

Let's be clear about one thing: you can't have confidence if you're negative. It just doesn't work. The former will inevitably eat away the latter. *Negative thinking erodes confidence, impairs performance, and inhibits taking full advantage of our God-given talents, abilities, and skills.* The good news is this: you can do something about negative thinking, which brings us to the next confidence lesson.

DEFINING SOME TERMS

Before I go into the details of how to "accentuate the positive and eliminate the negative," I want to take just a minute to define some terms that are at the core of what I am discussing. Every day—and in almost every sentence—we wantonly use words (and their derivatives) such as *mind*, *think*, and *feel*, never considering what their exact meanings are. *I think* and *I feel* are often used interchangeably, although in reality thoughts and feelings are very different. Understanding their differences is key to becoming more positive and less negative. Here are some definitions of *mind*, *thinking*, *thought*, *feeling*, and *emotion*.

Mind

Clearly the mind is where it all starts. What is the mind? The answer to this question depends a lot on whether one is a philosopher, a psychologist, or a neurophysiologist. Generally, *mind* is defined as "the totality of mental experiences of an individual organism"[2] which includes what a person thinks, reasons, perceives, wills, and feels.[3] Although this is a source of some intellectual dispute, a few synonyms for *mind* are *brain*, *intellect*, *mental faculties*, and *psyche*.

Thinking and thought

Webster's defines *thinking* as "the action of using one's mind to reason . . . and produce thoughts."[4] Conceiving, imagining, remembering, anticipating, reflecting, and planning are all forms of thinking.

A *thought* in scientific terms is "a few micromilliwatts of energy that flows through the brain."[5] However, the standard dictionary definition of *thought* is "what a person thinks, especially reasons, or something in the mind."[6] Ideas, beliefs, opinions, intentions, visualizations, and meditations are all thoughts.

Feeling and emotion

Webster's defines *feeling* as "an emotion or subjective response to a person, thing or situation that is positive or negative."[7] *Emotion* and *feeling* are often used synonymously. In fact, emotion is defined as "a reaction, both psychological and physical, subjectively experienced as strong feelings."[8]

Certain emotions—such as anger, fear, love, joy, and sadness—are considered innate, primary emotions, which means that we are born with them. Other emotions—such as hate, excitement, grief, pity, sympathy, guilt, envy, and shame—are considered secondary, or emotions that we learn.

Historically, thinking—all things intellectual, rational, logical, and reasonable—has been associated with the male gender. On the other hand, feelings—anything having to do with the vague, untidy senses—have been seen as mostly female business.

By the way, I am making a big deal about these definitions because most people are completely unaware of the differences between the words, let alone the pivotal roles they play.

THOUGHTS ARE UNBELIEVABLY POWERFUL

Consider the following:

• **Everything Created by Humans—both Good and Bad—Begins as a Thought**[9]

• Therefore It Follows That Your Thoughts Create Your Reality

Anyone who has ever taken a beginning college philosophy class will recognize the classic Descartean statement

I think; therefore I am.

I rather like what the more contemporary philosophers Henry Ford (Ford Motor Company) and Mary Kay Ash (Mary Kay Cosmetics Inc.) say about thoughts:

If you think you can, you can.
And if you think you can't, you're right.

• Your Personal Powers Are Shaped by the Ways You Think

According to Harvard Medical School's Herbert Benson, "It's how we interpret reality, [and] how our body 'sees' the concrete world around us, that is important."[10] What we feed our brains—new facts, life events, emotions, and especially positive, negative, and neutral thoughts and beliefs—gets processed as biochemical signals (also called neurosignatures) in our brains. These neurosignatures "rewire" the brain, which then sends out biochemical messages through the bloodstream to every cell in our bodies. Therefore, what we think and feel can be a major source of illness and health.[11]

For example, negative thinking (such as self-criticism and constant worry) have been found to affect such important bodily functions as the immune and cardiovascular systems, and have been linked to a variety of chronic diseases and even the common cold.

Most people are unaware of just how much negative, pessimistic, violent, or anxiety-producing information gets processed by their brains every day, and how that information affects them. Think about what you say to yourself, and what messages come through your brain from other people, newspapers, magazines, radio, television, and the movies. As Benson says, the body attempts to abide by and demonstrate the suggestions the mind gives it.[12] Sooner or later negative input begets negative personal effect.

• The Way You Think Is a Choice

You *can* literally and figuratively change your mind and your life.

The eminent psychologist Dr. Martin Seligman says that the idea that the way we think is a choice is one of the most significant findings in psychology over the last twenty years.[13] In fact, your thoughts are not merely reactions to events—they change what happens to you and your awareness and understanding of who you were, who you are, and who you will be.[14] Scientists have found, for example, that positive thinking (such as being enthralled with exciting ideas or thinking peaceful and calming thoughts) produces biochemical reactions that are similar to Interluken-2, a powerful anticancer drug, and Valium.[15]

The important message here is that you can and should be much more selective about what you say to yourself, what messages you choose to listen to from other people, and what you see and hear in your environment (including newspapers, magazines, radio, television, and the movies). Positive input begets positive personal effects.

• Your Feelings Are Effected by Your Thoughts and Actions

You create how you feel by what you say to yourself (your thoughts) and what you do (your actions), not the other way around. What's more important, you can substantially change how you feel — positively or negatively — by changing your thoughts and actions.[16]

Here is a quick demonstration of the power of thought:

1. Think of the happiest moment of your life. Remember and visualize the circumstances of what happened, what you saw, heard, smelled, touched, and thought and especially how you felt. Feel the rush of emotion: the excitement, the joy, maybe even the wonder of it all. Experience your body tingling, the goosebumps on your arms, and how you laughed and cried at the same time. Savor it.

2. Now think about one of the unhappiest moments in your life. Again, remember and visualize the circumstances of what happened, what you saw, heard, smelled, touched, and thought and especially how you felt. Feel the angst, the fear, and the horror of it all. Experience your throat tightening, your body tensing and generally feeling numb. Remember your tears.

3. Now go back to your happy memory and in your mind revive that experience. See how quickly you can feel one way and then another. Your thoughts really do change how you feel.

If you think negatively or act in ways that are not good for you there is the likelihood that you will feel bad and maybe even get sick.

On the other hand, if you think positively, or act in ways that add to or improve your life, you are likely to feel good.

• People Are Predisposed to Think Negatively

Despite all that has been said about the power of thoughts, negative thinking prevails in conversations people have with themselves. Like a dog running around with his nose sniffing the ground for gophers, our mind is always out there sniffing for the negative. We seem predisposed to say some pretty rotten things to ourselves. Do any of these sound familiar?

Who do you think you are . . . you can't do that . . . you're not good enough . . . you don't deserve it . . . don't even try . . . you'll never make it . . . somebody better than you should get it or do it . . . you can't say that . . . how stupid can you be . . . what will people think . . . settle down . . . watch out . . . be careful . . . it's too risky . . . it's too dangerous . . . you'll get hurt . . . bad things will happen to you . . . who are you kidding . . . they'll never forget that blunder, you've ruined it . . . you can't change, you're weak . . . you're basically selfish and you know it . . . you're just fooling everybody.

As I have talked with women about why they think they are negative, I have found that some are under the impression that negative self-statements are more akin to the truth and are more in tune with reality. Overall, people tend to believe the negative more than they do the positive, as can be seen in Ann Fairbarin's comment:

Got to see it, hear it, touch it, smell it, know it by our own senses to believe it — if it's good. But if it's bad — it's true.

Other women find negativity more comfortable or less threatening. Said one interviewee:

I feel more comfortable thinking negative things about myself because that makes me feel less selfish.

Still others profess that negativity is protective because it keeps them from becoming too arrogant, even staves off the "old evil eye." In what seems to me to be a cockeyed way of looking at the world, one woman told me,

If there's something I'd like to do that feels really self-indulgent, I often let myself feel guilty in advance. That way, when I do wallow in it, I don't feel like such a bad person; I've already paid for my sins with guilt.

For this woman (and I must admit others like her), guilt-in-advance becomes like a kind of secret badge of honor.

Where does all this come from? Practically from the day we are born, we are inundated with the negative. Most parents believe their job is to "stamp out" as much of their children's "naughty," inappropriate, or bad behavior as they can. Thus children hear "no, no, no," and "bad, bad, bad," much more than they hear "yes, yes, yes," and "good, good, good." Think back to all of the parental and grandparental and other grown-up "be care-ful's, watch out's, don't do this's, you can't do that's, tut, tut, tuts, and never, nevers" you heard. Is there a child alive who didn't hear one of these—often?

Parental Tut, Tut, Tuts

Don't count your chickens before they hatch.

You can't do that! Why? Because I said so!

Will you ever be a lady?

So life isn't fair.

Let me do it—you'll spill, or mess, or ruin it.

How could you do that? What were you thinking!

I'll give you something to cry about.

Just wait until the other shoe drops.

We don't want you to get a swelled head.
(Have you ever actually heard of a child getting a "swelled head" from too much praise or love?)

Nice girls keep their knees together, draw inside the lines, never say no, don't fight back, don't talk back, aren't loud, say "I'm sorry."

While some adults are outright mean and abusive, most intend to be protective and caring, but the endpoint is frequently the same: children come to think that they are bad, stupid, useless, incompetent, or not nice. Unfortunately learned negativity is passed along from one generation to another.

The same "accentuate the negative" philosophy is often carried out in schools, and certainly in the business world. Everyone notices when you have done badly. Housework is the classic example. Who notices when your place is a mess? Everybody. Who says "hip, hip, hooray" and thanks you when it's spic and span? Nobody. Who notices when a report is late and less than perfect? Somebody does! Who notices an on-time, fully crafted report? Maybe your boss does; but usually he/she takes it for granted and often doesn't take the time to say "good job" or "thank you."

Even experts find the negative more compelling than the positive. A study of professional publications from 1967 to 1995 by *Psychological Abstracts* found that there had been 48,366 studies on depression, 38,459 studies on anxiety, and 5,119 studies on anger, for a whopping total of 91,944 studies. By comparison there were only 1,710 studies on happiness, 2,357 studies on life satisfaction, and 402 studies on joy, a meager 4,469 positive studies.[17]

Every woman has the potential to think more positively about herself and her life. The reason to do this is very simple: being positive leads to having more confidence, and to better physical, emotional, and spiritual health. That's it.

THINKING MORE POSITIVELY

Becoming a more positive person starts with focusing your thoughts on what is positive.

Like an underused muscle, you may feel discomfort as you first begin to focus your thoughts on the positive. As with exercise, you need to start slowly, remind yourself to do it, and practice, practice, practice before it begins to feel natural. Similarly, you also need to do it for a while before you experience results. I assure you that with time and practice, positive thinking will get easier and feel good. As Abraham Lincoln once said,

> *If you want something you've never had before,*
> *you've got to do something you've never done before.*

Bear in mind that there is only one person in the world who has control over what you think and that's you. You have the right, the responsibility, and the power to say only those things to yourself that uplift, empower, and restore you. Why not try? You have nothing to lose!

FIVE STEPS TO FOCUS ON THE POSITIVE

The renowned Stanford University psychologist Albert Bandura has spent much of his professional life conducting research on how people's beliefs affect their overall functioning. In his view what works is:

1. Believe that you have control over your thoughts.
2. Choose positive things to say to yourself.
3. Consistently make positive choices in your everyday life.
4. Identify and find solutions to the life problems and personal challenges that repeatedly plague you.
5. Live by your own positive belief system.

People who do these things are more confident, less distressed, healthier, and happier, and they tend to live longer. Oh yes, they also share their happiness with others.

Let's look at these five easy steps in more detail:

Step 1. Believe that you have control over your thoughts

Hopefully, by now your eyes have been opened to the real possibility of gaining more control over your thoughts. Not only is it a documented fact that people possess the capacity to manage their own thoughts, but the extent to which they manage them dramatically affects how they feel and act, as well as whether they experience life events as benign or perturbing.[18]

Even though you may not fully believe it yet, begin saying to yourself:

> **I have control over my thoughts; therefore,**
> **I have control over my feelings, and**
> **Ultimately, I have control over my life.**

Step 2. Choose positive things to say to yourself

Yes, I do know that life is full of negatives, but that is a part of everyone's life. It is only a *part* of life, not *life* itself.

Yes, you have a negative part, with any number of weaknesses, bad habits, senseless fears, imperfections, and lacks. But those negative things are only a *part* of you; they are not *you*.

It probably feels a lot easier, even more natural, to notice, talk about, and ponder the negatives. Too many of us think about and act overwhelmingly on our negative side. How about giving the positive equal time and an equal chance?

Begin the Day by Asking Yourself

✓ What can I do to start my day off right? And then do it.

✓ How can I make this a good day? And then do it.

Paradoxically, people tend to resist asking themselves these questions exactly when they need them the most: when they're feeling down.

So that you will remember to start off your day with the positive, write the above two questions on two three-by-five cards and stick them in a few places that you see every morning: on your bathroom mirror, your daily calendar, or the console of your car. Or make the questions into "stickies" that pop up each time you turn on your computer.

Throughout the Day and Evening, Say Good Things to Yourself
Research shows that thought control is much more effective when people proactively focus on producing positive, wanted thoughts rather than trying to distract themselves from (or avoid) negative thoughts.[19]

> *Warning: Thoughts are remarkably powerful, but they are not omnipotent. Focusing on the positive is not a cure-all. Like everything else in life, to be effective, positive thinking needs to be based on reality and used with common sense.*

With that in mind, here are some ways to think proactively:

Affirm Your Right to Be and Do What You Want. Say
- ✓ I choose
- ✓ I want
- ✓ I won't hold back when
- ✓ I am
- ✓ I love being
- ✓ I am passionate about

Encourage Yourself as You Begin New Efforts or Face Challenging Situations. Say
- ✓ Yes, I can!
- ✓ I have time!
- ✓ It's never too late!
- ✓ Do it!
- ✓ Go for it!

Notice What Is Right and True About the World, No Matter How Simple or Profound. Say
- ✓ What a beautiful day!
- ✓ What a lovely flower!
- ✓ I love that song!
- ✓ That was an amazing talk!
- ✓ What an inspiring person!
- ✓ Now that's what I call service!

When You Have Done Well or Accomplished Something, Say
- ✓ Good for me!
- ✓ I'm really proud of me!
- ✓ Now, that's being healthy!

✓ I'm really getting on top of my life!
✓ That was just what I wanted!

When You Feel Agitated, Irritated, Scared, or Frustrated, Comfort and Quiet Yourself. Say
  ✓ It's really okay.
  ✓ Everything will be just fine.
  ✓ I'm not afraid.
  ✓ Slow down.
  ✓ Don't worry.
  ✓ Take a deep breath.
  ✓ I can handle this.
  ✓ Remember the following

> *Sometimes it's useful just to remember that nothing lasts forever.*
>
>   Anonymous

Every Day Give Yourself the Gift of Becoming Calm and Relaxed. Say
  ✓ Solace, peace, peaceful, soft, calm, still, sacred, quiet, spirit, patience, ocean

Step 3. Consistently make positive choices in your everyday life
Research also shows that positive thinking is increased by getting involved with engrossing activities. The same is true with regard to relationships. If you want to think more positively, choose to be with engaging people.[20]

The work of Joss, Spira, and Speigel of the Stanford Medical School suggests that even people who have frequent, perturbing thoughts because they have life-threatening illnesses such as cancer are greatly helped by occupying themselves in activities that give meaning and satisfaction to their everyday lives.[21]

Consider scheduling good things for yourself with the same priority, dedication, and precision that you schedule work commitments and medical and dental appointments for your children.

Quality Activities
Knowing what enthralls, captivates, and fascinates you is critical to having positive thoughts. Once again, I repeat: if you don't know what you like, then begin to find out now. Look, explore, and try out all kinds of things until you find something that touches your soul. The more you get into an activity, the more likely it will become absorbing.

The range and variety of absorbing personal, social, and recreational activities in which you might engage is infinite. *What* you do makes not a whit of difference. The only requirement is that you love it. Think about the times when you were doing something and lost track of time. What was it? How did you feel?

Quality People

Just as engrossing activities can have wonderful positive effects on you, so can wonderful people. Think about who applauds your positive thoughts, feelings, and actions. Who encourages you to become more of yourself? Who supports you to seek quality? Who appreciates and praises all the little and big things you do? Who says things and acts in ways that uplift and empower you? Who notices the positive and helps you to see it as well? Who cares about and loves you just the way you are?

Just recently, my husband, Mort, told me a story that demonstrates how much people around you can affect how you think and feel. One Monday morning, after having been away for a few days skiing, Mort called our office manager, Dianne Schultz, to check his schedule before he left for the office. He told Dianne how hard it was for him to get back into the work groove. As he put it, "I was really bitching and moaning!"

Before he could utter another word, Dianne said, "Mort, isn't that wonderful! If you feel that way, it means that you must have had a great time when you were away. That's awesome! You're just going to have to go skiing more often." Mort said that Dianne's positive take on his situation literally took away his negative breath. He immediately felt buoyed by her words and told her so. After he hung up, he told me the story.

Having people such as Dianne Schultz in your life is a perfect example of what I call making good people happen for you.

Quality Environments

Creating or changing your environments is another way to positively affect your thinking. Jain Malkin, one of the foremost health care designers in the country, is continually seeking ways to create more positive, healing environments for patients. Jain says that you don't need to be sick to seek out and create your own healthy environments. In fact, you can positively affect your thinking (which, as we have seen, can affect your health) by paying a little more attention to the settings in which you spend time.

Anthony Lawlor, author of *A Home for the Soul*, says that every space has the potential for "renewing and enlivening us . . . and nourishing our souls."[22] The qualities of a soulful setting are determined by such things as color, texture, shapes, objects, furnishings, art, noise (especially music), aromas, cleanliness, light, air quality, and views of plant life.

Lawlor also says that "soul is nourished by personal variety, quirks, and idiosyncrasies"—in other words, by all those things you identified in chapter 8 that have meaning for you, that honor your heart and that make a space feel "like home." Here are a few things that *A Home for the Soul* recommends for creating soulful spaces. While they are mostly meant for the home, they can also be adapted to certain work environments. As you read through the list, think about what small changes you might make to create positive, healing environments where you live and work.

- a seating arrangement (U-shaped) whereby people face one another to encourage conversation and storytelling
- extra deep, soft sofas and chairs to encourage people to enjoy themselves in relaxed, informal ways
- beautiful, soft cushions on the floor to make a room feel interconnected and whole
- music to enrich the mood of the day or the season
- a bookshelf (or bookshelves) filled with books to remind one of stories that have delighted, inspired, and informed
- a shelf, table, or sideboard with pictures of family, friends, celebrations, and major events (such as weddings, anniversaries, special birthdays, and graduations), as well as meaningful objects and mementos. These are wonderful places to show off your particular "quirks and idiosyncrasies."
- the presence of crackling flames and glowing embers in a fireplace; or if you don't have one or it's the wrong time of year, many lit candles
- soft lighting, especially if it is nighttime
- pieces of nature as in fresh or dried flowers, well-cared-for indoor plants, or even an arrangement of lovely rocks and stones[23]

Some people make soulful homes out of their workplaces. Take, for example, my English teacher friend, Carol Obermeier. This is what she has done with her classroom:

> *I used to fill my classroom with garage sale stuff, but that got to be a bit gamy after a while, if you catch my drift. Still, I loved the atmosphere it created and how it encouraged the kids. I teach a seminar class where we discuss Faulkner and Shakespeare and Joyce, et al. In any case, two summers ago I used the money I'd made teaching summer school, along with some funds our business manager provided (after I showed how much we'd save the school by not needing desks), and went to discount furniture places.*

After ordering three sets of living-room furniture in more or less complementary styles and fabrics (I tend to be eclectic in my decorating anyway), I headed off to find a rug to pull it all together, posters from various stores, vases, flowers, and a basketball hoop, small size. I lined the walls with pics and sayings from Eleanor Roosevelt, Sojourner Truth, and Mother Teresa, artwork from students, photos of current kids and grads, and posters from Hamlet, Dazed and Confused, Bette Midler, Antonia's Line, Martin Luther King, Mark McGwire, Barcelona, Who's on First, the Three Stooges in caps and gowns, a cardboard standup of Einstein, the Midwest Bill of Rights, Mia Hamm, Gabriella Reece, a poster of sheep with the notation that "this class is not a class of sheep," prayers, and all kinds of stuff. Of course, there are books galore!

The students at Parker [Frances Parker School in San Diego] see room twenty-eight as one of the senior privileges. The kids and parents tell me it's welcoming and warm and that it almost (believe it or not) has an old English study feel to it; some tell me it's nicer than their own living rooms. Most important, it invites open discussion of novels and plays. And once the students get to talking, the writing (which we do in the computer labs and at home) is much, much better! Faculty friends drop by to sit and take a breather. Some spend lunchtime in here grading papers. My children "show it off" to their buddies. It's really a lovely place, another home for me and my children, Sam and Lucy, and of course I hope for my students.

Humor

Herbert Benson affirms that one of the most effective medicines in combating negativity is humor.[24] Matt Weinstein (founder and emperor of Playfair, an organization that helps companies to improve morale and become more productive through the use of humor) says that while people have been saying for thousands of years that laughter is good medicine, in the last decade medical and scientific research has documented that laughter and play have a beneficial effect on physical health.[25] What's more, you don't have to be a comedian or even naturally funny to have more humor in your life.

I have already told you about creating an e-mail Humor Break with friends. Here are some other ways to bring humor to your life:

• Simply decide that you want more humor in your life and start looking for it. It's there.

• Many women tell me that they have difficulty remembering the punch lines of jokes. I sure do. But I've learned that if I write down jokes as I hear them (on whatever paper happens to be around), I have a much better chance of remembering and then sharing them with someone later.

• Every time you run into something that tickles you — a cartoon, a quote, a joke — tear it out, clip it, write it down. I have a card file of humorous things that I refer to dozens of times every day.

• Seek out friends who have a good sense of humor.

• Keep a watch out for humorous books, movies, and television shows. You might also keep a stock of videos on hand that are predictable negative mood breakers. Norman Cousins (author of the influential book *Anatomy of an Illness as Perceived by the Patient*) laughed himself into wellness by watching old Marx Brothers and other movies. Whoever tickles you (from Robin Williams, Billy Crystal, and John Cleese to Goldie Hawn, Bette Midler, and Whoopi Goldberg), why not buy a supply of his or her movie-videos and keep them on hand?

• Christine Forester, president of Catalyst, a corporate strategic design firm, is a master at finding clever, silly wonderful toys to give to friends for every imaginable appropriate and inappropriate occasion. She scours catalogs and goes to children's bookstores and toy stores for her many clever finds.

• Look for humor in everyday life, especially in things that happen to you.

One final suggestion — it doesn't matter if anyone else in the world enjoys your particular sense of humor. Just *you* enjoy.

Step 4. Identify and find solutions to the life problems and personal challenges that repeatedly plague you

In searching for ways to help people deal with negative thoughts, Albert Bandura found that the most powerful way to eliminate intrusive thoughts is to gain mastery over the annoyances, fears, threats, and stresses that repeatedly bring on those thoughts.[26] In other words, don't sit on problems, or ignore something that bothers you over and over and over again. Identify the problem and solve it!

Step 5. Live by your own positive belief system

As much as they can, confident women create and live by a positive belief system that serves as a guiding light for making authentic, honest, and fulfilling choices. Here is an example of one belief system:

1. My life belongs to me and no one else.
I am not on this earth to live up to other people's expectations.

2. I am responsible for identifying and meeting my own wants, desires, and dreams.
I don't have to wait for others to fulfill what I want, desire, and dream.

3. I can choose what my personal priorities are and act accordingly.
I don't have to live my life reactively, unthinkingly, avoidingly.

4. Only I can determine what I give to, and receive back, from others.
I don't ever have to tolerate disregard, mistreatment, or abuse.

5. I am responsible for, and competent to solve, my own problems.
I am not helpless.

6. I can seek out quality in all that I do.
I never have to accept shoddy treatment, work, or advice.

7. I can take good care of myself, including handling a broad array of people and situations.
The healthier and happier I am, the more I will be able to give to others.

To think more positively, you need to become ever so much more selective about what you do with your time, about whom you spend time with, and about your surroundings.

Now that you've learned about becoming more positive, let's take a Break.

THINK POSITIVE BREAK

Why Not:

Be easier on . . .

Be good to . . .

Be nicer to . . .

Think better of . . .

Be more responsible to . . .

Learn to forgive . . .

Believe in . . .

Make things happen for . . .

Create a positive environment for . . .

Take good care of . . .

Enjoy . . .

Be patient with . . .

Listen to . . .

Heal . . .

Look for the positive in . . .

Laugh at . . .

Carve out time for . . .

Allow others to give to . . .

Appreciate the wonderful things about . . .

Realize that it's okay to pay attention to . . .

Give to, nurture, even pamper . . .

Remember, your life belongs to . . .

Yourself

CHAPTER 11

Eliminating the Negative

Let us make the test. Say God wants you
to be unhappy. That there is no good.
That there are horrors in store for us
if we do manage to move toward Him.
Say you keep Art in its place, not too high.
And that everything, even eternity, is measurable.
Look at the photographs of the dead,
both natural (one by one) and unnatural
in masses. All tangled. You know about that.
And can put Beauty in its place. Not too high,
and passing. Make love our search for unhappiness,
which is His plan to help us.
Disregard that afternoon breeze from the Aegean
on a body almost asleep in the shuttered room.
Ignore melons, and talking with friends.
Try to keep from rejoicing. Try
to keep from happiness. Just try.

Linda Gregg
"Gnostics on Trial"
Too Bright to See

N o one is immune to periodic bouts of feeling down, fearful, anxious,
ineffective, upset, or discouraged. Everyone feels this way sometimes.
Life simply presents us with a continuing series of challenges that are
not easily controllable and for which we are not prepared. Yet when
negative thinking gets out of control, it can wreak havoc with our lives.
Negative thinking can make any situation or event into a disaster.

People are always thinking about something. Like background music in a movie, our thoughts are with us twenty-four hours a day, from the time we are born until the moment we die.

We think when we get up and while we brush our teeth, when we exercise and take a shower; we think on the commute to school or work; we think as we talk to people on the phone and use our computers; we think when we prepare and eat our meals; we think as we read to ourselves and to our children; we think when we're out with friends, when we attend concerts or lectures and watch TV; we even think while we're making love. As with movie music, we pay attention to just some of what we hear in our heads (according to neuroscientists 50,000 thoughts every day!)[1] but as we have seen in the last chapter, *what* we think profoundly affects every aspect of our lives.

NEGATIVE THINKING DEFINED

Negative thinking involves repeatedly focusing on what is painful, uncomfortable, flawed, difficult, complicated, and overwhelming. I give you the following information, first, to educate and inform you; second, to help you see that you are not alone, and finally, to prepare you for making some important behavior changes. Remember, knowledge is power.

Jonelle is a thirty-three-year-old account executive in New York City. In a telephone coaching situation not long ago, she said to me:

> *Marjorie, you'll never guess what happened. My boss just assigned me her niece as an intern for the summer. This is another case of I'm damned if I do and damned if I don't. If I take her on, I'll have a whimpering sixteen-year-old to watch over for two and half months. Like I don't have enough to do already. If I tell my boss I don't want to do it, she'll be really upset with me. This is her "darling" niece. As you know, summers are not exactly my favorite time anyway. I hate summers in New York! You're so lucky to live in San Diego. You have no idea how oppressive the heat gets here. My asthma acts up, summer clothes look terrible on me, and my hair flattens just as soon as I walk outdoors. And I have real trouble sleeping. Having "darling Jennifer" hanging around is going to make it unbearable. Oh God, I bet I won't even be able to take my August vacation! It's not fair. I don't understand — no matter how hard I try or how hard I work, I just get the problems and the shit! Everything seems to happen to me.*

Jonelle is a living example of someone who is a negative thinker: paying attention to and dwelling on what is wrong, not what's right; focusing on what's unpleasant, not what's nice; noticing what hurts, not what feels good; finding what's missing, not what's there; complaining about what the problems are, not seeing the opportunities; and pointing out the bad breaks, not counting her blessings.

Negative thinking centers Jonelle not on how she can take advantage of having an extra hand but on what extra *she* will have to do. Negative thinking tells Jonelle that she — of all people — shouldn't have to be burdened with the intern; like so much in her life, "it's just not fair."

Until just a few years ago, I had no idea how powerful negative thoughts were or how much control I could have over them. I now know that I can stop most of my negative thinking. I catch myself doing it every day. It takes some work and time, but there is no question in my mind that you too can get a handle on your negative thinking too. You can stop doubting, worrying, criticizing, finding fault, and feeling miserable. I'm about to teach you how to do it.

Negative thinking tends to run along a continuum of intensity from helpful to run-of-the-mill to moderate to out-of-control. The higher the intensity, the greater the impact.

<		>
Helpful	Run-of-the-Mill	Out-of-Control

HELPFUL NEGATIVE THINKING

Since confident women take positive "spins" on matters, let's take a positive, albeit paradoxical, spin on negative thinking by declaring that not all negative thinking is bad. Negative observations can be helpful if they are based on what is actual and/or real. In fact, negative thinking can serve as an early warning system when we perceive that somebody or something needs attention. These situations are negatives with a little *n*, helpful negative thinking.

Examples of Helpful Negative Thinking

• If you say to yourself, "The front tires on my car are threadbare," *that's not negative thinking*; that's noticing a condition that needs attending to and could have life-saving consequences. Getting angry at your husband or yourself for not having replaced them is *negative thinking*. Going out to purchase new tires yourself is *positive thinking and action*.

• If you say to yourself, "I noticed a mangy-looking guy hanging around the parking garage when I came in, and that scared me," *that's not negative thinking*; that's anticipating a possibly dangerous situation that you can find ways to avoid. Being scared all day is *negative thinking*. Calling the security people to check out that person and having someone accompany you to your car is *positive thinking and action*.

• If you say to yourself, "I don't like the way my hair was cut this time," *that's not negative thinking*; it's a statement about wanting something different or better. Fretting over it for the next month is *negative thinking*. Calling your hairdresser for another appointment to fix the "bad hair" situation is a *positive way of handling the situation*.

Helpful negative thinking is a gentle to moderate call for attention or corrective action.

RUN-OF-THE-MILL NEGATIVE THINKING

A second type of negative thinking involves all those pass-through-your-mind-quickly comments you make to yourself all day long. Although they are different for each person, they might include "I don't like this," "She annoys me," "I'm hot," "I'm cold," "I hate this elevator," "This stoplight is sure long," "The stock market is down again," "The budget seems off," "There's nothing on this menu that appeals to me today," and so forth.

Usually these thoughts are balanced by more neutral or positive ones, such as "I like this, "I just love her," "Gee, it's really cozy in here," "Hm, that's an attractive fellow," "There's that woman I see in the elevator every morning," "Amazing, I made the stoplight this time," "The stock market's up," "I like the menu today," and so forth.

Some run-of-the-mill negative thinking is normal; however, if it becomes a habit you should do something about it.

OUT-OF-CONTROL NEGATIVE THINKING

There is a third type of negative thinking—the extreme, exaggerated, highly destructive kind—that causes people enormous pain. Perhaps the most accurate way of describing this out-of-control thinking is to say that it is ordinary thinking run amuck.

The content of both ordinary and out-of-control thinking is the same. While not perfect, ordinary thinking is at least somewhat based on what is logical, rational, constructive, appropriate, real, and actual. By contrast, out-of-control negative thinking is characterized by flawed, illogical, distorted, irrational, fantasy-based, and inappropriate if not crazy ideas. Most important, out-of control negative thinking knocks the psychological wind out of you.

Cognitive therapists Aaron Beck and David Burns call out-of-control thinking—which negatively distorts and misinterprets events—cognitive distortions. They categorize negative thinking in this way:

Cognitive Distortions[2]

1. *All-or-Nothing Thinking:* You see everything in black and white terms.
"I really blew it with that cute neighbor," "I'm such a loser," "I'll never be able to get a good guy to date me." Something or someone (including your-self) is all one way or another, either smart or stupid, desirable or not desir-able, right or wrong.

2. *Overgeneralization:* You make one mistake and project that this is the beginning of a never-ending pattern.
"I really flubbed the presentation this morning," "I'm never going to be able to speak in front of groups," "I always screw up some way, somewhere, some-how." You define one isolated event as an ongoing personal deficiency.

3. *Mental Filtering:* You pick out one or a few negative details and allow them to color everything else.
"My professor told me that the first part of my paper needs a lot of editing; obviously, I can't write." You dwell on the one piece of negative feedback someone gives you and ignore all the positive.

4. *Accentuating the Negative:* You discount successes, positive experi-ences, and positive feedback and choose to focus on losses, negative expe-riences, and negative feedback.
"I still have fifteen more pounds to lose," ignoring the fact that you have *already lost ten pounds.* You disqualify the positive and allow only the neg-ative to count.

5. *It's-All-My-Fault Thinking:* You find personal fault or take responsi-bility (often apologize) for "anything and everything," even things that aren't under your control.
"Oh dear, John doesn't seem to be enjoying the concert. I should never have invited him." You see yourself as responsible for external events and/or other people's discomfort, dissatisfactions, or problems.

6. *Catastrophic Thinking:* You take ordinary mistakes, setbacks, or events and make them into catastrophes by exaggerating their seriousness.
"Suzie got a B minus on her test. She's never going to get into a good col-lege." You interpret things with the worst-case scenario; furthermore, you think and act as if it were the truth.

7. *Life's-Not-Fair Thinking:* You think that your situation is really unfair at best, tragic at worst.
"Why do I always have to be the one who gets sick?" You exaggerate the

importance of your problems. Everybody else is luckier, happier, healthier than you, had better parents, and so on.

8. *Jumping to Conclusions*: You arbitrarily jump to negative conclusions that are based on flimsy evidence.

"Janice is angry with me because I, not she, was chosen to go to the retreat." You conclude that someone will react or is reacting to you negatively, based on a look, a word, or the lack of a word.

9. *Emotions Are the Truth*: You assume that your negative feelings are the truth.

"I feel awful about not going to that party; I really did something wrong." You feel any kind of negative emotion—guilt, resentment, anger, anxiety, helplessness—and presume that it is right and real.

10. *Ruminating*: You brood on something or somebody and go over it in your mind at length and in depth.

"Eric seemed really charmed by that woman the other night. I wonder if he's unhappy with me. I've gained some weight. It wouldn't surprise me if he was attracted to her and for that matter many other women. I wonder if he's having an affair. If he isn't, he probably would like to. I would really be devastated if that happened. I would just die." These thoughts continue on and on and on throughout the day and the night. You chew on something repeatedly and at length, focusing on negative implications, projections, and conclusions.[3]

Which of these traps do you get caught up in?

> *Reality rarely turns out to be as bad as we imagine it to be.*
>
> Anonymous

Out-of-Control Thinking Is Like a Wildfire

From working with people in my private practice, I have found additional defining characteristics of out-of-control thinking. It's like a runaway wildfire, accelerating into and melting everything that gets in its way.

Often out-of-control thinking starts with just a spark of a thought, such as noting that *once again your husband has forgotten to do something you asked him to do.* Before you know it, the original thought—his forgetting something—abruptly gets whipped up by your mind, and *you remember back to all the things over the years that he's forgotten: picking up the cleaning, half of your grocery lists, your birthdays, the kids' birthdays, you name it.*

Then at night, as you lie in bed, your thoughts melt from one negative to another, even jumping to subject matters that are unrelated or irrelevant. *You begin to think how his forgetfulness is just another indication of his insensitivity and lack of caring. You remember your parents' last visit and how he was less than gracious.* Then your thoughts jump back to yourself. *You begin to feel upset at your husband for not being as affectionate as you would like him to be.* When he reaches out to you, your negative thinking spreads into this arena: *why is it that when you want to be held and cuddled, all he ever wants is sex? Has he forgotten about your needs too?*

You never quite know when out-of-control thinking will get ignited, how long it will last, or where it will go. It moves on real and authentic threats as well as imagined ones. If they are not addressed, negative thoughts breed feelings of irritation, then frustration, then resentment, then anger, and then sometimes rage.

Predictable Times When Our Thinking Runs Amuck

There are certain times in our lives when we are more vulnerable to having our thoughts run amuck. Some of these include:

- having "a bad day" or a "bad" interaction with someone, and/or a series of bad days or bad interactions
- being tired, sick, or getting sick
- a family member (especially more than one) being sick or having problems
- before, during, and even after a stressful situation, crisis, or emergency event
- experiencing something that we have never experienced before or a situation for which we are not prepared
- experiencing hormonal changes during premenstrual days or postpregnancy or menopausal times

BELIEFS ARE NOT THE TRUTH!

A great deal of our negative thinking is based on beliefs that are unfounded, inappropriate, outmoded, or just plain false. After all, beliefs are not the truth! They're not even fact. As Julia Cameron, author of *The Artist's Way*, says, "The world was never flat, although everyone believed it was. [Neither] are [you] dumb, crazy, egomaniacal, grandiose, or silly just because you falsely believe yourself to be."[4]

You might want to examine your own belief system and reflect on ways that it is flawed. Here are the ten typical female negative beliefs based on the old Female Code of Conduct. As you will recall, many women think and act in self-negating ways because they are trying to be the proverbial nice, unselfish **Good Woman,** as well as the thin, fit, desirable **Beautiful Woman,** as well as a polite, unimposing **Ladylike Woman,** as well as the overresponsible, do-it-all **Superwoman.**

BELIEFS WOMEN HAVE ABOUT THEMSELVES

NONCONFIDENT THINKING	REFUTATION OF THE BELIEF	CONFIDENT THINKING
1. *I have to put other people's needs, desires, and preferences before my own.*	When you always put others first, you become a victim or a martyr and create the circumstances for becoming unhappy, resentful, and/or depressed.	Confident women balance their own needs with the needs of others.
2. *I am nothing if I am not thin, beautiful, and fit.*	"To seek after beauty as an end is a wild goose chase—because it is to misunderstand the very nature of beauty which is the normal condition of a thing being as it should be." Ade Bethune	Confident women treat their bodies with care and respect.
3. *It's not nice for me to get angry, disagree, confront, or protest. If I do, others might get uncomfortable, dislike, disapprove, reject, or retaliate against me.*	Sometimes "being nice" actually means that you're being "chicken." "Real courage is speaking your mind about what's in your heart." Carol Gilligan	Confident women are open and direct with their anger and express it appropriately.
4. *I am responsible for others' (especially my husband's, children's, and other family members') happiness and comfort.*	When you assume responsibility for other people's moods and comfort, you rob them of their own responsibility.	Confident women allow others to be responsible for their own happiness and comfort.
5. *I feel self-indulgent, silly, and childish if I play, laugh, and have fun, especially on my own.*	"Smiles, humor, silliness, laughter, and play are the very best medicine." Dr. Herbert Benson	Confident women seek out the humorous and playful aspects in themselves, in situations, and in others.

6. *I shouldn't challenge thoughtless, unkind, disrespectful, or even abusive treatment from others because it won't do any good anyway and might even make things worse.*

In healthy relationships one person does not yell at, act disrespectfully, put down, or hurt the other.

Confident women form nourishing rather than destructive relationships and stick up for themselves on occasions when things go awry.

. . . .

7. *I hate change, new things, different things, and risks; therefore I have to endure energy-draining work, activities, and relationships.*

"Our doubts are traitors, and make us lose the good we oft might win, by fearing to attempt."
                    Shakespeare

Confident women see life as an adventure and seek out new and better ways, ideas, and experiences.

. . . .

8. *I'm not comfortable asking others for help because it's not worth the embarrassment or possible rejection I might feel if I get turned down. Besides, I can probably do it better, faster, and more easily myself.*

The major barrier to women getting help at home and in the workplace is that they don't ask for it. Successful women increasingly depend on others to do for them.

Confident women are equally comfortable in giving and receiving, as well as being asked and asking for what they want.

. . . .

9. *I need to have someone stronger and smarter than I am to help me solve difficult problems, make decisions, and take care of financial matters.*

"God helps those who help themselves."
                    Algernon Sidney
"I'm not afraid of storms, for I'm learning how to sail my own ship."
                    Louisa May Alcott

Confident women accept responsibility for themselves and for being the cause and effect of what they want.

. . . .

10. *I can't be alone. I have to be married.*

"If the right man does not come along, there are many fates worse. One is to have the wrong man come along."
                    Letitia Baldridge

Confident women are not afraid of being alone and enjoy men who are best friends and add to their lives.

Women also have beliefs about how other people "should" behave that are a source of negative thinking. Here they are:

BELIEFS WOMEN HAVE ABOUT OTHERS

NONCONFIDENT THINKING	REFUTATION OF THE BELIEF	CONFIDENT THINKING
1. *Other people are responsible for my happiness and unhappiness.*	"Happiness is a do-it-yourself job." Alfred A. Montapert	Confident women understand that only they can make themselves happy.
2. *I know the way things ought to be, including how others should think and act.*	Often we don't know what's best for ourselves, so how can we possibly know what's best for others?	Confident women treat others with respect and dignity.
3. *It's good for me to point out, correct, and remind people of their faults and mistakes.*	Loving someone is accepting him or her exactly as he or she is.	Confident women appreciate that everyone has his or her strengths and weaknesses.
4. *The people I love should love, approve of, and appreciate me in the ways I need and want.*	Love is never owed, it is a gift that comes from the heart.	Confident women don't feel that anyone owes them anything, including love, approval, and appreciation.
5. *The people with whom I am close should know what I want and need and help me get it.*	Only we are responsible for knowing and getting what we want from life. If others choose to help us, that is icing on the cake.	Confident women live actively and proactively and assume responsibility for getting what they want.

WOMEN'S SPECIFIC TYPES OF NEGATIVE THINKING

Before discussing how to handle negative thinking, I want to mention four specific types of negative thinking that are characteristic of women: excessive worry, perfectionism, and thoughts that lead to unreasonable guilt and resentment. I'll bet you'll find yourself in at least a couple of them.

Excessive worry

[Worry] . . . that was a snake that would lay eggs in my brain.

Faith Sullivan
The Cape Ann

Worry, worry, worry! There isn't anything in the world about which we don't or won't seem to worry: marriage, kids, looks, money, other people, jobs, traffic, the weather. In its ordinary-thinking version, worry is a reflection of who and what we are interested in or care about.

Excessive worry is the epitome of ordinary thinking run amuck, and it seems a proclivity much more common in women than in men. If you question this, think about the last time you heard a man say, "You know, I really worry about . . ."

Here is an example of excessive worry. (The cognitive distortions and characteristics are noted in bold.)

A woman and her boyfriend (or husband) break up. While HE picks himself up and begins exercising more and dating (rarely bothering to think about what went wrong), SHE immediately tries to figure out what happened and why.

SHE desperately wants to understand (**UNPREDICTABLE, INTRU-SIVE RUMINATION**), so SHE repeatedly relives the entire relationship, sometimes even thinking back to how she felt during the breakup of previous relationships (**MENTAL FILTERING**). SHE remembers every detail of what HE said and did, and what SHE said and did that might give her a clue about what went wrong, especially what SHE did wrong (**IT'S-ALL-MY-FAULT THINKING**). If someone should point out to her that HE has been emotionally abusive to her, rather than acknowledging this, SHE wants to understand why he would possibly want to act that way. What could she have done (or now do) to help him understand his behavior?

SHE also begins to think that something is fundamentally wrong with her ("What is it? Am I just not sexy enough, or pretty enough, or cool enough, or smart enough? Is there another woman?") (**EXCESSIVE, DESTRUCTIVE CATASTROPHIC THINKING**). SHE begins to think that SHE will never, ever find someone to love again (**OVERGENERALIZATION**). Eventually, her thinking projects twenty, thirty years into the future, when she imagines herself to be alone and unloved (**LIFE'S-NOT-FAIR THINKING, SELF-DEFEATING THINKING**).

You can't be confident if you worry excessively.

Let's move on to the next form of ordinary thinking run amuck, perfectionism.

Perfectionism

If you can't say somethin' nice, don't say nuthin' at all.
> Thumper
> from the Disney
> movie *Bambi*

If you can't do something purfect, don't do nuthin' at all.
> Thumper's perfect
> girl-cousin

Perfectionism is another example of ordinary thinking run amuck. The ordinary thinking version of perfectionism is when you balance having high standards for some things with having lesser standards for others. For example, you may like having your home neat and clean most of the time, but do not want to obsess about unmade beds or a handful of messy closets and drawers. Perfectionism is when you have unreasonably high standards and unrealistically high expectations for yourself and/or others. Nothing is ever good enough, and nothing ever really satisfies you.

According to Judith Rodin, women with perfectionistic standards also tend to be more dissatisfied with their own bodies and to feel fatter — regardless of what they actually weigh — than less perfectionistic women.[5] This is not surprising since bodies are the central arena in which women's dissatisfaction with themselves gets played out.[6]

When you're a perfectionist, you:

- feel compelled to accomplish, but rarely experience joy in what you do
- dread making mistakes, making decisions, and being a beginner. You also hate any feedback, since much of it contains words of disapproval or criticism.
- are defensive when confronted with flaws and/or weaknesses
- play it safe rather than take risks
- always compare yourself to others and are critical of them as well
- try to flawlessly juggle all aspects of your life but never take time for yourself

- often feel inadequate and inferior in spite of many successes, accomplishments, and "wins"
- assume that, if what you do isn't perfect, it's a failure

When things go wrong, female perfectionists blame themselves and loathe their faults, flaws, or imperfections. As you might guess, men are much less likely to engage in such self-loathing. They usually place blame on external sources—the situation or other people.

The fantasy of perfectionists is that, if they do everything "right," there will be a magical time when all is well or done, and one can finally be happy. Since perfection is unattainable, it never happens. The irony, according to behavioral scientists, is that when perfectionists pull back a bit, expect less of themselves, and relax, they often do more or better.

You can't be confident if you have excessively perfectionistic standards.

> *We forget that . . . the only standard of perfection we have to*
> *meet is to be perfectly ourselves.*
>   Anne Wilson Schaef

The next form of ordinary thinking run amuck is guilt.

> *I used to feel guilty if the cat had matted fur.*
>   Sue Patton Thoele

Guilt

Guilt, guilt, guilt! There isn't anything in the world about which women aren't willing to feel guilty.

Freud brought the word to our attention, but it's women who have given it the prominence that it holds in our lives today. Harriet Lerner, author of *The Dance of Anger,* says that "our society cultivates guilt feelings in women such that many of us feel guilty if we are anything less than an emotional service station to others."[7]

Guilt feelings develop when you don't live up to your or other people's expectations, thus finding yourself wrong, bad, inadequate, or undesirable. These expectations are what produce the many *can'ts, shoulds, have-tos, ought-tos, need-tos,* and *musts* in your life.

Because guilt is so uncomfortable, people tend to assume that, like a facial mole, it is a useless and bad thing, just waiting to be covered up or excised. But having a healthy sense of guilt is actually a good thing. Willard Gaylin, the author of *Feelings,* goes so far as to say that guilt is a "noble emotion"[8] because it lets you know when you have acted in an unnecessarily hurtful or unfair way, or when you may have violated your personal standards. After all, psychopaths, like serial killer Ted Bundy, never experience guilt feelings.

Some guilt feelings are valid and appropriate, but many are not, depending on the source and merit of the standard. What's not good is when excessive guilt-provoking thoughts take over your life, when ordinary thinking runs amuck. That's what happened with this twenty-something, twenty-pound-overweight woman, who told me:

> *Oh my God, after I had an argument with my mother last night, I must have eaten two dozen cookies. I absolutely have no self-control* (**ALL-OR-NOTHING THINKING**). *I'll never be thin* (**OVERGENERALIZING**). *I'm nothing but a big, fat pig* (**MENTAL FILTERING**). *I can never stay on a diet* (**ACCENTUATING THE NEGATIVE**).
>
> *Everybody else I know is really good about controlling their eating and they're thin and gorgeous. I'm such a loser. I keep trying to lose weight, but once I start, I feel miserable, and then I eat everything that wasn't on my diet and gain MORE weight. No really good man is ever going to want to date, let alone marry me* (**CATASTROPHIC THINKING**).
>
> *I just don't understand it. Why can't I be like normal people? It's not fair that I look at food and it jumps on me* (**LIFE'S-NOT-FAIR THINKING**). *I'm just going to end up being a big, old, fat bag lady* (**OVERGENERALIZING**). *When I'm in the gym, I can see what people are thinking about me* (**JUMPING TO CONCLUSIONS**). *If I feel so guilty about this weight stuff, I must really be a mess* (**EMOTIONS ARE THE TRUTH**). *I'm so miserable, all I can think about is how much I weigh* (**RUMINATING**).

As Harriet Lerner points out, other people (especially those to whom we are closest—husbands, parents, and siblings as well as children) often use guilt-inducing tactics to challenge us when we begin doing more of what we want and less of what *they* want. You start hearing accusations that you are "selfish," "crazy," "man-hating," "over-emotional," "immature," "unfeminine," "neurotic," "irresponsible," "ungiving," "cold," or "irrational."[9] These terms are inappropriate name-calling. Let the person know, in a responsible way, that you find this kind of talk unacceptable.

> *Show me a woman who doesn't feel guilty and*
> *I'll show you a man.*
>
> Erica Jong

Most important, if you think someone is trying to make you feel guilty, consider this provocative yet truthful statement: no one else can *make* you feel guilty. People can try to make you feel guilty, but you are the only one who can choose your reaction — including whether you're going to feel guilty.

You can't be confident if you engage in excessive guilt-provoking thoughts.

Let's move on to the last form of ordinary thinking run amuck — resentment.

Resentment

Resentment opens no door and breeds no courage.
                                                    Susan Glaspell

While guilt develops from trying to meet your own and other people's expectations, resentment most often develops from (1) other people not living up to *your* expectations, and (2) others' intense pressure for you to do something or perform. Resentment also develops in a backhanded way, when you expect other people to take care of you because you fail to take care of yourself.

The ordinary thinking version of resentment occurs when somebody says or does something that doesn't seem quite right. Usually it's a momentary event. You deal with it, or you don't. It happens, and it's over.

Lingering resentment is yet another animal. This seething, hurt/anger (even hate) develops over time when someone doesn't do or say what you think they should (usually without your ever having questioned them). Lingering resentment occurs when your standards for what is right, fair, responsible, and caring are violated; thus, you feel wronged or injured. With resentment, the *shoulds, have tos, ought tos, need tos,* and *musts* are on the other shoe, "meant for thee and not for me."

When push comes to shove, resentment *never* works. It makes you feel bad; and it *never* changes the behavior of the person who has brought it on. Carried to its extreme, resentment becomes hate, which, as we all know, is often much worse for the "hater" than for the "hatee." The late theologian Harry Emerson Fosdick captured it best when he warned that "hating people is like burning your own house down to get rid of a rat."

Resentment also has a boomerang effect. If you feel resentful because you're not getting enough of another's time, love, or help, resenting that person is likely to generate more negative reactions — more of what you *don't* want — rather than what you do want. You can't be confident if you are filled with resentment.

Now it's time to find out how you can handle your negative thinking.

SEVEN STEPS FOR HANDLING YOUR NEGATIVE THINKING AND CHANGING YOUR BEHAVIOR

It's never too late—in fiction or in life—to revise.

Nancy Thayer

The seven steps for handling negative thinking and changing behavior are:

1. Increase your awareness of your negative thoughts.
2. Stop negative thoughts and replace them with positive ones.
3. Observe and describe your negative thoughts.
4. Diagnose your negative thoughts.
5. Find solutions.
6. Educate yourself and get help.
7. Reward the new thoughts and/or behaviors.

Perhaps the best way to demonstrate how to handle negative thinking is to tell you about Paula, a forty-something executive who lives in La Jolla.

Paula's story

Like many middle-aged women, Paula did not come to physical exercise easily or willingly. She said that in her day, "there weren't any girls' sports save for high school gym classes." Aside from her father's golf games, Paula said "no one I knew—especially women—ever exercised." Then she went on:

> From the time I first met my husband many years ago, Al has been an inspired, consistent exerciser who was always "suggesting" that I exercise too. But I never seemed to be able to find a form of exercise that I liked, let alone one that I would do consistently. I was very negative about the whole thing.
>
> For years I would wake up in the morning, lie in bed, and think, "Oh God, I should exercise today." When I got out of bed, I would then say to myself, "I can't exercise now. I need to get breakfast, get the kids off to school. Maybe there'll be time before work."
>
> Of course, there was never any time then, nor was there time in the afternoon. In the middle of a workday, who in her right mind would drive someplace to exercise, take forty-five minutes to an hour to do it, shower, take another half hour to fix her hair, and then drive back to work? No way.
>
> What about the late afternoon or evening? That's when I did grocery shopping, errands, dinner, laundry, helped the kids with their homework, and so on. Forget it.

I read somewhere that joining an exercise class was a good way to exercise. So I joined a gym. Sometimes I went two or three times a week for a week or two, but then something would always happen. I would get sick, one of the kids would get sick, I would go out of town. I'd get out of the habit (which wasn't really a habit), and invariably it took me a few weeks (sometimes months) to get back to it.

Next I heard that fast walking was a good thing to do. I thought to myself, "I can do that!" So I started walking around our neighborhood. But as I walked down the highly trafficked streets, I kept thinking that the car exhausts must be doing as much damage to me as the "good oxygen" and physical benefits I might be getting from the walk.

Always I would be thinking, "I hate this. How can people say they love it? What a waste of time! There's so much that I could be doing right now. This does not feel good. I hate getting so hot and sweaty. I hope no one I know sees me. How long have I been doing this? (Usually five minutes.) How soon can I stop? Wouldn't it be great if I could just do it once and get it over with for the rest of my life? I'm never going to get into this exercise thing."

About once a year I would become very resolute about getting into a regular exercise routine. In a burst of enthusiasm, I would inevitably overdo it and end up with blisters, shin splints, sore muscles, and the like, any of which were legitimate excuses to stop exercising for a while.

Let's use Paula's story to see how you can get a handle on your negative thoughts.

> *Our ability to create the conditions of life most dear to us—*
> *realizing our hopes, dreams, goals and aspirations—depends*
> *on having control over events we initiate ourselves and over*
> *those that come into our lives unbidden—the seeming stresses,*
> *obstacles and disappointments.*
>
> Dr. Kenneth Pelletier[10]

Step 1: Increase your awareness of your negative thoughts
The first step to handling negative thinking is to become aware that you have negative thoughts.

Awareness is the first step to eliminating or changing your negative thoughts. Just as many people stop exercising to do a pulse check, take a moment or two each day to do a "thought check."

Listen to what you say to yourself as you carry on your daily activities. Some women have told me that they frequently become aware of their thoughts when they are walking or running or working out at a gym. Others have said they experience them during church (or temple) services. Still other women say that keeping a journal (or even jotting down short phrases or sentences in their Day-Timer) helps them. Notice what and how much you think is negative, how much is neutral, and how much is positive. If nothing else, observing your own thoughts will be informative.

There is no magic formula for how many negative thoughts are too many. Only you can determine that.

> *For years Paula was unbelievably negative about exercise, but she wasn't aware of the specific negative thoughts. The thoughts just were there. As far as exercise was concerned, she thought she was just dealing with the "reality" of not being a natural athlete and feeling overwhelmed with too much to do in her daily life.*
>
> *She told me that one day as she was fast-walking down a busy street, mumbling and grumbling about hating to do it, all of a sudden a lightbulb went off in her head. She said, "I remember this moment like I remember the instant when I heard about Kennedy being killed. For some reason, I suddenly realized that I was being unbelievably negative about exercise. That was the day I began to deal with exercise differently."*

If, during your thought checks, you find that you are "accentuating the negative," Step 2 will help you handle your negative thoughts.

Step 2: Stop negative thoughts and replace them with positive ones

The second step to handling negative thinking is to:

A. Believe that you can stop your negative thoughts.
B. Say "stop!" when you catch yourself thinking negatively.
C. Quickly replace your negative thought with a positive word or phrase such as "calm" or "this is good."

A. *Believe That You Can Stop Your Negative Thoughts.*

To tell you the truth, before I did the research for this book, I wasn't aware of the amazing power of thoughts. If anything, I was skeptical about all of the "positive thinking" hoopla. But having read renowned psychologist Albert Bandura's work and his careful evaluation of others' research, I am now convinced that believing in your ability to control your own negative thoughts is critical to actually *doing it*. As he says, "Self-belief does not necessarily insure success, but self-disbelief assuredly spawns failure."[11] If you want proof beyond these words, please refer to the works cited in the bibliography of this book.

B. Say "Stop!" When You Catch Yourself Thinking Negatively.
Simply saying "no" or "stop," "cancel," "delete," "erase," or any other word that feels right for you, is different from telling yourself not to think about something. Trying to suppress your thoughts by telling yourself not to think about the content, as in "Quit thinking about chocolate cake," is not only ineffective but may exacerbate the problem. This is because the very negation of the thought contains the thought (of that luscious chocolate cake). The very thoughts you try to suppress are the ones most likely to come back and haunt you even more. Daniel Wegner, author of *White Bears & Other Unwanted Thoughts*, says that through repeated suppression, even situations in which the thought-suppressions occur become reminders of those unwanted thoughts. And the more times and situations you try to suppress a thought, the more reminders there are of it.[12]

C. Quickly Replace Your Negative Thought
with a Positive Word or Phrase.
Repeat one of your favorite positive words, such as "solace," "calm," "peace," or one of your favorite positive phrases, such as "This is good," "Good for you!" or "Get positive!"

Becoming absorbed in positive thoughts and positive activities, says Wegner, escapes the paradoxical activation that takes place with negative suppression. Positive thoughts and activities not only draw one's mind away from negative thoughts but replace them with new positive associations.[13]

> *Paula not only became aware of her negative thoughts, but because of some work that we had been doing, she also came to believe that she could change them.*
>
> *Once she became aware that she was being negative, she then began paying attention to the specific thoughts she was having. As you recall, some of what she was saying to herself was "Oh God, I should exercise today. I hate this. What a waste of time" and so on. The first thing she did was stop saying those things to herself. Paula told me that she simply said the word "stop."*
>
> *Finally, Paula began replacing her negative thoughts with positive ones. She said, "Good for you! You're going to do it this time! Look at what a beautiful day it is. Hey, you're getting healthy."*

Bonus Suggestion: Put Aside Specific Time to Worry.
Many negative thoughts are not so easily controllable. As we have seen, many women engage in ruminating thought patterns that plague them all the time. Cognitive psychologists suggest that when you face this kind of negative thinking, you might want to take another step.

Put aside a specific time to "worry." Rather than allowing your negative thoughts to come and go throughout the day and night, postpone your worrying to a particular time and place each day. For example, simply say, "Stop! I'll get to these things at nine o'clock tonight." Then at nine o'clock sit down for a half hour to deal with your thoughts. Experts say that chronic worriers who use this mode of thought control spend much less time worrying and overall are less distressed than people who don't.[14]

Step 3: Observe and describe your negative thoughts

The third step to handling negative thinking is to observe and describe your negative thoughts. Ask yourself two questions:

A. What am I saying to myself?
B. What am I feeling?

Very often our thoughts, however fleeting and elusive, offer the keys to figuring out what is going on and eventually dealing with what is going on. To better deal with your thoughts and feelings, write them down. Don't worry about writing complete sentences or writing in good form. Just write.

A. *What Am I Saying to Myself?*

To answer the question "What am I saying to myself?" Paula wrote down the following:

> *I'm really having a hard time with this exercise thing. I don't seem to be able to find anything that I like. I wonder if there is anything I like or at least that I don't hate. I don't have any time. There is no good time. I don't seem to be able to underline{keep it going}. I hear it's supposed to be good for me; I read that all the time, but it sure doesn't seem to do me any good. I don't like to underline{exercise in front of other people} because I look so terrible and feel so awkward.*

B. *What Am I Feeling?*

To answer the question "What am I feeling?" Paula wrote this:

> *I really underline{don't feel like exercising}. I wish I didn't have to do it, but because of the underline{family's history of heart disease} and my own underline{creeping}*

weight gain, I know I'd better. I feel *guilty* when I do it because of the time it takes—and guilty when I don't because of what I'm not getting done. I have foot problems and can't stand those *big, clunky, uncomfortable running shoes.* I feel jealous of all those women who do it and don't make a big deal about it. I wonder what their secret is. How did they get that way? I feel safe walking on busy streets, but I *hate the traffic* and the *noise* and the *unattractiveness* of it all. I like places where it's *peaceful and uncrowded,* but if no one is around, I feel edgy and *unsafe.* One of the things that worries me is *being chased by dogs.* I feel like a failure.

Once you have written down your thoughts and feelings, go back and underline what appear to be the key points.

See Paula's underlines in the two paragraphs above.

Note: *Getting enough information about your thoughts and feelings to go on to the next diagnostic step may take more than one sitting. So don't be in a hurry. Write as much as you can.*

Step 4: Diagnose your negative thoughts

The fourth step to handling negative thinking is to diagnose the problem (or problems) by asking yourself these questions:

A. What is the problem that needs to be solved here? What's bugging me? What am I worrying about?
B. What's keeping me from doing something about the problem?
C. Is this a one-time situation or an issue that comes up frequently?
D. How are my thoughts cognitive distortions?

A. *What Problem Needs to Be Solved?*

Researchers have found that the most powerful way to eliminate negative thoughts is to remove their cause—in other words, to solve the problem, remove the threat, or calm the stressor.[15] While this may seem like one of those easier-said-than-done things, the same researchers also urge us to remember that "there are few problem situations in which there is absolutely nothing people can change."[16]

Paula's underlinings in her thoughts and feelings about exercise are significant clues as to what her real problem is.

WHAT IS THE PROBLEM:
Because of my family medical history and "creeping weight gain," I know that I need to create and keep an exercise program. So far I haven't been able to do this.

WHAT BUGS ME:
I haven't found anything I like to do.
I hate exercising in front of others.
My shoes are uncomfortable.
I don't feel like doing it.
There's too much traffic.

WHAT WORRIES ME:
I'm afraid of being alone in places where no one else is around.
I'm afraid of being chased by dogs.

B. What Is Keeping Me from Doing Something About the Problem?
I don't have enough time.
Things that get in the way.

As you will see, all of this information was useful for the solution phase of problem solving.

C. Is This a One-Time or All-the-Time Pattern?
Some negative thinking is situational and hence short-lived. Other negative thinking is habitual and often involves dealing with the same issue over and over again.

This is what Paula wrote down about her exercise problem:

> *Since I have been unsuccessful in starting and maintaining an exercise program all of my life, I would say this is an all-the-time problem, not a one-time negative-thinking issue.*

D. Are Any of My Thoughts Cognitive Distortions?
I asked Paula to examine the thoughts and feelings she wrote down to look for any cognitive distortions. Here are some of the cognitive distortions she found:

- *There was an **overgeneralization** as I felt jealous of "all those other women" who seemed so easily to find and do exercise that they liked.*
- *Clearly I engaged in **accentuate-the-negative thinking** as I went on and on about all the stuff I dislike about exercise.*
- *I also engaged in some **catastrophic thinking** as I let my fears about being alone and barking dogs affect what I was going to do.*
- *Finally, I allowed that **emotions are the truth** to get the best of me when I acceded to "not feeling like exercising."*

Step 5: Find solutions

The fifth step to handling negative thinking is to find ways to solve the problem identified in Step 4 by developing a goal and then (A) dividing the goal into subgoals or (B) identifying the barriers and solving them.

A. Develop a Goal

> *When you have a great and difficult task,*
> *something perhaps impossible,*
> *if you only work a little at a time,*
> *every day a little, without faith and without hope,*
> *suddenly the work will finish itself.*
>
> Isak Dinesen

Isak Dinesen (the pen name of Karen Blixen, the Danish author who is best known for her book *Out of Africa*) knew instinctively what psychologists now teach people facing difficult or intimidating tasks: specify the large task and then break it down into easily accomplished subtasks.[17]

Paula wrote down this goal:

My goal is to create and maintain an exercise program.

B. Crossing the Barriers to Reaching Your Goal

Using much of the information that she had generated in Step 4, Paula identified these barriers and solutions to create and maintain an exercise program.

BARRIER #1: I HAVEN'T FOUND ANYTHING I LIKE TO DO.
SOLUTION
When it came right down to it, the kind of exercise I really did like was walking, even fast walking. Creating the "right circumstances" for myself, I eventually began to add some running.

BARRIER #2: I HATE EXERCISING IN FRONT OF OTHERS.
SOLUTION
I found that by walking down side streets and in parklike areas, I was virtually away from most people.

BARRIER #3: MY SHOES ARE UNCOMFORTABLE.
SOLUTION
Over the years I had developed a couple of foot problems that made walking not an easy or comfortable thing to do. I researched and

found a wonderful athletic shoe store that helped me to find the most amazing walking/running shoes that aren't the least bit clunky. That solved my problem and made the walking much more pleasant.

BARRIER #4: I DON'T FEEL LIKE DOING IT.
SOLUTION
I have to admit that there are still many times when I don't feel like exercising. I know that I have to ignore those feelings. Now I get up, put on my exercise clothes and shoes, and just do it. Usually by the time I'm five or ten minutes down the road, I feel good and I'm getting into a groove.

Remember that thoughts and actions can change your feelings.

BARRIER #5: THERE'S TOO MUCH TRAFFIC.
SOLUTION
By walking down side streets and in parks, I almost totally avoid traffic, noise, and everything that used to annoy me. In fact, I now seek out beautiful, interesting, pretty places to walk.

BARRIER #6: I'M AFRAID OF BEING ALONE IN PLACES WHERE NO ONE ELSE IS AROUND.
SOLUTION
Most of my fears about being alone are not well founded. Nevertheless, to assuage those fears I always walk in areas where I feel safe.

BARRIER #7: I'M AFRAID OF BEING CHASED BY DOGS.
SOLUTION
I consulted a veterinarian friend about what I should do to keep from being chased by dogs. For one, I avoid places where I know they will be. If I'm feeling particularly anxious, I sometimes carry a small can of a Mace-like dog repellent.

BARRIER #8: I DON'T HAVE ENOUGH TIME.
SOLUTION
I have made exercise one of my top priorities. By doing it first thing in the day, I don't have to worry about having time. I make the time. In fact, I take it one step further: I say to myself that because it is so important to me, not exercising is not an option.

As the saying goes, people *make* time for what is important.

BARRIER #9: THINGS GET IN THE WAY.
SOLUTION
*Most of the time I exercise, so when I fall off track, I don't beat myself
up for it; I simply say that this is what happens sometimes and just
get back on track. Sure, things still get in the way. I try not to let that
happen, but distractions are a part of life.*

Everyone goes through cycles of starting, getting distracted, and relaps-
ing into old nonexercising ways. Faultless self-control is what perfectionists
seek.

As you can see, the problem of not exercising was not just one problem
but a combination of many problems or issues. When Paula was able to see
what those different issues were and address them one by one, she was able
to solve the exercise problem.

Step 6: Educate yourself and get help
The sixth step to handling negative thinking is to become more knowledgeable and get good help.

A. *Become Knowledgeable*
There are many ways of becoming more knowledgeable, including reading books, doing research on the Internet, attending lectures, and taking
short courses and classes.

*Paula read the manuscript for this book and a number of books that
I recommended to her. She also made use of the growing resources
on the Internet. Finally, she took advantage of numerous seminars
on women's health that hospitals offered in her area. Most important, she made exercise one of her top priorities.*

B. *Get Good Help*
Good help comes in many different forms. Sometimes it means consulting
someone whom you trust—a good friend or colleague—to help you sort
through negative thinking and/or brainstorm solutions. Other times it
means consulting a storekeeper as you look for a product that helps you
deal with a problem (for example, Paula's walking shoes). At times you may
want to consult a professional therapist for help in sorting through a problem that seems too complicated for you to solve on your own.

Select a therapist with great care. Be a good consumer of services, and shop around. One of the best ways to find good help is to ask trusted people for their personal recommendations. You don't have to actually see their therapists if you don't want to, but their suggestions are a good place to start your search. What's useful is for you to interview potential therapists on your own via the phone or in person to ask questions and see if you like them. After you've done your research, carefully select a therapist.

Here are some characteristics to look for in a good therapist. Someone who:

- has excellent credentials
- is knowledgeable about the psychology of women
- is respectful of and sensitive to you and your particular concerns
- is aware of what she/he knows and doesn't know; and is open to referring you to other exceptionally good resources when your issues are outside her/his areas of expertise
- you find pleasing to be with, someone with whom you feel very comfortable and sense you can trust

Martin Seligman, the former president of the American Psychological Association, adds that it should be someone who

- can look at what is going on now in your life and what you can do to correct it
- requires you to assume responsibility for your problem and to commit to the hard work of making your life better.[18]

Confident women know that getting help is a form of competency.

Step 7: Reward the new thoughts and/or behaviors
The seventh step to handling negative thinking is to applaud or reward your new ways of thinking or behaving.

———

As you make progress in dealing with your negative thoughts, don't forget to say positive things to yourself, especially when you make major behavioral changes. This can be as simple as mentally applauding yourself by saying: "Hip hip hooray for me!" Or it might take the form of a small gift—that new book you've heard people raving about or dinner out or a day away at a spa.

As you might guess, Paula did all of the above.

TIME TO MOVE ON

I hope that the knowledge and techniques you have learned in the last two chapters will help you to move from self-doubt and negative thinking to self-confidence and positive thinking. Remember,

You are what you think and say to yourself.

In the next chapter we're going to deal with feelings and especially how you can use them as cues to who and what is not working in your life.

———

Now, I think you deserve a Humor Break.

HUMOR BREAK

I love deadlines.
I especially like the whooshing sound they make as they fly by.

DOUGLAS ADAMS

Duct tape is like the force.
It has a light side and a dark side and it holds the universe together.

CARL ZWANZIG

Research is
what I'm doing when I don't know what I'm doing.

WERNER VON BRAUN

A conclusion is
simply the place where someone got tired of thinking.   ARTHUR BLOCK

A synonym is a word you use
when you can't spell the word you first thought of.   BURT BACHARACH

Blessed are the meek,
for they shall inhibit the earth.   ANONYMOUS

If at first you don't succeed, then you're running about average.

JENNIFER JAMES

Love thy neighbor as thyself . . . but choose your neighborhood.

LOUISE BEAL

If you knew how often I say to myself: to hell with everything; to
hell with everybody. I've done my share; let the others do theirs
now. Enough, enough, enough. I have had enough.   GOLDA MEIR

The women's gate to hell is filled with women who have said, "I
thought that he would change if I just loved him enough."

ANONYMOUS

The trouble with the rat race is that even if you win,
you're still a rat.   LILY TOMLIN

CHAPTER 12

Trusting Your "Gut"

We cannot
listen to what
others want us
to do
We must listen
to ourselves
We don't need to
copy other people's ways
and we don't need to
act out certain lifestyles
to impress other people
Only we know
and only we can do what
is right for us. . . .

> Susan Polis Schutz
> To My Daughter with Love

Feelings and *emotions* are used synonymously to describe all those elusive, spontaneous, subjective responses we have in our heads—and experience in our bodies—that reflect our most personal concerns, deepest commitments, and heartfelt needs and desires.

FEELINGS HAVE TWO REPUTATIONS

Over the last few decades, feelings have come to be seen in either of two ways: either as (1) *the epitome of female silliness*—trifling and irrational responses (compared with the more rational male thought processes), or (2) *self-evident personal truths that are beyond question*—coming from the "I feel it, therefore, it's the truth" school of thought promoted by some psychotherapists and a fair number of New Age and self-help advocates.

The reality is that feelings are neither silly nor wise, neither truth nor fabrication, neither right nor wrong, neither good nor bad. Feelings are definitely not facts, and they're certainly not who you are. They just are.

Most feelings come and go and often fade with time, while others stick around to "bake" in our minds. While researchers from California to Massachusetts are busy pondering the nature and meaning of feelings, little is really known about them. What we do know is that feelings reflect our relative state of comfort or discomfort, contentment or turmoil, and are the key to understanding what is going on in our lives.

> *Emotion doesn't travel in a straight line. Like water, our feelings trickle down through cracks and crevices, seeking out the little pockets of neediness and neglect, the hairline fractures in our character usually hidden from public view.*
>
> Sue Grafton

EMOTIONS ARE CONTAGIOUS

Emotions are contagious. When you walk into a room, have you noticed how quickly you "catch" the tension or the laughter of the other people there? How easy it is to start crying when you see another's tears, especially if it's someone about whom you care. Because of this empathic quality, some people think that others share their feelings. They are wrong. While everyone has feelings, the feelings you experience are yours alone; your feelings are unique, idiosyncratic, and no matter how well you describe them to others, in the end they are still personal and private. No one can feel exactly as you do, even when you share the same facts or experiences. Likewise, no one can *make* you feel something. You alone are responsible for your own feelings.

Even though feelings are not the be-all and end-all of our lives, they do perform an extraordinarily useful function. They are, among other things, inner guides about our choices. They are "messages from our soul"[1] about whether we are getting what we want.

POSITIVE FEELINGS

> *She who is sorrowful*
> *can force herself*
> *to smile,*
> *but she who is glad*
> *cannot weep.*
>
> Elma Lagerlöf[2]

There are differences in intensity among positive feelings: a little bit of feeling admired is nice, a fair amount of feeling desirable is good, an abundance of feeling happy is even better. But the quantity of positive feelings does not seem to affect their quality. According to one of the foremost experts on feelings, Willard Gaylin, "when we feel good, we simply feel good."[3]

When positive feelings arise, most women are ready to welcome them as they would a bouquet of flowers. However, some women find it less easy to do so. For example, the day that Warner Books bought my book *The Superwoman Syndrome* was one of *the* most exciting days of my life; but rather than enjoy the headiness of it all, I found myself feeling overwhelmed and scared by my joy and excitement. Then I began to feel guilty for not feeling good! Although I don't do this anymore, I know that millions of other women go through similar experiences every day.

To explain the inability to "feel good about feeling good," one need only understand that women sometimes think that having positive feelings is selfish. And we know that for women selfishness is anathema. If you are among the women who continue to engage in this practice, let me suggest that you do something now to stop this nonsense for yourself—and everyone near and dear to you. Feeling good is not narcissistic; in fact, health researchers have found that the hallmark of health and well-being is having a predominance of positive feelings over negative feelings.

Do everything you can to create positive feelings. Go back to all those things that you said you were interested in and wanted to do in chapters 5 through 9. Do the things you love, spend time with fun, nurturing people, find activities that really turn you on, visit amazing places, create warm and cozy spaces, read marvelous books, and listen to thrilling music. You'll feel good as a result of doing these things. As I have said over and over, feelings are controlled by thoughts and actions. So right now start thinking and acting more positively: your feelings will follow along. And when those good feelings arrive, savor them.

We don't often have words at our fingertips to capture what we're feeling, and as far as I am aware, there is no easily accessible inventory of feelings. So here is a list of positive feelings, A through Z, to which you can refer. (Later on I'll give you a list of negative feelings.)

POSITIVE FEELINGS, A THROUGH Z

A	ambitious, alert, assertive, able, affectionate, authentic, alive, assured, admirable
B	brave, balanced, beautiful, blessed, bold, bright, brilliant, buoyed
C	capable, competent, creative, curious, centered, courageous, cherished, content, compassionate
D	delighted, defined, deliberate, dependable, deserving, desired, determined, dignified, directed
E	elated, excited, energetic, engaged, eager, easygoing, efficient, elegant, enthusiastic
F	fortunate, focused, funny, fascinated, fashionable, feminine, festive, fit, flexible, free, fulfilled
G	good, generous, gracious, genuine, giddy, glorious, graceful, grateful, great, gutsy
H	happy, healthy, handy, hardy, helpful, hip, honest, hopeful
I	important, independent, imaginative, included, insightful, inspired, intelligent, interested
J	joyful, jolly, jazzy, jovial
K	kooky, kind, knowledgeable, knowing
L	lovable, lusty, lucky, launched, leisurely, likable, lively
M	merry, motivated, magical, mature, mellow, mischievous, modest, moved
N	neighborly, nice, normal, natural, neat, nostalgic, novel, nurturing
O	open, outgoing, optimistic, on fire, organized
P	powerful, pretty, playful, positive, productive, pampered, passionate, peaceful, persuasive, popular, praised, proud, purposeful
Q	quiet, qualified, quick
R	resourceful, real, resilient, relaxed, radiant, reasonable, recognized, refreshed, relaxed, relieved, renewed, respected
S	serene, satisfied, successful, smart, sexy, self-assured, spontaneous, safe, secure, strong
T	talented, tranquil, triumphant, tender, terrific, thankful, thrilled, touched, trusted
U	unstoppable, understanding, understood, unique, up, useful
V	vigorous, valuable, valued, versatile, victorious, virtuous, vital
W	worthwhile, well, wild, wacky, warm, wealthy, welcome, whole, wise, worldly
X	x-cited, x-ceptional
Y	young, youthful
Z	zestful, zany, zingy, zippy

Confident women embrace their positive feelings.

NEGATIVE FEELINGS

Negative feelings are another thing again. As Gaylin says, "in sharp contrast to positive feelings, there are infinite ways of feeling badly, all discrete and different."[4] He also notes that in contrast to positive feelings, "the quantity of negative feelings alters their quality."[5]

Let's take anger as an example of how feelings grow and intensify, sometimes exponentially. Particularly among men (because anger is an emotion women are taught is inappropriate for them),

- anger often starts out as simple annoyance
- then becomes irritation
- and if not caught, can mount into hostility
- which propels into rage
- which then can explode into violence.

Suffice it to say, because *all* feelings are legitimate, feeling angry is legitimate; but what really counts is what a person does with his or her strong feelings such as anger. Negative feelings offer us incredible opportunities for making right what is wrong in our lives. This chapter is all about how to do that.

Negative feelings can be very confusing. Like unannounced houseguests, they sometimes appear from "out of nowhere" and in numbers that you don't expect: shock, excitement, annoyance, self-consciousness, and anxiety can all show up at the same time. (They also frequently hang around longer than you want.) At times we don't know how we really feel until days, perhaps years after something has happened. As I've said, many women didn't know how they felt about being sexually harassed until they watched the Clarence Thomas hearings—many, many years after the actual harassment incidents took place.

It's not good to stuff your negative feelings

Many women are uncomfortable with and/or frightened by their negative feelings, especially jealousy, disappointment, anger, envy, and fear. Women have told me that they're scared that these feelings will overwhelm them or get out of control. One very common approach is to leave them alone, or "stuff" them. But researchers say that no matter how painful, silly, stupid, mean, or ugly you think your feelings are, sooner or later stuffing them away will lead to their reemergence in unwanted, undesirable ways or in physical symptoms.

Ironically, when you try to put a lid on "inappropriate" or "unaccept-able" feelings, they often accumulate and gain power. Someone can say or do something that "hurts" you and you let it pass by—you put it in the back of your mind. You do this over and over and over again, day in and day out, month in and month out, year in and year out. Usually this happens when the people causing us pain are those closest to us (as in husbands or boyfriends or mothers or fathers) or people with whom we have to deal on a regular basis (like colleagues and bosses). The slights, put-downs, forgot-ten promises, criticisms, irritating habits, or gross misbehavior accumu-lates, and after a while that pocket gets awfully full.

Then some little incident occurs, and you become an emotional vol-cano. You blow up and can't understand (or sometimes even remember) what it was all about. Afterward you feel just awful, and the people around you think that you're a little nuts. From years of observing this female predilection to "stuff, stuff, stuff, and then the unexpected blowup," I have come to the conclusion that this behavior may be one of the reasons why women have gotten the reputation for being hysterical and overemotional.

How about letting your feelings all hang out?

Spilling your guts is just exactly as charming as it sounds.
                                                    Fran Lebowitz

Another common approach to negative feelings is to tell *everybody* about *everything* we feel. While it's useful to give *ourselves* permission to feel whatever we feel, that doesn't mean that it's useful or constructive for us to express our feelings to the world or even to people with whom we are close. As author Esther Hautzig says, "Feelings are untidy."

The current cultural bias toward expressing strong emotions probably began sometime in the 1950s and 1960s, when certain therapists encour-aged patients to confront their emotions and express them. This was sup-posed to help people get over their respective birth traumas, early childhood abuses, and so forth, with the result that the patient could then feel better. Fortunately in the 1980s we had other psychologists such as Carol Tavris to straighten us out. Among other things, Tavris noted in her book *Anger* that informing others how bad we feel by "blowing off steam" doesn't really make us feel better at all; if anything, that behavior often makes us feel worse. Furthermore, contrary to current public opinion, telling people off doesn't help get rid of strong feelings; it frequently inflames them.[6]

Mixing freedom of speech with the notion that manners are outmoded gives many people the impression that there's something positive about public displays of strong emotions. Just turn on the TV to observe talk show hosts who encourage their guests and audiences to tell everyone "how they really feel." It's not a pleasant sight to behold.

Willard Gaylin says that "letting it all hang out"—that rather vulgar yet descriptive expression for talking about all of your feelings—should be seen as a form of public littering much akin to dropping a dirty Kleenex on the sidewalk.[7] He and other thoughtful people suggest that each one of us has a responsibility to preserve our dignity and be selective about what we say to others until we have some constructive way of expressing ourselves.

Holding back much of what you feel is being protective not only of yourself but of the sensitivities of others. In the end, feelings should serve as relevant and important pieces of information about our actions and should not become the actions themselves.

Uncomfortable feelings are not necessarily bad

Uncomfortable feelings are not as menacing as you might think; in fact, they can be a powerful tool for fixing what's not working in one's life. Frequently uncomfortable feelings develop as women engage in any of the Seven Negative G's: they *give away* too much of themselves, they *give in to* what they don't want, they *give over* to others' manipulation, they *give up* their dreams, they *give way* to the stresses of life, they *give back* more than is needed, and they *give ground* to friend and foe alike. These G's are often the negative face of something quite positive among females—their predilection to care, nurture, connect, serve, and make peace. But when the "gives" get out of control, more often than not they leave women feeling resentful, ripped off, guilty, exhausted, addicted, and sometimes ill.

Confident women are able to step back and become aware of their uncomfortable feelings, identify what those feelings are—including what they are trying to communicate—and then decide what actions to take. In other words, confident women learn to trust their "gut."

Lara's story

Young in age yet wise beyond her years, Lara is a classic example of someone who used her uncomfortable feelings to figure out what was going wrong in her work life. After she graduated from an Ivy League college, Lara's first job was as a junior programmer at XYZ, a high-tech computer company in Minneapolis. Here is some of what she told me:

> *Life as a computer programmer has been up and down for me. When I first came to XYZ, I worked directly with one person, Mel, a company VP, but my official manager was another person, Ken.*

Mel and I got along wondrously—like two peas in a pod. While he was a vice president in the company and I was a junior programmer (JP), there was no hierarchy in our relationship. When I came to him with my ideas, he always treated them as if they were just as valid as his. Some of the best times I ever had at the company were when he and I would retreat into a conference room and just brainstorm. We'd throw up ideas, build on them, and always come up with new and better ones. We were a great team. Mel was much higher up in the company flow chart, but he was someone I respected, liked, and learned from. I always felt like he had my interests at heart.

Ken was another story. From the day I started working for him, he struck me as slippery. Questions I asked would be diverted. Suggestions I made would be dismissed or forgotten. I always felt as if Ken's first priority was making himself look good. He would promise things like time off or raises, then not follow through. Time and again he would tell us junior programmers that he would get us what we needed (new programs, better computers, better Internet connections, even basic necessities like chairs to sit in!), but nothing ever happened until a JP took it upon himself or herself to go directly to the company person who was in charge of meeting that particular need.

So what happened to me at XYZ? The company decided to create a new technical support service. I told Ken that I would like to take on that position since I had been doing some of the work anyway. Ken was thrilled to have someone already in the company who wanted to do the job. I asked him for a raise and a title change, which I deserved, since I was due both in my current position.

From the very onset of my new position, Ken was difficult. I should have anticipated this based on his previous behavior, but I thought if I worked hard enough, he would come around. He told me that he couldn't make me a manager because I was inexperienced and had just a couple of years with the company. (That response should have set off a big alarm!) But because he wanted to fill the position as soon as possible, he asked me if I would start and then he'd get around to a raise and new title later. He also said that he would retroactively pay me for the salary increase when all the paperwork was done. Well, skip ahead four months—no raise or title change in sight. In fact, nothing happened except that the work piled up, and because of Ken's constant blocking, I was the only one there to do it.

Work days that used to end at six now went on to seven, eight, nine, and ten, and still I was falling behind under the increasing workload. I had no time to think about ways to structure and develop the department (ostensibly what I was supposed to be doing), and when I did write up a proposal, Ken (1) criticized me for "working outside of the box," and (2) told me just to focus on getting my work done.

Furthermore, at every turn — at meetings, in personal remarks, or in e-mails — I was admonished for trying new ideas or offering suggestions to improve the department; in other words, by trying to be better than Ken wanted me to be, I was making life more difficult for myself. He obviously feared any positive changes that I might bring about, because that would have been a direct threat to his making those changes and reaping the benefits. All the while, I was sinking.

So how did I feel? I felt (1) powerless to do anything to change my situation in the company, (2) disrespected, (3) put down, (4) caged in, (5) not supported, (6) not trusted, and (7) treated as if I were valueless.

I longed for the days when I was working with Mel, having fun, being supported, feeling productive and smart, liking and being liked. I remembered the day I cried as I told Mel I had decided to take the new position. Now I was crying almost daily because I hated my situation. I was frustrated, unhappy, overworked, and stressed out. I felt just awful.

It wasn't until I decided to take a week away from work with a bunch of my former college roommates that I realized how unhappy I was, and how it was affecting the rest of my life. Away, I was able to relax. I spent time with good friends and remembered what it felt like to feel good. I remembered how it felt to be supported when times were tough. I slept in and remembered how it felt to not be tired. I played tennis and volleyball and remembered what it felt like to move my body and not sit in front of the computer for twelve hours a day.

When I came back to my job after vacation, I was changed. I decided not only that I wanted to be happy and feel good, but that I also had the right to do that. I decided that my suffering probably wasn't going to benefit anyone in or out of the company (except maybe Ken). So I started looking for alternatives. Within the company I could go back to programming, but that would be a step backward. Besides, my old position had long ago been filled.

I started looking outside the company, consulting friends. On a whim I contacted an old college buddy of mine who was working at another computer company in Chicago. The day after I e-mailed him my job inquiry, I got a note back saying "How soon can you start!!?" He was excited at the possibility of having someone with my talents and intellect working with him. He was a project development officer for his company and wanted me to join him. I had never done his particular kind of work before, but he told me not to worry, that I was smart and would pick it up in no time.

Wow! What a difference! I felt as though the world was opening back up to me again. I hadn't been in a good work situation in months, so I wasn't feeling very confident about my own abilities. In spite of having graduated cum laude from my college, in just four short months I was almost convinced that I wasn't smart, didn't have any talent, was an emotional disaster, and couldn't think well on my own.

But I knew back in the depths of myself somewhere that I could find that confident, smart, talented woman that my college friend knew and was hiring. Needless to say, I jumped on the opportunity. Hello, Chicago!

Let's take Lara's situation and see what we can learn about how to put your negative feelings to productive use.

WHAT TO DO WITH YOUR NEGATIVE FEELINGS

There is a process for using your negative feelings, and it involves these seven steps:

1. Get away and calm yourself.
2. Become aware of, identify, and describe your feelings.
3. Figure out what your feelings are trying to communicate.
4. Ask yourself if you want to express your feelings.
5. Ask yourself, what actions can I take?
6. Take the action.
7. Reward your positive thoughts and actions.

Step 1. Get away and calm yourself

When we're in the middle of a lot of negative feelings, we're so overwhelmed by them—and the situation causing them—that it's difficult to have any perspective. We need to get away and calm ourselves. In everyday life that may simply mean going to another room, taking a walk alone, or finding a spot to sit and think.

Many women have difficulty getting their heads clear if they are around other people. So if you are a married woman and/or have children and have been plagued by negative feelings for a while, you might need to get away by yourself or with a friend. (Maybe take a weekend away to one of those favorite places you identified in chapter 5.) Yes, you can do it. It's healthy for you to do it. Think of these words as if they were a doctor's prescription.

For Lara, it meant going away for a week with her college friends. When she got away from her work and especially from her boss, she was able to realize how unhappy she was—and how it was affecting the rest of her life.

Lara also did something that we talked about in the last chapter: she created a positive situation for herself, she went away with positive, nurturing people, and she got involved in a lot of activities that she loved. These actions helped her to calm down, get a better perspective on her feelings, and figure out the reasons behind them.

After just a week Lara's batteries were charged again and she was able to set herself on a corrective path.

Step 2. Become aware of, identify, and describe your feelings

Observing our own feelings can tell us much about our mental life.
William James

When you're feeling bad, sometimes you get so caught up in those bad feelings that it seems impossible to figure out what they are. Ask yourself these two questions and then write down your answers:

- What or how am I feeling right now?
- When did I start feeling bad?

Most of us were not taught by our parents how to name our feelings—quite the contrary, daughters were told that we shouldn't or didn't have the negative feelings we were experiencing. So many women have difficulty putting names to what they feel. By naming your feelings, you open the door to more accurately diagnosing why you feel the way you do. As Albert Ellis, the rational-emotive psychologist, says, "The more aware you are of your feelings, the greater the chances for your getting rid of them."[8] To this I add getting rid of them *constructively* rather than *destructively*.

Sometimes keeping a diary of how you feel is useful. You don't have to do it for a long time—a week is usually long enough. You can keep track of your strong emotions in entries that look something like this:

Lara's Negative Feeling Diary[9]

Day/time	Trigger	Intensity of Feeling (on scale 1–10)	Duration	What Happened/ How You Felt
1/10 8:00	Boyfriend snapped at me	4	2 minutes	Sam called to say that he wouldn't be coming over. I got upset, and he said he couldn't do anything about it.
10:00	Woman in elevator at work crowded in front of me	2	15 seconds	Brief encounter, no big deal.
11:00	Supervisor avoided my calls.	8	2½ hours	It took me 2 hours to get the supervisor to talk to me about project. I felt frustrated, ignored, and stuck. When I finally spoke to him, he was curt, unhelpful, arrogant, and attacking.

Fortunately, Lara was able to sort out what her negative feelings were. To the question "What am I feeling right now?" as you know, she answered: "powerless," "not respected," "put down," "caged in," "valueless," "frustrated," "unhappy," "overworked," tired out," and "just awful." To the question "When did I start feeling bad?" Lara was able to identify that her bad feelings had begun when she started working for Ken.

In case you have difficulty identifying your negative feelings, here is a list to help you along.

NEGATIVE FEELINGS, A THROUGH Z

A   angry, annoyed, afraid, agitated, anxious, ashamed, abandoned, apprehensive, abused

B   blue, bored, burdened, burned out, bad, betrayed, beat, bewildered, bitter, blamed, blocked, bullied

C   caught, confused, constricted, crippled, closed

D   depressed, dissatisfied, discouraged, dumb, dull, defeated, defensive, disgusted, drained, dangerous, dark, dependent, deprived, distracted

E   embarrassed, energyless, exhausted, edgy, empty, envious, evil, excluded, exploited, enraged

F   foolish, frustrated, fearful, frightened, (like a) failure, fake, flaky, fooled, frail, frantic

G   guilty, grief-stricken, greedy, gloomy, gray, grim, gross, grouchy

H   hating, hopeless, hunkered down, helpless, hurt, hostile, hesitant, handicapped, harmed

I   insecure, incompetent, irritated, indecisive, ill, inadequate, intimidated, immobile, inferior, irritable, ignorant, insignificant, invalidated, insulted

J   jealous, jaded, jilted, jittery, judged, jumpy

K   keyed up, kicked, klutzy, knocked down

L   lonely, (at a) loss, lacking, lax, lazy, left, let down, limited, listless, lost

M   misunderstood, melancholy, miserable, mad, managed, manhandled, marked, mean, meek, moody

N   negative, nervous, nagged, neglected, numb, naive, nasty, naughty, needy

O   old, overloaded, overwhelmed, obligated, odd, off balance, offensive, opposed, oppressed, outraged

P   pressured, purposeless, pessimistic, panicky, powerless, pitiful, pained, paralyzed, passive, pawed, peculiar, persecuted, pessimistic, picky, prejudiced

Q   quaky, quarrelsome, queasy

R   resentful, rejected, raped, raw, ravaged, rebellious, reckless, regretful, remorseful, replaced, reproached, resigned, restrained, righteous, robbed, rotten, ruined, rushed

S   sad, stressed, shamed, selfish, sorrowful, shy, silly, stupid, silenced, self-righteous, subordinate, sapped, scattered, screwed, self-conscious, shaky, sheltered, shocked, sick, silly, stuck

T   tense, timid, threatened, tactless, taken advantage of, torn, tested, thoughtless, tight, troubled, tumultuous, turned off, thwarted, trapped

U   upset, uncomfortable, unhealthy, uptight, uncertain, unattractive, unlucky, unappreciated, undeserving, unhappy, used, ugly, unable

V   victimized, vacant, vague, vetoed, vicious, violated, violent, vulgar

W   worried, worthless, weak, whiny, worn out, worn down, wan, wanting, weepy, wary, wasteful, watched, wavering, whipped, wicked, wishy-washy

X   xenophobic

Y   yucky, yellow

Z   zilch, zombielike

Step 3. Figure out what your feelings are trying to communicate

Sometimes our negative feelings send out small signals telling us that something is awry. Other times the signal is much louder and warns us that we are in real emotional or physical danger. Sometimes our negative feelings are false alarms, the source of which is often the same cognitive distortions and specious belief systems that pollute our negative thinking. Different from thoughts, though, our feelings come as vague, amorphous, coded messages that often need to be deciphered before we can do anything with them.

To help decode your negative feelings, ask yourself these questions. (Again, write down your answers.)

WHY AM I FEELING THIS WAY? WHAT IS GOING ON HERE? WHAT ARE THE FACTS OF THE SITUATION?
I like what Carol Dressler, president of a Silicon Valley executive search firm Dressler Associates, asks herself when she feels uncomfortable: "Is this really what I want to do, or am I doing this because someone else wants me to?"

Write down exactly what circumstances are causing you to feel bad. Where are you? Is anybody else involved? What happens? Who says what to whom?

WHAT ARE MY FEELINGS TRYING TO TELL ME? AM I DOING ANYTHING TO CONTRIBUTE TO OR DISTORT THIS SITUATION?
Take a look at the feelings you have identified, and analyze them for ways that you may be distorting what is going on. What messages are your feelings sending you? Are you setting limits? Have you done anything that violates your own or other people's sense of appropriateness or respect? Go back to the "Cognitive Distortions" and "Beliefs Women Have" lists in chapter 11 to see if any of them apply now.

WHAT SITUATION(S) AM I IN WHEN I FEEL ———?
Look at how you are feeling, and assess when and where those feelings arise. Are they present all the time, in some situations, or in one situation?

WHO AM I WITH WHEN I FEEL ———? IS HE OR SHE SAYING OR DOING SOMETHING THAT AFFECTS HOW I FEEL?
Ascertain if and when your negative feelings develop around certain people. Is someone stepping on your emotional toes? If the answer is yes, then identify who they are and what they are saying.

When people communicate with us in negative ways, we know we feel bad, but it's often difficult to sort out exactly why. Our reactions to what they have said can be so confusing. We all know how inexact communications are. Sometimes what someone says leaves us feeling wary or uneasy; there's something going on, but we're not quite sure what. At other times, people's words leave us with a sick feeling in the pit of our stomachs, or feeling blindsided, startled, and shocked. To help you better understand and diagnose negative words, here are various ways that people communicate that can, in turn, affect how we feel.

NEGATIVE COMMUNICATIONS GRID

ANOTHER'S WORDS	LABEL	HOW YOU FEEL
"You look fat in that dress." "This food is terrible." "Why the hell don't you just shut up!" "The whole department is going to suffer because of you." "Tom's wife is a really good cook. Wouldn't hurt you to try, would it?" "Why don't you stand up to your boss? You just want everybody to love you."	ATTACKING, CRITICIZING, JUDGING (assailing with unfriendly or bitter words, pointing out faults)	Devalued, judged, hurt, rejected, unappreciated, not respected, unsafe to be yourself, wounded
"That's not the way to do it!" "I will not stop. You'll listen to what I have to say and like it. You can't tell me what to do!" "You're going off your diet again! Are you ever going to exercise?" "Why did you buy that TV? Do you always have to pay the highest price? Where do you think the money's coming from?"	BADGERING, BULLYING (harassing, annoying, browbeating, belittling, insulting)	Negated, judged, condescended to, discouraged, useless, guilty, inadequate, powerless, undermined, pressured, childish, stupid

ANOTHER'S WORDS	LABEL	HOW YOU FEEL
"Why can't you be more sexy?" "Hellllloooo! Will you stop with that incessant talk, talk, talking on the phone. I don't care who it is."		
"You really made a mess of things." "Why do you think I work my tail off? For fun? No! For you and the kids." "You just hold on to things—you never let go!" "You make me depressed." "You don't care about anything except yourself."	BLAMING and ACCUSING (charging or finding fault or placing responsibility for)	Startled, judged, criticized, guilty, devalued, misunderstood, undermined, mistrusted, wrong, bad
"You have no right to get angry with me." "You waste all your time trying to make stupid things perfect." "I don't want you to spend time with those people anymore." "Why do you need a new dress? Especially such an expensive one?" "You always have to be right, don't you?"	CONTROLLING and BLOCKING (trying to restrain or direct influence over)	Criticized, dismissed, invalidated, judged, minimized, misunderstood, treated like a child, unacknowledged, unappreciated, unimportant
"Don't mind me. I'll just go to the movie alone." "If you cared about me, you'd make the time." "You're making a big deal out of nothing." "You know my friends' daughters-in-law bring their grandchildren over to see them all the time."	GUILT-SLINGING (charging one with a breach of conduct)	Blamed, controlled, criticized, judged, pressured, unforgiven, mistrusted, guilty, selfish

"I know you're a mother, but do you think it's fair to others that you leave the office so early?"

. . . .

"There's nothing to be afraid of. Why are you such a baby?" "Don't you think your friend is taking real advantage of you?" "You don't know what you're talking about. You're just being duped." "It's not hot; it's just warm." "I'm not the one with the problem; you're just overreacting."	INVALIDATING (weakening or destroying the cogency of)	Wrong, out of touch with reality, negated, condescended to, controlled, invalidated, judged, misunderstood, not supported, discouraged, not heard

. . . .

"Here we go again, Miss Perfect. I've had it with your complaints." "Don't be such a baby." "You're crazy." "Bitch!" "You really are selfish!"	NAME-CALLING (using offensive names, especially to win an argument or to induce rejection or condemnation)	Bullied, condescended to, criticized, dismissed, hurt, invalidated, uncared for, undermined, unloved, insulted, bad

. . . .

"You take too long to do things." "What's the matter with you?" "You have nothing to complain about." "You look like a mess." "Your paper is bad."	PUTTING DOWN (disparaging, belittling, humiliating, squelching, degrading)	Blamed, condescended to, criticized, invalidated, judged, not respected, ridiculous, foolish

. . . .

"Do this, and this, and this, and this." "Get me some coffee." "I want you to have dinner ready at seven every night." "Here. Write this report for me."	TELLING, ORDERING (ordering or directing)	Bugged, annoyed, condescended to, frustrated, minimized, very resentful, uncared for, coerced, stressed, put upon, not respected, childish, angry

ANOTHER'S WORDS	LABEL	HOW YOU FEEL
"I need you to go get some gifts for me."		
"You'll do it and you'll like it!" "You better stay out of my way." "I'm warning you . . ." "I'm not going to put up with this much longer."	THREATENING (expressing an intention to inflict evil, injury, or damage)	Thrown off balance, unprepared, surprised, shocked, fearful, hurt, mistreated, not cared for, scared, worried, unsafe
"You think you work hard? Well, tell me who earns the real money in this family." "You shouldn't feel bad about what happened." "I don't care about how you feel." "You're too sensitive. I have a right to say whatever I want." "Listen, quit making such a big deal about a little flu."	TRIVIALIZING (saying that someone or something is of little worth or importance)	Empty, criticized, dismissed, invalidated, judged, minimized, misunderstood, unacknowledged
"I can't believe you waste your time on that group." "Spending the weekend with you is so boring." "You don't know what you're talking about. You're wrong." "That's a flimsy excuse." "Who do you think you are!"	UNDERMINING (subverting or weakening insidiously or secretly)	Caught off guard, disdained, discounted, blamed, criticized, dismissed, invalidated

While it's useful to be aware of how people's words trigger many bad feelings, it's also useful to take the advice of Deborah Tannen, author of *You Just Don't Understand*: "misunderstandings can arise, and with them tempers, when no one is crazy and no one is mean and no one is intentionally dishonest. We can learn to stop and remind ourselves that others may not mean what we heard them say."[10]

WHEN HAVE I FELT THIS WAY BEFORE?

It's very useful to know if and when you have experienced these strong negative feelings before. The answer to this question will often lead you back to certain kinds of situations and/or certain people.

IS THERE SOMEONE WITH WHOM I CAN TALK WHO CAN HELP ME GAIN SOME PERSPECTIVE?

Sometimes it's beneficial to enlist the help of a trusted friend to fig- ure out what's going on. If that person is not readily available, you might do what Los Angeles real estate developer Dana Goodman does: she asks herself, "If my best friend came to me with the same feelings as I have now, what would I tell her? Okay, that's what I need to tell myself." Other times you might want to talk with a trained therapist. Whatever works for you is what you should do. Experiment by talking to various people until you find one who can really help.

Once again, let's return to Lara and see how she answered these questions.

WHY AM I FEELING THIS WAY? WHAT IS GOING ON HERE? WHAT ARE THE FACTS OF THE SITUATION?

Lara wrote: "Why am I feeling powerless, disrespected, put down, caged in, valueless?"

Her reasons were pretty clear: She was feeling miserable because Ken was undermining her efforts, not following through on his promises, not giving her what she needed, criticizing her efforts, and blocking any positive changes she wanted to make.

WHAT ARE MY FEELINGS TRYING TO TELL ME?

The answer to this question was also clear: Lara's feelings told her that she was frustrated, unhappy, overworked, and tired out.

AM I DOING ANYTHING TO CONTRIBUTE TO OR DISTORT THIS SITUATION?

Lara had spoken to Ken on numerous occasions about correcting the various situations that were leading her to feel bad, but these efforts seemed to have a boomerang effect: he became defensive and even more critical of her.

WHAT SITUATION AM I IN WHEN I FEEL SO UNHAPPY?

Lara saw that her unhappiness was directly related to her taking on the technical support position and working for Ken.

WHO AM I WITH WHEN I FEEL UNHAPPY?
The answer to this question was obvious: Ken.

WHEN HAVE I FELT THIS WAY BEFORE?
Lara looked back on her life and determined that she had never experienced the frustration and unhappiness she was experiencing with Ken and the XYZ job.

IS THERE SOMEONE WITH WHOM I CAN TALK WHO CAN HELP ME GAIN SOME PERSPECTIVE?
After consulting the personnel manager in her company and other junior programmers, Lara was able to see that her contributions to the problem were minimal. Everyone agreed that Ken, not Lara, was the problem.

Step 4. Ask yourself if you want to express your feelings

As we have already seen, there are many nonproductive ways of addressing negative emotions. Certainly complaining, blaming, lecturing, accusing, and attacking another person are among the least fruitful. These actions predictably exacerbate and complicate whatever is going on. But deciding to talk with someone about your feelings can be an effective move. As I have noted, this does not mean "letting it all hang out."

"I" Language

The most responsible way of getting your feelings across to someone is to use "I" language. You may recognize the term "I" *language* from things you have heard about parent effectiveness training. Thomas Gordon and other parenting experts teach "I" language as a nonjudgmental way of speaking to children and adults.

Most of us used "I" language when we were very young. Watch a three-year-old as she talks about what she wants: "I want ice cream! I want to go play!" There is no mistaking her desires. As we move through childhood, though, the "I's" slowly seem to disappear. As girls grow up watching mothers, older sisters, and other women, they often learn to get their needs met indirectly. They begin to replace "I's" with "you's" and say things such as "Wouldn't *you* like to go to the beach today?" when that's where they want to go, or "I bet *you'd* like to go out for a Big Mac" when that's what they want to do. After a while many girls get what they want and what other people want so mixed up that they are no longer able to figure out what their true wants and desires are.

We lose our "I's" in other ways as well. One of my clearest memories from high school is my first high school English paper that had red marks through every "I" I had written. Not only had the English teacher, Mr. Palmer, completely marked up my paper, but at the end he wrote, "Who cares what *you* think or feel? Who do *you* think you are, somebody important or some authority?" Ouch! Believe me, from that point on, I almost never used the pronoun *I* in writing papers. As you can tell from this book, however, somewhere along the way I found that it really was okay.

"I" language is made up of three parts and sounds like this:

- **When you A** [describe the action],
- **I feel B** [identify your feelings]
- **because C** [identify the consequence of the action].

Here is a real-world example: Your daughter has gone over to her friend's house after school without informing you. You say to her:

Ineffective Communication	*"I" Language Communication*
"You are just the most inconsiderate, thoughtless girl I know. How dare you go to Judy's house without telling me! You're grounded!" (These are attacking, threatening words.)	"When you went over to Judy's house and didn't phone me [A], I felt really worried [B] because I didn't know where you were or why you weren't home [C]."

Here's another example: Your husband is very upset with you because you don't want to go with him to visit some of his friends. He says to you, "I can't believe you! You don't care about anything except yourself!" You reply to him:

Ineffective Communication	*"I" Language Communication*
"How dare you say that! I've gone with you to places I haven't wanted to go thousands of times!" (These are defensive words.)	"When you tell me that I don't care about anyone but myself [A], I feel judged and put down [B], because I do care about you. I just don't want to go to the Nielsens' house this weekend because I'm exhausted [C]."

Here's a work example: A colleague screams at you, "I just hate when you treat everybody else like dirt around here. I'm not going to put up with your disgusting attitude anymore!"

Ineffective Communication	*"I" Language Communication*
"How dare you talk to me that way! You can't tell me what I can or can't do." (These are hostile words.)	"Phyllis, when you tell me I treat people badly and call me names [A], I feel hurt and upset [B] because I wasn't aware at all that what I said was disrespectful. Tell me more about what you mean [C]."

Most of us have knee-jerk reactions to negative things people say to us. "I" language gives us an opportunity to "cut off at the pass" potentially escalating, negative interactions and avoid fights and arguments. When you say "I feel . . ." instead of "You are . . ." or "Why do you . . ." it restores a kind of rationality and judgment to a conversation. It also helps you to not act out your strong negative reactions.

Here are some other examples of how "you" is used that are not effective:

"You never . . ."
"You always . . ."
"You should . . ."
"You make me feel bad."
"It's your fault."

Acting out our bad feelings can take any number of forms, including (1) pouting, (2) silence or withdrawal, (3) sarcasm, (4) defensiveness or reactive criticism, (5) negative body language, such as making faces, (6) rudeness, (7) playing the martyr or victim, (8) slamming doors or throwing things, (9) swearing, or (10) drinking too much. These behaviors do not stop other people; they irritate and arouse them.

Using "I" language does take some getting used to — and practice. If you would like to learn how to effectively use this technique, there some books in the bibliography to which you can refer. You can also take an assertiveness/communication training class, or seek out a counselor/executive coach who is an expert on the technique.

Let's go back to Lara again.

On numerous occasions Lara spoke to Ken. She used proper "I" language and was as respectful as she could be. The real problem was that Ken was almost always disrespectful of her and never properly used "I" language.

Step 5. Ask yourself, what actions can I take?

As with so many of the suggestions I have made in this book, the best way to deal with a problem is to become active, not to sit back and wait for it to become solved by others or fate. As you look at what you have said about your uncomfortable feelings, what possible options do you have for dealing with them? Ask yourself: What do I want to do and when?

Basically there are three ways of looking at a situation:

• **You can change your attitude about the situation or person**
(that is, change the words you use to describe what is going on and accept the situation as it is or the person as he or she is)

• **You can change the situation**
(that is, change the circumstances that are bothering you the most and accept the circumstances you can't change. But don't fall into the trap of thinking that you can change another person. That is one of the most prevalent, self-defeating attitudes you can have. Even if it's in their best interests, you cannot change other people. *It never works.*)

• **You can change situations**
(that is, go on to something or someone else)

Here is how Lara approached the question of what to do and when:

CHANGE YOUR ATTITUDE ABOUT THE SITUATION OR PERSON
Lara first looked at the option of changing her attitude about her job and Ken. She told me that she tried "every which way" not to feel overwhelmed by the requirements of the job and not to dwell on how much she disliked Ken and how he treated her.

While she loved working at XYZ and liked many of the people, the nature of the job as defined by Ken made it impossible for her to feel anything but powerless, disrespected, put down, caged in, and valueless. So changing her attitude was not an option.

CHANGE THE SITUATION
For all of the above reasons, Lara could not change the nature of her work situation. Her position was completely under Ken's thumb. Not surprisingly, even though she tried to be "nice" to Ken, "confront" him, even "ignore" him, she could not change him. So changing the situation or person was not an option.

CHANGE SITUATIONS
After Lara went away on her vacation, she realized that she needed to get out of that work situation. First she tried to find another posi-

tion within XYZ, then looked outside the company. That's when she was offered the job in Chicago. For Lara, the best option was chang-ing situations.

Step 6. Take the action

We've already discussed how to develop an action plan. To summarize what this involves: Remember what's important, get clear about your goals, break your goals into subgoals including dealing with barriers, then create a "to do" list with due dates attached.

LARA'S ACTION PLAN
Once Lara decided that she was going to accept the job offer in Chicago, she created a series of "to do" lists including: "Things I Need and Want to Do to Leave XYZ" (with a timetable), "Things I Need to Do to Find Housing in Chicago" (again with a timetable), and "Things I Need and Want to Do to Get Settled in My New Job."

As I have worked with various women, two questions often come up with regard to taking action: What if the option I choose doesn't work? and What if I fail? This is how I answer those questions.

If your first option doesn't work, try another. Who says that a first try is always supposed to work anyway? If nothing else, *some* parts of it usually work. As the saying goes, "Nothing ventured, nothing gained." Think of all the first tries in life: first drafts, first kisses, first bicycle rides, first cooking ventures, first attempts at finding cures for diseases, first rocket launches. How many of them have succeeded straight away? Keep in mind that when something doesn't work, the information generated from the failed attempt is often the key to what will work the next time around.

What if you fail? Let me remind you that no one is perfect. As with the previous question, if one option fails, then you always have the choice to try another. Like everything else in life, the process of using your feelings to determine what you're going to do takes practice. Of course you might fail. But remember, there is no failure in trying, only failure in not trying.

Step 7. Reward your positive thoughts and actions

Don't forget to acknowledge and reward your positive thoughts and actions. Why? As I've said many times before, you're more likely to con-tinue thinking and acting positively if you do. One woman told me that she has a group of old friends who help one another to celebrate "victories — little and big." As she said, "It's so simple. We feel good to see one another happy. So each one of us wins when one does something good."

Lara was very pleased with herself for getting on top of her bad work situation. She effectively used her negative feelings as a springboard for corrective action. What's more, she did not dwell on her regrets at leaving the XYZ, although she had made many good friends there. Rather, she moved very quickly into celebrating her new position and the renewal of her friendship with the Chicago friend. What's most important, she rediscovered the confident, smart, talented woman she knew herself to be.

A year later Lara is still in Chicago, enjoying her new work and moving in a career direction totally different from what she was headed for at XYZ. It appears that she has also met "the love of her life." So you see, negative feelings can be the start of something very, very good.

Obviously, not all negative feelings need to be examined through this comprehensive process. The seven steps are especially useful for handling feelings that are particularly strong or seem to hang around for a while. To get used to the process, you might first use the process with something simple, such as uncomfortable feelings that might develop in a phone call from a friend. Then you can go on to more complicated feelings, such as those involved with being a working mother. Or you might take a look at the exasperation you feel about a needy, dependent brother or sister. Or maybe you're feeling blue because it's your birthday and there's no one around to help you celebrate. Or perhaps you want to deal with fears about an upcoming career move. Potentially all negative feelings can be dealt with by using this seven-step process.

The most important thing to know, though, is that you can do something about those feelings and situations. Don't give in to your feelings; use them. It's simply a matter of deciding which ones, how, and when.

HANDLING NEGATIVE OR DESTRUCTIVE COMMUNICATIONS

Obviously there are an infinite number of situations and people around which negative feelings can develop. In one arena, however, women seem to have the most difficulty handling their feelings and knowing what to do: facing someone's disrespect, upset, or anger with them. This is a real confidence-buster and the number-one issue among women who ask me for help.

Over and over women describe what happens to them. Here is an example:

I just hate it when someone snaps at me, puts me down, picks at me, or "tells" me what to do. All I do is choke on it and feel miserable.

It's like my mind freezes. And if someone really gets mad at me and yells, well, forget it. I feel so startled and confused that I become paralyzed. I don't know what to say or do. Usually I end up either saying nothing or blurting out something defensive or stupid. After it's over, I have fantasies about what I might have said, like whipping out some witty, razor-sharp retort.

As you probably are aware, none of the above reactions work very well. To say nothing is essentially to reinforce the negative behavior, while to blurt out something defensive is to invite a more elaborate explanation of why the person feels the way he or she does. Even though it might momentarily feel good, reeling off witty retorts is likely to raise the power stakes and escalate into further negative interactions. I assume that none of the above is what you want.

Destructive communication defined

When faced with negative words, women have difficulty sorting out the difference between ordinary communication and *mis*communication (and sometimes stupid mistakes), and knowing when they cross over to destructive or abusive communications. The rule of thumb is this:

Destructive and/or abusive communication is when a communicator's intentions, attitudes, words, and behaviors are disempowering, disrespectful, and/or devaluing.

All of the words and types of behaviors I identified in the "Negative Communications Grid" on pages 231 through 234 fit into the destructive or abusive category.

Please know this: no one has the right to say or act toward you in ways that are inconsiderate, insensitive, disrespectful, critical, hostile, sarcastic, imposing, manipulative, dictatorial, bossy, rejecting, controlling, or abusive. It is your *right and responsibility* to respond to these behaviors in constructive ways.

Constructive ways to handle negative communication

You cannot make yourself feel something you do not feel, but you can make yourself do right in spite of your feelings.
                                                              Pearl S. Buck

Here are some constructive ways to handle difficult negative communications:

Prevent and Avoid

Confident women prevent and avoid destructive and/or abusive communications by choosing to be with people who do not engage in these kinds of behaviors. They are very careful to keep close relationships with only those people who treat them with respect, care, and concern. As I have said before, you can usually eliminate disrespectful people from your life. If you can't (because of circumstances beyond your control such as being related to, living next door to, or working in close proximity to them), you can limit and control the amount and type of time you spend with them. You can also have a lot of control over the communication that takes place.

Choose to Deal With or Not

While no one should allow anyone to speak to them in a disrespectful or abusive way, you must remember that in many situations people inadvertently say or do stupid, inconsiderate, or thoughtless things. In many cases, it probably makes sense to ignore them. After all, if we felt a need to act on every annoyance or twinge of hurt, we'd drive ourselves and everybody else crazy. That's called hypersensitivity. And of course, you always have the alternative of using "I" language.

If you have difficulty deciding whether to let a remark pass or to deal with it, go back to my old formula of assessing something on a scale from 1 to 10. Let's say that your father blurts out that he thinks you should drive more carefully. Fathers do that kind of thing. Even if he is correct, how you take his words will depend upon how his words make you feel, the tone of his voice, the attitude he exhibits, his intentions, where you are, and whether this is the first or the fiftieth time he's said it. If you are only slightly irritated by his words, then simply consider the source, let it roll off of you, and go on with your driving. If you find that you are feeling more than slightly irritated, then you can ask yourself, on a scale from 1 to 10, how annoyed you are. If it's below 8, then forget about it. If it's 8 or above, then you can choose to deal with the issue, using "I" language.

Don't Waste Time Trying to Figure Out Why People Act Badly

Whether it's your boss yelling at you, your sister blaming and attacking you, or your husband using hostile words—if you get a sick feeling in the pit of your stomach (a true 8 or above), then you know it's something you need to deal with. Anger is what people feel; aggressive acts are what they do.

Sarcasm, insults, blame, attack, and hostility are all inappropriate, aggressive acts that serve no good purpose.

As I have said before, women often want to understand and be understood; therefore they have a knee-jerk tendency to want to know why someone would be sarcastic or insulting or blaming or attacking or hostile toward them. This often becomes the stuff about which we ruminate—and you know from a previous discussion how ruminating is bad for us. Wanting to know the reason for someone's aggressive behavior is both self-destructive and a waste of time.

Martin Seligman, the eminent expert on emotions, has a fascinating explanation for why the overt expression of anger is bad for everyone.

Anger Is Bad for Everyone

• Overt anger is not "the truth." While some people are under the impression that it's honest to tell the object of their anger what they think, there is a difference between honesty and the truth. Anger may *feel* honest to the person experiencing it, but it colors how they view the world, causing them to see it in hostile and threatening ways. Therefore, the judgments that people make when they are angry are frequently far off the mark.

• Anger aims for revenge and restitution. It is a moral emotion that is filled with self-righteousness, and it imposes a protective, self-interested lens on the eyes of the person experiencing it. Even more important, anger fuels violence. Out-of-control anger ruins many lives, and its effects are devastating, often more potent than the effects of schizophrenia, alcohol, depression, and even AIDS.

• Overt anger is unhealthy for the person experiencing it. It produces high blood pressure and heart disease. For example, in a number of studies the angriest people had five times more heart disease than the less angry.[11] Anger also exacerbates depression.[12]

• Anger damages relationships and is especially destructive for children. Serious turmoil between parents can be the most devastating event that children experience, and it has lasting effects. Children who observe their parents fighting can end up as "unbridled pessimists" who experience more depression. They may see bad events as permanent and pervasive and feel themselves to be responsible.[13]

Yes, anger in some form is always with us. It's a fact of life. As I said above, it's not the fact of anger but what we do with it that's important.

There are alternatives to expressing anger and other strong negative emotions. There are more effective ways of dealing with how we really feel.

Positive Actions for Negative Emotions

Anger and conflict are inevitable; fighting is a choice.
Anne Wilson Schaef

We've already seen how you can deal with your own negative emotions. Now let's turn to how you might deal with the negative emotions of others.

• To Deal With or Not to Deal With.
First ask yourself whether you want to deal with the remark. If not, go on with what you were doing. If you do, then proceed to the next step.

• Get Ahold of Yourself.
Breathe deeply. Then stand or sit tall, hold your head high, and look the person straight in the eye. Think to yourself that you are going to speak calmly, firmly, competently, and clearly. Tell yourself that you accept full responsibility for what you want in your life. Do *not* whine, cry, plead, try to explain yourself, or act like you are worthless, defeated, or unimportant. Do *not* allow yourself to fall into the trap of acting like a victim or a martyr.

• Use Humor.
If you can and it's appropriate, try saying something of a humorous nature. That's often enough to defuse a tense situation.

• Respond.
Depending on what was said, you might respond with "I" language or one or more of the following comments or questions:

For Mild-to-Moderate Negative Communications
- "Tell me what you mean."
- "I don't understand. Give me some examples."
- "I want to think over what you've just said. I'll get back to you this evening (or in a few hours or tomorrow)."
- "I'll discuss this with you when you're calmer."
- "This is what I think. . . ." "This is what I would like from you. . . ."
- "This is how I feel. . . ."
- "I love you, but I care about me too. This is what I need to do to take care of myself."

– "I'm sorry that you're having this problem. Is there something that you would like me to do to help?"
– "No, I don't want to do that."
– "Your attitude and tone of voice make me very uncomfortable. I'll talk with you when you calm down."

For Hostile, Threatening, Abusive Communications
You must set limits directly and firmly with whoever is speaking to you in these terms. This is *not* the time for "I" language or for mincing words.

– "I don't have to respond to angry words."
– "Stop it! I don't want you to talk to me like that. I don't deserve to be criticized (blamed, attacked, put down, called names)."
– "This is as far as I go. I will do this. I will do that. I will not tolerate . . . This is my limit."
– If you want to talk that way, that's your business. But you can't do it in front of me. Either you stop, or I'll walk away."
– "I'm going to see a counselor. Will you join me?"
– "Your behavior is inappropriate."
– "I want to be asked or consulted, not told what to do. I don't follow orders."
– "You may not raise your voice to me. I don't want to listen to this kind of talk from you."
– "If you don't stop, I am leaving the room (house)."
– "Stop that kind of talk right now."

> *Violence is the last refuge of the incompetent.*
> Salver Harden

Confident women know that becoming more competent in handling their feelings is the harbinger of positive change.

———

Most of this chapter has been about ordinary people with ordinary feelings. If you should experience any extremes in your feelings, you should definitely contact a health or mental health professional. In the appendix of this book is a quick preliminary self-test for you to take to evaluate whether or not you may be depressed. Also, the comments I have made regarding negative communications from others are meant for ordinary circumstances.

If you are experiencing any kind of physical or emotional abuse, see a health or mental health professional or call a domestic violence hot line right now. Again, in the appendix there is another self-test for you to take to evaluate whether or not you are being abused.

Inner awareness is the beginning of outer change.

Anonymous

Before we leave this chapter, here is a Thought Break.

THOUGHT BREAK

No matter how much you care, some people just don't care back.

It takes years to build trust, and only seconds to destroy it.

You can do something in an instant that will give you heartache for life.

You should always leave loved ones with loving words, because you never know if it's the last time you'll see them.

Two people can look at the exact same thing and see something totally different.

No matter how hard you try to protect your children, they will eventually get hurt.

It's hard to determine where to draw the line between being nice and standing up for what you believe.

Maturity is more about the types of experiences you've had than about the number of birthdays you've celebrated.

No matter how good a friend is, you're going to be hurt every once in a while and you must forgive.

It isn't always enough to be forgiven by others; sometimes you have to forgive yourself.

Either you control your attitude or it controls you.

You have a right to be angry, but that doesn't give you the right to be cruel.

It's not what you have in your life that counts, but who you have.

You are responsible for what you do, no matter how you feel.

Your background and circumstances may influence who you are, but you are responsible for who you become.

ANONYMOUS

CHAPTER 13

Taking Control of Your Life

I'D PICK MORE DAISIES!

If I had my life to live over,
I'd try to make more mistakes next time.
I would relax. I would limber up.
I would be sillier than I have on this trip.
I would be crazier. I would be less hygienic.
I would take more chances, I would take more trips.
I would climb more mountains, swim more rivers,
and watch more sunsets.
I would burn more gasoline.
I would eat more ice cream and less beans.
I would have more actual troubles and fewer imaginary ones.
You see, I am one of those people who lives
prophylactically and sensibly and sanely,
hour after hour, day after day.

Oh, I have had my moments
And if I had it to do over again, I'd have more of them.
In fact, I'd try to have nothing else.
Just moments, one after another.
Instead of living so many years ahead each day.
I have been one of those people who never go anywhere
without a thermometer, a hot water bottle, a gargle, a
raincoat, and a parachute.

If I had to do it over again, I would go places and do things.
I'd travel lighter than I have.
If I had my life to live over, I would start barefooted
earlier in the spring and stay that way later in the fall.

I would play hooky more.
I wouldn't make such good grades except by accident.
I would ride on merry-go-rounds.

I'd pick more daisies!

Nadine Stair
(age eighty-five)

John Farquhar, the director of Stanford University's Center for Disease Prevention, says, "We are what we do; we become what we have done."

Think about that statement for a minute. Make it personal: "I am what I do each day." What do you *do* every day? Now think ahead to when, God willing, you are eighty-five years old. What will you have *done* that will make you feel most proud? What will be your *I would haves*? When you are gone, how will people remember you? What will your tombstone say?

A few years back, I asked myself these questions. The first thought that popped into my head was: "Here lies Marjorie Hansen Shaevitz — she did a lot . . . of chores and errands." Unfortunately, this was both a literal and metaphorical description of my life at the time. Every day, every month, every year melted into one never-ending "to do" list.

Like so many other women then and now, I was engaged in a kind of female machismo in which I perceived that keeping busy, doing more (faster), and feeling stressed meant that I was a successful woman. Whenever I spoke with one of my female friends, we always ended up in a friendly competition of "I can stuff more into my life than you can."

Some make things happen.
Some watch things happen.
Some ask, "What happened?"
Anonymous

WHY WOMEN DO AND OVERDO

Many women incorrectly think that compressing the largest number of things into the smallest number of minutes is the most efficient way to use their time. Frankly, I think some women become addicted to the adrenaline stimulated by their maddening pace. Women from all age groups and backgrounds have told me that they can't stop to think or organize or change what they do because they already have too many demands on their time. Finally, some women are under the impression that, if they just work hard and long enough, someday everything will get done and they can relax. Of course, that time rarely comes. Usually it takes a major life crisis or a serious illness to get women to change their ways and be more self-responsible.

Beginning about twenty years ago, women started wanting to "have it all" — marriage, a family, a successful career, a beautiful home, an active social and/or volunteer life, and regular church/synagogue involvement. When I coined the term *Superwoman Syndrome* in the early 1980s, women came to hear me speak about the topic so that they could learn how to do more and be more efficient — in other words, how to become a better Superwoman! Oh, how disappointed they were when I told them that this was unhealthy! Rightly so, many women today don't want to have anything to do with Superwoman — both the term and the behavior are seen as suspect, if not politically incorrect. However, women's actions often belie their healthier thoughts. I see women doing more now than when I first wrote the *Superwoman* book. If anything, their behavior hasn't changed; it's gotten worse.

Every year the standard for what women should "be and do" is raised. Directly and by implication the media tell us that we're still supposed to be nurturing, yet also relentless in proving our work mettle. We're told that our career aspirations should be equal to men's, in spite of continuing to bear an inordinate share of family and household responsibilities. We read that it's okay to get old, but only if we look like Jane Fonda, Goldie Hawn, or Cher. It goes without saying that we need to be attractive so that the "right" kind of man will want to marry and stay with us. We can thumb through any magazine to see how our home is supposed to look: not only "cleaner than clean" but decorated as if it has just come out of the pages of *House Beautiful* or *Architectural Digest*. Everyone knows that the meals we serve should be low in fat, high in fiber, nutritious, and delicious. But if we really want to impress company, the food should also look as if it has been Martha Stewart–designed on the plate. One of the strongest messages we get is that our children should not only be beautiful and well mannered but also involved in enough activities (and AP courses) to get accepted into an Ivy League college. Shockingly, the path to the Ivies today seems to begin in preschool. Finally, if any of the above are neglected, then the woman in question is surely deficient, inefficient, incompetent, or a failure. Like sleepwalking automatons, women try to be everything to everybody and end up doing it all except for taking good care of themselves. Rarely do they stop to think about or evaluate what they're doing. They just keep going and doing. (And as a result, the behavior women model is mimicked by their children — many of whom do not know how to "play" or sit at home and daydream or just be.)

> *No woman chooses evil because it is evil; she only*
> *mistakes it for happiness, the good she seeks.*
> Mary Wollstonecraft Shelley[1]

The question must be asked: What is all this for? What does the frenzied lifestyle — running around, flying here and there, rushing to and fro, having exhausting days and sleepless nights — do for us? Okay, so we're just doing what we're supposed to be doing. Okay, so we're working in order to support or help support ourselves and/or our families. My guess is that we're also doing all this because (at least on an unconscious level) we think it's going to make us happy.

HAPPINESS

As I was writing this book, I took some time to grapple with the question "What is all this for?" It led me directly to the subject of happiness.

Notable women have had some intriguing things to say about happiness. For example, Anna Pavolva, the great Russian ballerina, said, "I thought that success spelled happiness. I was wrong. Happiness is like a butterfly that appears and delights us for one brief moment but soon flits away."

What happiness is not

Every day we are bombarded with advertising messages that declare that happiness is, not elusive or transient as Pavolva suggests, but immediately available and ceaseless. If we are to believe Madison Avenue, happiness is just around the corner in a big fat check (as in winning the lottery), a purchase (as in that sleek, fancy car), an experience (as in going on a cruise), a "look" (as in having perfect skin), or a man (as in a handsome, rich guy). Happiness is everywhere! And what fools we are not to get as much of it as we can. The impact of all this hype is rather alarming.

Of late, I have been struck by how many women in my private practice say they are worried about not feeling happy all the time. Some women have actually said to me, "Oh my God, I'm not happy! What's wrong with me? Should I be on Prozac?" Some women even report feeling guilty about not being happy. These are not depressed people, nor are they narcissistic; they're just misguided. Expecting to be happy all the time is at best unrealistic and at worst destructive—causing us to feel depressed. The truth is that no one is *always* happy.

Happiness is not wealth

Likewise, expecting to gain happiness by becoming "rich and famous" is uncertain and precarious. Counter to what most people believe, research says that there is a very weak relationship between the acquisition of material things, the accumulation of wealth, and the attainment of fame, on the one hand, and satisfaction with one's life, on the other. Billionaires in America are only infinitesimally happier than those with average incomes.[2] In fact, "beyond the threshold of poverty, additional resources do not appreciably improve the chances of being happy."[3] Think of all the unhappy lottery winners, miserable celebrities, and "poor little rich girls" you have read about in the newspapers over the years.

Having worked with women of great wealth in my private practice, I have seen that money and happiness do not necessarily go hand in hand. In fact, for these women money posed more problems than it solved. They worried about whether people, especially men, liked them for themselves or for their money. Because they didn't *have* to earn a living, they were frequently at loose ends as to what to do with their time; they jumped from one unfinished project to another. Every single one lacked focus and meaning to her life.

This latter issue is at the crux of a study Kenneth Pelletier conducted at Stanford University on fifty prominent individuals (including women participants such as artist Laurel Burch, Congresswoman Claudine Schneider, philanthropist Eileen Rockefeller Growald, and AT&T vice-president Dorothea Johnson) who represent the prototype of professional success and prominence. In looking at what constitutes a healthy, happy lifestyle, Pelletier found that the key to well-being was not material abundance but, rather, moving beyond materialistic and competitive concerns to "altruistic or self-transcending behaviors based on a sense of higher purpose and/or spiritual values."[4] As with everyone else, what the rich and famous *do* that has meaning and purpose seems to determine whether they experience life as happy, healthy, and worthwhile.

Happiness is not thin

I would be remiss if I didn't once again mention that women associate happiness with having a thin, beautiful body. Judith Rodin, one of the country's leading authorities on body image, says that "while twenty years ago appearance was felt to be an issue, today national surveys show that we have never been so preoccupied and dissatisfied with our bodies."[5] Too many women think that if they could just lose a certain amount of weight and/or have a certain look, then they would be happy. But health experts tell us that this is far from the truth. Women who are obsessed with their self-perceived imperfect bodies often contribute to their own unhappiness by not doing nice things for themselves — until they have a body that they think is deserving of good treatment.[6]

Rodin opines that "bodies do matter . . . caring about your body is normative. But preoccupation and obsessive worrying are normal responses pushed to the extreme by a society that places too great an emphasis on how the body looks."[7] Research shows that: (1) The more you focus on your body, the more aware you become of its flaws and the more you try to be like some unrealistic ideal. Increased body focus hurts, not helps, us.[8] (2) The practice of thinking you need to lose weight before taking good care of yourself is self-defeating. Healthy, effective weight loss actually happens as a result of self-care: doing things to feel good often enables one to take control of weight.[9] (3) When people stop feeling ashamed of their appearance, they gain time and energy to find out what they really want and need and to fulfill those wants and needs, a key to becoming a happier person.[10] (4) Women who do not define themselves totally as their bodies, but instead identify a variety of roles, activities, experiences, and personal contacts that matter to them, are more likely to experience greater happiness. As Rodin says, "it is much easier to add joys to our life than [it is to] subtract pounds."[11]

Rather than trying to change our bodies, health experts suggest that we change our actions. They urge us to stay away from people and activities who lead us to feel bad about ourselves and our appearance, including:

- People (including friends and relatives) who care *only* about looks and appearance, either ours or their own.
- People who belittle us or our appearance.
- People who make negative comparisons to media ideals in magazines, inane television shows, movies, and other sources of images. As Rodin says, "if you can't stop comparing, then stop looking."[12]
- Activities that inflame our body anxieties and insecurities, such as joining gyms where everyone else seems to be a part of the beautiful people crowd, attending bikini-clad party or vacation settings, and the like.[13]

Like having great wealth, being thin and beautiful isn't all that it's made out to be. Rodin says that "more often than not, [thin and beautiful women] are tormented by uncertainties of who they really are, worried whether people will like the real them, and insecure that without their looks they would have nothing."[14]

The fact is that no matter how hard we work to avoid it, the aging process eventually catches up with us. There comes a time when, even for the thinnest and the most beautiful women, youthful looks are no longer a possibility or a reality. That's normal, and that's life. As I have said many times before, we women are so much more than how we look. When it comes to appearance, I love Lynne Alpern and Esther Blumfield's perspective:

> *If you go through life trading on your good looks,*
> *there'll come a time when no one wants to trade.*

Happiness is not other people

I've already discussed the implications of thinking that other people are responsible for our happiness. Perhaps it's best summarized by the thought that if you depend on another to make you happy, you will be endlessly disappointed. As the late Agnes Repplier once said, "It isn't easy to find happiness in ourselves, but it's impossible to find it elsewhere."

Alas, while happiness comes to us some of the time, life's challenges seem to be with us almost all the time.

Let's face it, life is difficult

At the beginning of his best-selling book *The Road Less Traveled*, M. Scott Peck reminds us that there is a never-ending supply of problems, burdens, and difficulties — life is difficult. This is one of life's great truths, according to Peck, but most people don't see this truth and instead incessantly complain about the enormity of their problems as if life were easy, as if life *should* be easy. He goes on to say that it's all too human for people to think that *their* difficulties represent a uniquely unjust affliction, and that *their* difficulties have somehow been especially visited upon them or else upon their families — and not upon others.[15] The aforementioned "I have more 'stuff' to do than anyone else" is one version of this kind of thinking.

What is it that makes life difficult? Life is difficult, Peck declares, because of the emotional pain (such as worry, anger, frustration, loneliness, guilt, and anguish) that ensues from having to deal with our daily challenges. Every person has a choice either to moan and groan about what they have to face — their pain and troubles — or to accept, act on, and deal with it.

Once we truly accept that life is fraught with

- ongoing problems (we or a family member has a chronic health issue),
- everyday difficulties (the dishwasher or refrigerator or washing machine breaks down),
- annoying situations (the freeway ride is taking longer and longer),
- ordinary burdens (the bills need to be paid),
- minicrises (the water pump in our car has just burst), and
- megacrises (lost jobs, lost loves, the childcare person has just quit)

. . . and that this is normal, then we can get on with addressing our challenges and spend more of our time and energy on the positive aspects of our lives. When we finally do this, Peck says, life no longer seems so difficult. Real life involves an ongoing parade of major and minor challenges that are interrupted by moments of serenity and contentment.

Confident women recognize and accept that happiness is both transient and elusive and that life is fraught with everyday problems and challenges.

WOMEN AND CHANGE

Action may not always bring happiness, but there is no happiness without action.

Albert Camus

Perhaps the biggest barrier that women have to feeling happy is their reluctance to address challenges and make positive changes. Women — much more than men — are prone to chew on something, to brood about it, and in their minds to obsess over it. Again much more than men, women tend to say "I can't," "I shouldn't," and "There's nothing I can do." *When women feel overwhelmed by their lives and are hurting, their propensity is to want to talk about it, not to do something about it.*

Because girls are raised to be more passive, they learn to live with difficult situations for far too long for their health and well-being. Because girls are raised to be more dependent, they are discouraged from solving their own problems and making their own choices. As a consequence, many females engage in a lot of wishful thinking, including wanting someone else to make decisions for them, hoping that someone else will "make it all better," and expecting someone else to change. More than anything else, these propensities compromise a woman's ability to overcome obstacles and take control of her life.

We can overcome most obstacles

God changes not what is in a people, until they
change what is in themselves.

Koran

According to Mihaly Csikszentmihalyi (pronounced "CHICK-sent-me-high-ee"), a professor of psychology at the University of Chicago, people don't want to admit it, but the ability to overcome most obstacles is within their own hands.[16] This is as true for women as it is for men. Translated to "I" language, that thought becomes "*I* have the ability to overcome most obstacles." Yes! Know it, believe it, and say to yourself, "I have the ability to overcome most obstacles" over and over again. The next time you hear yourself say, "I can't," remember that more often than not "I can't" really means "I won't" or "I didn't" or "I don't want to," not "I am unable to."

Confident women take ownership of their lives in spite of what life brings them, good or bad. They learn to handle a broad array of people and situations and find resources to help them do so.

Some facts about happiness

So if happiness is neither wealth nor fame nor material possessions nor good looks, what is it? We know from Kenneth Pelletier's work that engaging in meaningful activities often leads to feelings of happiness. What else will get us there? As I looked through the literature for characteristics and actions of happy people, this is some of what I found:

1. Happiness Is Doing.
Over and over, the leaders of the new field of positive psychology declare that one's quality of life depends, not on happiness alone, but on what one does to be happy.[17]

2. Happiness Is a Side Effect.
The research of one of those leaders, Martin Seligman, has revealed that "happiness . . . develops as a side effect — of mastering challenges, working successfully, [and] overcoming frustration and boredom."[18]

3. Happiness Is a Life Fully Lived.
In his book *The Pursuit of Happiness,* social psychologist David Myers says that happiness is not specific to any age or gender and is not even dependent on physical wellness. Even the most tragic of physical injuries or illnesses, he finds, does not necessarily inhibit one's delight in living. Rather,

happiness comes from "a life fully lived,"[19] in other words, from taking advantage of all our God-given talents and abilities and pursuing them to the nth degree.

4. Happiness Is Having Goals and Using Your Mind.

Apparently having goals is an integral part of leading a happy life. Furthermore, positive psychology experts say, if a person does not use her mind to the fullest in pursuing those goals, then the good feelings she has, including happiness, are just a fraction of the potential she might reach.[20] Happiness, then, is also using your mind.

5. Happiness Is Feeling Good About Your Work.

Csikszentmihalyi's work suggests that "in terms of the bottom line of one's life, it is always better to do something you feel good about than something that may make you materially comfortable but emotionally miserable."[21]

6. Happiness Is "Flow."

Csikszentmihalyi has also identified "flow" as one of the highest forms of happiness. "Flow" occurs when you focus your "heart, will, and mind" on what you are doing, you forget yourself in the activity, it goes on effortlessly, and you enjoy it so much that you don't want to do anything else. "Flow" can be experienced when you are working or studying or volunteering or involved in some creative project or hobby such as gardening, writing, or painting. Some people experience flow when they are involved in certain sports.[22]

7. Happiness Is Being Connected.

Wellesley College's Stone Center researchers have found that women feel happiest when they are well connected to the main people in their lives, including "doing for" them (that is, supporting them, empowering them, taking care of them, doing nice things for them, and the like).[23] Myers adds that happy women (and men) spend as much time focusing on the well-being of others as on themselves, but they also know how to receive as well as give.[24]

8. Happiness Is Having a Spiritual Orientation.

Myers also says that a happy person is likely to have a spiritual orientation to his or her life.[25]

9. Happiness Is Having a Good Attitude.

I would be remiss if I didn't mention Csikszentmihalyi's wonderful insight for making the most of the humdrum aspects of our lives. There are many things in life we must do and don't like doing, he says, such as paying bills, taking care of household chores, and going to meetings. Some activities are unavoidable—those that we can't eliminate or manage to get help with—and no matter how ingenious we are, we still must do them. So the choice, he says, is either to do these activities against the grain, grumbling about the imposition—or to do them willingly, with gusto. In both cases, he says, we're stuck having to do the activity, but in the second case the experience is bound to be much more positive.

10. Happiness Is Having Control of Your Life.

Successful people feel that they can affect the course and destiny of their lives. In a study of prominent executives, City University of New York researcher Dr. Suzanne Kobasa found that happy, healthy individuals have a sense of personal control over their lives.[26]

> *All things being equal, we may expect the scientist [or artist or housewife or executive] who is happy, secure, serene, and healthy to be a better scientist than if she were unhappy, insecure, troubled and unhealthy.*
>
> Abraham Maslow

So what can you do to bring more happiness to your life? To better master the problems and challenges you inevitably face? To gain control over your life? I have spent the last ten years looking for answers to these questions, and in the last couple of years I have queried hundreds of women for their ideas and suggestions. The remainder of this chapter summarizes the best of what I have found.

I can't promise you a rose garden

First, it's important for you to know that I can't *promise* to make you happy or to make your problems go away. No one can do that. Also, I can't promise that my suggestions will be easy or comfortable for you to implement. Personal inertia is always a strong force to contend with, and even good change can be uncomfortable at times. As you know, all actions carry with them consequences—some pleasant and others not so pleasant.

> *Logical consequences are the scarecrows of fools and the beacons of wise men.*
>
> Thomas Henry Huxley

CHANGE

Edward Deci, a University of Rochester psychologist and author of the best-selling *Why We Do What We Do,* has great insight into the circumstances under which people are most likely to make positive personal changes. First of all, he identifies *what doesn't work.*

What doesn't work

When it comes to personal change, what doesn't work is doing something

- because someone who is in a one-up position over us threatens to punish us if we don't
- because someone else (or even our own selves) is pressuring us to do it[27]
- because internalized *shoulds, oughts,* and *have-tos* that come from outside values and rules motivate us[28]

I am impressed by the brilliant common sense of Deci's explanation. According to Deci, when a person does something because of an outside threat or pressure or an internalized *should,* one of three behaviors results:

1. Rigid, dutiful compliance
(doing what we are told because we are told to do it)[29]
2. Half-hearted adherence
(doing what we are told with minimal effort or standards)
3. Outright defiance and rebellion
(doing the opposite of what we are told, just because we have been told to do it)[30]

Compliance and adherence, Deci says, produce change that is not likely to be maintained, while defiance blocks change in the first place.[31] He offers three examples of how compliance, adherence, and defiance get negatively played out.

1. Compliance.

The best-selling author Michael Crichton went to medical school to please his family. As Deci says, Crichton's family thought that growing up to be a doctor was exactly the right thing for Michael to do, the thing he ought to do, and for a long time Crichton believed it himself. But after many years of training Crichton chose not to practice medicine but to do instead what he really wanted to do: write. This decision horrified Crichton's family and cost him much training for a career he did not want.[32]

2. Half-hearted Adherence.

A young man went into his family's business because he thought he "should," but in his heart he didn't really want to. As Deci describes him, the young man literally spent years whining and complaining about how badly things were going, and coming up with a million excuses. As you might expect, the business eventually failed.[33]

3. Defiance.

A lawyer's son didn't want to become an attorney, even though there was family pressure to do so, and instead got into trouble with the law. As another example of defiance, Deci mentions a minister's daughter who, under pressure to become more and more pious, became a vocal, dyed-in-the-wool atheist. Pressure (parental, spousal, professorial, or supervisorial) is experienced as control, Deci says, and the internal response is often, "You can't control me; I'll show you who's in charge here!"[34]

What does work

According to Deci, effective behavioral change is most likely to occur "when people accept themselves, take an interest in why they do what they do, and then decide that they are ready to do something differently."[35] Some of the elements that are likely to contribute to personal change involve doing something:

- because of a true personal desire to change and a readiness to commit ourselves fully
- because of feelings deep inside that our actions are our own choice
- because we are interested in it, engaged in it, and find it personally important
- because we believe it will lead to a desirable outcome[36]

Some notable examples of people effectively changing their behavior (and their lives) include Michael Crichton's decision to leave medicine to write novels, Sally Ride's decision to leave NASA to teach college students, and the late Princess Diana's decision to forgo other activities to focus on her passionate interests—AIDs and land-mine removal. While these changes were momentous for the individuals involved, Deci's ideas apply equally to the most mundane everyday changes one might make, including deciding to exercise every morning before work, deciding to schedule Thursday evenings with a good friend, or deciding to take a pottery class.

Of course, sometimes all of the positive elements of change are not in place and it's in our best interest simply to act. After all, actions do change feelings. Deci's major message is not that we need to have everything perfectly in place before we act, but that the decision to act should be ours alone, not someone else's.

Others' reactions to change

One of the likely consequences of change is that some people will not like it. Frankly, such people may be the toughest part of the change process. Please, please don't let that deter you. Remember, even if it's your husband (lover, significant other, boyfriend) or children or parents or boss or best friends, you are not on this earth *just* to please other people or to do what others want or are comfortable with.

Even if you wanted to, it's impossible *never* to irritate, annoy, or displease anyone. Obviously you want to act responsibly toward others. Obviously you don't want to purposely do things that will hurt others. If, in being responsible to yourself, however, you happen to step on someone else's overly sensitive toes, remind yourself that "it's not my job to make everybody happy." If they are normal, healthy people, they will adapt and eventually get over it and respect you.

An out-of-control lifestyle wherein pressures and stresses eat at your body and your mind does no one any good. Decreased resistance to illness, sleep problems, eating disorders, irritability, high blood pressure, and many other physical and emotional symptoms are the result. David Reynolds, a proponent of a form of positive psychology called Constructive Living, says that "when you don't do anything to change what is happening [to you], when you don't build or learn or move or oppose or educate or otherwise respond to your circumstance, you are in for trouble unless Fate steps in and turns the burner down for you."[37]

TAKING CONTROL OF YOUR LIFE

Erratic uncontrolled lifestyles produce erratic
uncontrolled people.

David K. Reynolds

Here are some actions that you can take to get control of your life:

1. Eliminate unimportant, nonessential activities and events.
2. Act on your priorities.
3. Let someone else do it.
4. Become a "solution nut."

1. ELIMINATE UNIMPORTANT, NONESSENTIAL ACTIVITIES AND EVENTS

The first major step toward regaining control of your life is to engineer your everyday actions so that you spend more and more time on meaningful, rewarding, energizing experiences, and less and less time on the nonessential, meaningless, space-absorbing, energy-draining ones.

For the most part, our lives are on automatic pilot. Every day we engage in and repeat patterns of behavior that we have developed over the years. Not surprisingly, we don't pay very much attention to what we actually do, let alone evaluate what we have done. Each one of us leads what Plato called the "unexamined life."

In the course of an average day, it has been estimated that one-third of what we do is what we have to do and one-third is what we do willy-nilly because we have nothing better to do. Only one-third of our time is spent doing what we want to do.[38] (Since these estimates are for people in general, I would venture to guess that women spend even less than a third of their time on what *they* want to do.)

I don't know about you, but many women tell me that—particularly at home—they often start one thing (like preparations for dinner), only to find something else that needs their attention (the buzzer on the dryer rings, so they run off to pull out the dried clothes and fold them), which then gets interrupted by something or somebody else (the phone rings), during which they see something else that is calling for action (the beds haven't been made), and then they remember what was left behind (dinner preparations). Women end up starting a dozen different things, finishing some and leaving others half done; none of them are important, but all of them take a lot of time. This pattern is repeated in the workplace. Not that we should go crazy organizing every aspect of our lives; but I do think that women pay a price for living a totally reactive life.

Finish it

> *Efficiency is getting things done; effectiveness is getting the right things done.*
>
> Anonymous

One easy rule of thumb to begin using is this: When you start to do something, don't allow yourself to get distracted—finish the task. (But sometimes it makes sense not to start some tasks at all.)

To break out of our mindless ways and gain ownership over our lives, women would do well to pay attention to what they are doing and in the process eliminate unimportant, extraneous activities and events. You can add quality to your daily existence by making choices, rather than falling into doing whatever happens to you, or whatever someone asks of you, or or whatever comes to your attention. By consciously choosing what you do for a while, the pattern will soon become a habit about which you won't have to think.

Here are some ways for you to make conscious, deliberate choices:

To eliminate it or not to eliminate it?

To evaluate the importance of some activity or event, ask yourself these questions:

> **Do I really want to do this?**
> **Is it really necessary?**
> **What will happen if I don't do it or it doesn't get done?**
> *or*
> **What will happen if I don't go?**

• Example 1

At work you receive a notice that your professional association is having a guest speaker next week. The topic is of medium interest to you.

Mindless way of dealing with it:
You put it on your calendar without thinking and go.

In-control way of dealing with it:
You ask yourself:
  Do I really want to do this? No
  Is this really necessary? No
What will happen if I don't go? Nothing.

Mindful action:
You don't go.

• Example 2

You get a call from an old friend who is coming into town for the weekend. She invites you to go out to lunch at her hotel.

Mindless way of dealing with the old friend:
You meet her for lunch even though you have to scramble for child care and postpone a repairman appointment.

In-control way of dealing with her:
You ask yourself:
  Do I really want to do this? Yes, but lunch is going to be difficult.
  Is this really necessary to do? No, but I really want to do it.
  What will happen if I don't go? I'll miss seeing my friend.

Mindful action:
*You ask your friend to meet you at your house for deli-bought sand-
wiches. She says yes, and it all works out.*

To delay it or not to delay it?

Another situation that women often face is feeling pressured to do something immediately that could easily be done later. For this situation, ask
yourself:

Does this really have to get done right now?

• Example 1
You open the refrigerator while making dinner and see that it needs to be
cleaned out.

Mindless way of dealing with the refrigerator:
*You clean out the refrigerator, including the bins and the assorted
half-full jars that are sitting in the side door shelf. Then you decide
to clean out the freezer as well. Dinner is delayed half an hour.*

In-control way of dealing with it:
You ask yourself:
Does this really have to get done right now?
No, not unless something has spilled all over everything or crea-
tures have started growing on the food!

Mindful action:
*You wait until the weekend to clean out the refrigerator or delegate
the task to someone else (spouse, child, house cleaner).*

• Example 2
In the middle of writing a report, you put some papers back into a file and
notice that the file drawer needs organizing.

Mindless way of dealing with the file drawer:
*You take out all the files, replace those that are damaged, and cre-
ate new ones. The report doesn't get finished, so you take it home
to finish that night.*

In-control way of dealing with it:
You ask yourself:
Does this really have to get done right now? No.

Mindful action:
You make a note to yourself that the file drawer needs attention and finish the report (or you ask your secretary to clean out and organize the file drawer).

When to say yes and no

Many of us get into time trouble, not because of the things that we *don't want* to do, but because there are too many things we *think we want* to do. With so many invitations and possibilities open to us these days, we simply get seduced by all the opportunities! We don't want to miss seeing our friends or going to the great concerts that come to town or turn down invitations to join important boards or throw away opportunities to be in a play or deny ourselves the advantages of a professional club. But as with all things in life, including our favorite desserts, too much of a good thing can make us sick. The difficulty then is not just saying no, but in deciding when to judiciously say yes.

There is a very easy, handy technique for making a decision about whether to do something. And I must say that of all the techniques I have come upon over the last ten years, this one has made more of a difference in my life (and in the lives of my friends and clients) than any other.

Here is the technique. It involves asking yourself two questions, then answering them by assigning them a number on a scale from 1 to 10. (1 = no way, negative; 10 = absolutely yes; there's nothing I'd rather do.)

Two Questions to Know Whether to Say Yes or No
  Question 1: How much do I want to do this?
  (Rate the activity or event from 1 to 10.)
  Score: _____

  Question 2: Given everything else that is going on in my life, how important is it that I do this?
  (Rate the importance from 1 to 10.)
  Score: _____

Now add up the two scores:
  Sum of scores: _____

If the sum of scores from the two questions is 13 or less, don't do it. If the sum is 14 or more, then do it and enjoy yourself!
  It's as simple as that. That's all there is to it.

Here is how Sandy, an advertising executive who is a single mother, used the Two Questions technique.

After hearing me give a talk at a local hospital, Sandy called for an appointment to get my help in "getting better control of her life." One day as she was finishing up a session, she blurted out that she had to rush off to her children's school because the new principal was going to give her first speech. Since Sandy was on the parents' board, she felt obligated to go.

Sensing that Sandy wasn't all that keen about going to this event, before she could open the door to leave, I asked her if she would like to evaluate her decision. I told her that it would just take a couple of minutes. In spite of being in a hurry, she said yes. I explained the Two Questions technique to her, and together we went through it.

First I asked Sandy, "How much do you want to go hear the principal tonight? Give me a number between 1 and 10." I urged her to be really honest with herself about her answer and to think about how she really felt. Sandy said, "I'm really feeling bushed. This has been a very hectic week. To tell you the truth, how much I want to go is about 4." I said, "Good. Let's go on to the next question."

I then asked Sandy the second question: "Given everything else that is going on in your life, how important is it that you go hear the new principal tonight?"

On the side of attending the event, Sandy felt that it was important to support the new principal, particularly since Sandy was one of the parent leaders. Since this was the principal's first public appearance, Sandy was worried that, if she didn't show up, the principal might take offense. Sandy had two children at the high school, and she didn't want to do anything that might negatively affect the principal's feelings about her and especially her kids — after all, college recommendations were just around the corner.

On the side of not attending, Sandy was feeling tired. She had to go out of town the next morning and had to complete packing and preparations for the trip. Finally, with a thousand people at the event, the principal might not even notice that she wasn't there. Having heard all this, I then asked her to give me a number for how important it was that she go to the principal's speech that night. Sandy answered, "6 or 7."

I added her previous 4 to her 6 or 7 and told Sandy that her score was 10 or 11, below the "go for it" mark. She looked at me and seemed relieved. As she was leaving the office, she said, "Wow, thanks for doing this with me. I'm definitely not going tonight. It would never have occurred to me not to go, had we not evaluated the decision with that technique."

Dealing with invitations and requests

Stress is when your head says no and your mouth says yes.

Anonymous

Another technique, I have found, is very useful in helping women to gain control of their lives. It concerns face-to-face (or telephone) invitations and requests. Frequently, the technique helps women say no.

If saying no is difficult for you, you're not alone. Researchers have found that saying no is much harder for women than for most men. Carol Gilligan, the Harvard psychologist who wrote *In a Different Voice*, says that women are ever so much more concerned about the impact of their decisions on others, especially saying no to someone.[39]

Many women have told me that, since they take it personally and feel rejected when someone says no to them, they don't want to cause others to feel rejected by saying no. To this concern, I remind women that feeling rejected is a choice, both on their own part and others' parts. Other women have said that they don't like to say no because of the potential anger it might arouse in other people. To this concern, I remind them that we cannot control others' feelings, including their anger. Of course, we can do everything possible to act responsibly toward others — including not purposefully hurting or offending them — but short of this we cannot control their reactions.

Finally, some women don't say no because it never occurs to them to do so. "Yes" is their programmed, automatic response. To this I say, it's in your best interests to begin paying attention to what you say and do.

How to say no graciously

Here is a proven way to say no graciously and effectively. (Of course, it will probably not apply to an assignment you receive from an instructor or a boss.)

1. To begin with, NEVER, EVER say yes automatically to anyone who asks for your time or energy.
(And for goodness' sake, don't volunteer!)

2. Graciously thank the inviter for the invitation and say that you will get back to him or her within a specified amount of time (ten minutes, a half hour, a few hours, even tomorrow).

Tell the inviter that you need to check your calendar or consult someone else who might be involved.

By the way, this maneuver gives you some distance from the person or a situation so that you can gain perspective and decide with no pressure if you want to accept the invitation.

3. Decide whether you want to accept the invitation.

Don't forget, if you have trouble deciding, you can use the Two Questions method. Also keep in mind that you always have at least three alternatives:

- Saying yes, if you really want to do something.
- Making a counteroffer, if you want to say yes but the time or date or circumstances are not good for you.
- Saying no.

4. If you decide to say no, get back to the inviter, again graciously thank him or her for the invitation, and with no apologies or excuses say no. If you decide to say yes, go for it!

5. After saying no (or making a counteroffer), reward yourself for that behavior with a positive thought such as "Good for me!" "I did it!" "I'm finally getting control of my life!"

And for goodness' sake, *don't* beat yourself up for saying no. Replace any guilty or anxious thoughts with positive ones.

Here is an example of how to say no graciously. Mary Ann is a Northern California schoolteacher in her late twenties. I met her not long ago at a health conference at which I was speaking, and she told me about her "telephone problem." I asked her to explain.

Mary Ann's life is jam-packed with a husband and little boy at home, children and parents at school, and many, many friends. "Sometimes," she said, "I begin to think of my telephone as the enemy." She described how from the moment she arrives at home, "the phone rings off the hook, and the callers are pretty much people who want something from me: you know, either to bake something, or do something, or go someplace, or help them with a problem. I could just scream!" Could I offer her some help for what to do about all of these phone requests? I asked her to describe the last "request" she had received. "Mrs. Ellis," she replied, "one of my room mothers, asked me to bake six dozen chocolate chip cookies for the parent bake sale." When I asked Mary Ann what her reply was, she said, "Well, yes, of course! I didn't want to hurt her feelings."

I told Mary Ann about the "How to Say No Graciously" technique, and we used it to go through the chocolate chip request.

1. To begin with, NEVER, EVER say yes automatically to anyone who asks for your time or energy.

First I instructed Mary Ann to NEVER, EVER say yes automatically to anyone who asks for her time or energy. She said, "Great, I won't."

2. Graciously thank the inviter for the invitation and say that you will get back to him or her within a specified amount of time

Mary Ann and I went through what her response might have been. She could have said something like: "Mrs. Ellis, thank you so much for thinking of me for the bake sale. I really appreciate it, and I am so impressed with what the Mothers' Club is doing for the school. Listen, I'm not really sure what the schedule is next week; I think that midyear reports are due. I'd like to check with the principal and get back to you about the cookies tomorrow after school."

3. Decide whether you want to accept the invitation.

I asked Mary Ann if she had really wanted to say yes to Mrs. Ellis. Her reply was, "Gee, I never really thought about it." So I asked her to consider the question right then and there. Her reply didn't surprise me. She said, "Mrs. Shaevitz, I hate baking. No, I really didn't want to do it at all, but I didn't think I had a choice."

As you can imagine, I told her that there is always a choice to any question or request. But of course, there are consequences to any response. The consequence of saying yes is having to bake six dozen cookies. The consequence of saying no is possibly causing Mrs. Ellis to be upset. Another possibility was for Mary Ann to counteroffer to buy six dozen cookies rather than bake them herself. She said that she liked that idea.

4. If you decide to say no, get back to the inviter, again graciously thank him or her for the invitation, and with no apologies or excuses, say no. If you decide to say yes, go for it!

We played through how getting back to Mrs. Ellis might sound. Mary Ann could say: "Hi, this is Mary Ann Pratt. As I promised, I'm getting back to you about the cookies for the bake sale. When I spoke to the principal, I found that midyear reports are due next week. I can't bake six dozen cookies, but I'd be happy to bring six dozen bakery cookies. How does that sound to you?"

5. After saying no (or making a counteroffer), reward yourself for that behavior with a positive thought such as "Good for me!" "I did it!" "I'm finally getting control of my life!"

I urged Mary Ann to reward her "good behavior" with a "Good for me!" I also reminded her that it's nonproductive to feel guilty, and we talked about that for a few minutes.

Remember, if we continue to berate ourselves for not doing something, we might just as well do the activity in the first place!

> Confident women have learned to eliminate unimportant, nonessential activities and events.

2. ACT ON YOUR PRIORITIES

> *Be assured that you'll always have time for the things you put first.*
>
> Liane Steele

Knowing who and what is important to you is a major part of getting control of your life. Back in chapter 6 you identified your favorite, most important people. Then in chapter 9 you identified what's important in your life. (If you didn't do these exercises before, now would be a good time to go back and do them.) These people and things and activities are your priorities.

Keep a list of your priorities in front of you

In the hustle-bustle of everyday decision-making, we often fail to take into account our priorities. It's not so much that we intend to do this—it's more a matter of "out of sight is out of mind." Therefore, we have to consciously remember our priorities. A good first step is to write them down on a few three-by-five cards. The number of cards depends on the number of places you want to post them in order to remind yourself of them. You might, for example, place one card on the monitor of your computer. You might staple another to your calendar. Another might go into your wallet. Another could be taped near your desk phone, and so on. Placing these cards at strategic locations will help remind you where and with whom you really want to spend your time and in what directions you want to make decisions.

Compare the ideal with the reality

Now look at your calendar for the next month or months. Compare your priorities against how you have actually allocated your time. Is there a match? If your answer is yes, then good for you. If your answer is sort of or no, then get your behavior to match your priorities better by scheduling regular time for the people and things you hold dear. For example, many working mothers carve out the first half hour after they arrive home to play with (or talk to) their children (and not answer the phone or open the mail or check messages or get dinner started). Other women have told me that Sunday mornings are set aside as inviolable family time. As for what's important, a number of women take the first hour of every morning to act on their top priority, whether it be writing a novel or taking an exercise walk. Others carve out time to go back to school. Still others red-line one day a month for doing nothing. *Yes!* They really do that!

As you look at your calendar to make sure that your priorities get your time and attention, you might also check to see if there are any activities you want to eliminate.

> Confident women know who and what is important to them
> and make sure that how they spend their time reflects that.

3. LET SOMEONE ELSE DO IT

When there's something to be done, if a woman can't eliminate it, she usually jumps right in and does it herself, especially at home. Not long ago I gave a talk on the subject of delegating to staff people at the University of California at San Diego. After I made the above statement, one of the highest-ranking women at the university came up to me and said:

> *Marjorie, you're so right. You know, at work I have no problems with delegating. At work I would never think of waiting for someone to volunteer to help me. At work I would never hope that someone would notice that I needed help. At work I would never mince words and say things like "Oh, do you think, if it's not too much trouble, that you might do something for me?" At work I would*

*never feel hurt if someone wasn't totally enthusiastic about doing
something I asked. At work I would never expect to have to do everything! At work I would never hesitate to delegate or hire someone
to help me out with a project. But at home—I do all of those
things! What's more, I didn't even realize I did that until I heard
you say it.*

It is still uncommon for a woman at home (who works outside the home)
to ask herself, "Who else can do it?" If you really want to gain control over
your life, you need to ask yourself this question frequently and every day.

For many women, a major barrier to getting help is that they fail to ask
for it. Another common barrier is that they don't ask effectively. Hinting,
hoping, blaming, getting angry, and guilt-slinging do not do the job.
When you think about it, most women have few effective role models to
draw upon: Their mothers usually didn't ask or asked ineffectively, and
their fathers often simply ordered or told others what to do (which elicited
those compliant, reluctant adherence, or defiant reactions we just talked
about).

There are three major ways to address the question "Who else can do
it?" They are: delegating, bartering, and hiring and/or buying help.

How to delegate

To delegate effectively, here are some steps to follow:

1. Decide what task you want to delegate.
2. Determine to whom you want to delegate the task.
3. Delegate the task by:
   a. Describing it (including the elements of what, when, where, why, and how),
   b. Listening to any reply,
   c. Responding to the reply.
4. Follow up on the delegation by:
   a. Thanking the person for doing the task, and/or
   b. Describing what needs to be done in order to do the task appropriately.

Let's see how this might play out in real life. Imagine that it's early evening
and you are preparing dinner. You have two children, a boy and a girl.

1. Decide what task you want to delegate.
   *You decide that you would like to have one of your children set the
   table for dinner.*

2. Determine to whom you want to delegate the task.
Since your daughter is showering, having just come home from soft-ball practice, you decide to ask your son, Jimmy.
3. Delegate the task by:
   a. Describing it (including the elements of what, when, where, why, and how)
You say something such as "Jimmy, the table needs to be set [what]. I'd really like to have your help [why]. We're going to eat dinner around six o'clock, so I'd like to have it done in the next fifteen min-utes [when]. We're going to eat in the dining room tonight [where] instead of the kitchen. Since we're having soup, please put out soup dishes and soup spoons along with everything else [how]."
   b. Listening to any reply
Jimmy responds to you by saying, "Mom, I'm in the middle of my math homework. Why can't Madeline do it?"
   c. Responding to the reply
You respond to Jimmy's reply by saying, "Okay, but if I ask Madeline to set the table, then I will ask you to do the dishes after dinner." Jimmy walks into the kitchen and says, "I'll set the table."
4. Follow up on the delegation by:
   a. Thanking the person for doing the task, and/or
   b. Describing what needs to be done in order to do the task appro-priately.
After Jimmy has set the table, you go into the dining room to see how he has done. You see that he has forgotten a few things, so you say to him, "Hey, Jimmy, thanks for setting the table. I just noticed that you forgot to put out napkins and the salt and pepper shakers. Would you please do that now?"

That's all there is to it. You can use this technique with both children and adults. Don't worry if it doesn't work perfectly the first time around. As with anything, it takes practice to work out the bugs and make the tech-nique your own. If you have a hard time with this technique, you can always buy a book on the subject or some audio- or videotapes, or even take a class at a local college. But if you have trouble getting the hang of it, don't give up; get some help.

What If Someone Says No?

Right about now you might be thinking, "Well, this is all fine and well, Marjorie, but what if someone says no to me? What do I do?" That's a good question because people say no all the time. First of all, I want to remind you that to all questions there are two answers: yes and no. Many women get so upset when people say no to them that they practically fall apart. Some end up never asking the person — or anybody — for help again. That's not exactly effective. But there is an alternative. Here is how it goes:

Let's say that it's evening, and you are about to go to bed. You remember that some important dry cleaning needs to be picked up tomorrow, so you ask your husband to do it. He says no. What do you do?

1. Find Out Why

Most people usually don't just say no, they also offer a reasonable explanation. But sometimes people do respond with just the single word *no*, without explaining why. This response is both confusing and frustrating, but the major thing lacking is information. If someone simply says no, then in a nonattacking way, you should try to find out why he or she has responded so abruptly. For example, you could say,

> *Gee, Bob, I was really hoping you could help me out. Do you mind telling me why you can't pick up the cleaning?*

To this your husband might reply,

> *I'd like to help you out, but I can't. I have a meeting after work.*

2. Offer an Alternative Suggestion

One response to your husband's saying no would be to offer an alternative suggestion. For example, you could say,

> *Okay, if you can't do it after work, how about stopping by the cleaners in the morning on your way to work?*

Your husband might say yes to this, or he might say no; but at least you've made a good try. One word of caution: Offering more than one or two alternative suggestions is not likely to work well. If you keep at him with ideas, he'll begin to feel like you're bugging him (translation: controlling him, telling him what to do). At that point you might want to come up with a solution that doesn't involve him, such as asking a parent or friend or sibling who lives close to the cleaners to do it for you. Or if it's a real emergency, pay for the cleaning over the phone with a credit card and then have a taxi company pick it up for you.

What If Someone Doesn't Follow Through?

Another problem that frequently arises is someone says yes but then doesn't follow through with what they have been asked. What should you do? To begin with, don't assume that the person has not followed through because of some ulterior motive. Often there is a good explanation. Again, the best way to handle this situation is simply to ask for more information.

Let's assume that husband Bob has not brought home the cleaning, even though he agreed to it.

> *Bob, last night you agreed to pick up the cleaning. Is there a reason why you didn't? What happened?*

Bob might respond in any number of ways. He might say that he got a traffic ticket on the way to work and forgot; the cleaning wasn't ready when he got there; or any number of other things. Having identified the reason, you can then proceed with whatever makes sense.

What If Someone Responds Inappropriately?

Finally, someone may respond to your request for help in an unreasonable way: They may thoughtlessly forget, or tell you to "bug off." This is a good time to use all your "I" language skills. (Refer to chapter 12 for help with that.)

To an inappropriate response, you might say,

> *Bob, when you forget to pick up the cleaning after you've said you would [describing the action], I feel frustrated [identifying your feelings] because now I don't have my special dress to wear, and you don't have your tux [identifying the consequence of the action].*

Let's assume that you and Bob work out this problem in one way or another. Things do have a way of getting worked out.

Bartering

Bartering is a system wherein one person exchanges a product or service for another person's product or service. For example, you might bake six dozen cookies in exchange for a friend providing two days of after-school child care. Surprisingly many women all over the country use the barter system in one form or another. It's especially useful for people who don't have a lot of extra cash on hand. Most women are very informal about their exchange arrangements, and that informality usually works out. But if you get involved with some kind of complicated bartering, to avoid misunderstandings you and your bartering partner might want to write down exactly what products and or services are being offered by each person.

Here are some products, services, and other things that women are bartering (I'm sure that you can think of many more):

What You Can Barter

Products	Services	Other
•Meals	•Tutoring	•Room and/or board
•Food products (such as breads, cakes, cookies, homemade baby food)	•Cooking	•Use of a car
	•Haircutting or mani-curing	•Use of garage
	•Child or elder care	•Use of a storage area
	•Erranding	•Use of a computer
•Homegrown vegeta-bles and fruits	•Bookkeeping	•Use of an office
•Homegrown flowers	•Grocery shopping	
•Handmade clothing	•House cleaning or gardening	
•Handmade jewelry	•Word processing	
•Art pieces	•Carpooling	
•Used clothing	•Writing or editing	
•Used household items	•Pet-sitting and vaca-tion house-sitting	
	•Meeting service people (telephone person)	

Hire it or buy it

If I were to ask you right now why you don't hire someone or some service to take care of your household chores, errands, or other work, your answer would probably be typical of what many other women say:

> No, I can't.
> No, I don't have the money.
> No, it's too expensive.
> No, it's too much of a hassle.
> No, I wouldn't know where to even begin.
> No, I don't have time; it's easier to do it myself.

While some of these answers may contain elements of truth (no money, a lot of hassle, easier to do myself), when push comes to shove, they are mostly used as excuses for not getting outside help. Even high-income, highly successful women today put up incredible resistance to spending money on what women have traditionally done for themselves or their households. For a variety of emotional rather than logical or financial reasons—and even if husbands are encouraging of such behavior—women resist "buying it" with a passion that outweighs any reasonable explanation.

Why? Part of it, I think, stems from women feeling guilty about spending money on themselves (or on what they perceive is their responsibility). Some women have told me that they don't spend money on outside help because they want to avoid being criticized or accused of being lazy, a spendthrift, or self-indulgent. But as Letty Cottin Pogrebin once said, "If it's okay to hire someone to fix the toilet, it sure as hell should be okay to hire someone to clean it."

Women need to think about how to conserve their time and energy for the priorities in their lives. Paying other people to do things is an appropriate way to do this. I can't tell you how much to spend; that's something that you and your family will need to determine on your own. But I urge you to do it. And remember, you can buy parts of a person's time, or parts of an important meal such as Thanksgiving, or hire someone for a few hours of service. You don't have to hire a full-time housekeeper (although that's a fine thing to do), or have your Thanksgiving dinner catered (also fine if it's what you want), or hire a handy person for a full day.

Services You Can Hire

Other women use a wide range of services: answering service, baby-sitting service, bartending service, bookkeeping service, catering services, children's party service, cleaning service, companionship service (for elderly or homebound), diaper service, dog-walking service, driving services (for children or elderly), drugstore delivery service, errand service, home repair service, in-home personal grooming services (hairdresser, masseuse, manicurist, exercise coach), gardening service, house-sitting service, laundry and cleaning services that pick up, messenger service, milk delivery service, package-wrapping and -mailing service, painting service, party service, pickup and delivery service, pool service, rug- and furniture-cleaning service, secretarial service, shopping service, travel service, tutoring service, wardrobe consultant, window-cleaning service.

If you decide to "buy it," remember that the goal in hiring a service is to save you hassles, to give you more time, and/or to preserve your energy for the people and things that are important to you. You will want to hire a service that makes your life easier, not more complicated or difficult. Be careful to choose individuals who are not only competent, prompt, reliable, and honest but *nice!* Over and over the women I interviewed for this book told me that one of life's great lessons is to stop hiring people who are a pain the neck.

Confident women learn how to delegate, barter, or hire good "help."

4. BECOME A SOLUTION NUT

Over the years I have noticed that the most interesting, confident, competent women I encounter have become what I call Solution Nuts. In everyday terms this means that they are always "on the make" for good ideas and suggestions, excellent products, outstanding service and professional people, and helpful hints — every single one of which helps them to get better control over their lives. These women not only seek out solutions but are very generous in sharing their finds with others. More important, Solution Nuts seem to have such fun doing what they do.

If you are not a Solution Nut now, please join the club. It's not difficult to become one. Step one is to open up your eyes and ears to whatever solutions are out there. Pay attention to and write down any ideas you see or hear.

Step two is to keep track of these ideas: in a box, in a binder, in a manila folder, in a folder on your computer, or all of the above. On my Mac I have a folder called "Competency and Resources." My array of topics surely is random and a little crazy, but perhaps some of the files will give you an idea about what kinds of information you can collect: air-conditioning information, attorneys, best books, best cookbooks, cable TV, cats, Christmas poinsettias, cleaning services, computers and printers, cosmetics and personal stuff, fleas, garage door openers, hurricane alerts, movers, physicians, pruning fruit trees, running shoes, Spanish language lessons, upholsterers, wine, writing resources.

Step three is to find a group of people who enjoy sharing solutions with one another. Many of my friends share their new solution finds through e-mail. You can do this in a more formalized way, too. For example, the women at a Women's Healthcare Roundtable that I attend devote part of each meeting to sharing ideas about such varied topics as how to handle different work situations, how to pack a to-die-for carry-on bag, which airlines provide the best service, who is the best cleaner in town, and so on. While there is real substance to the talks and information that the Roundtable deals with, I think that the favorite part of every meeting is "solutions time."

Confident women look for and find solutions for everything they do.

The quality of your life is determined by one thing: what you *do* with every minute of every hour of every day. Regardless of your circumstances, age, or health, your happiness depends on your actions and your actions alone. Frankly, if your life is stressful, dull, meaningless, or out of control, it's useless to blame your family, society, or even history.

From this moment on you can take ownership of your life by making positive choices about what you do right now, with whom you spend time right now, and where you choose to be right now. Yes, you can do that, and you can do it as of right now.

> *When each day is sacred*
> *when each hour is sacred*
> *when each instant is sacred*
> *earth and you*
> *space and you*
> *bearing the sacred through time*
> *you'll reach*
> *the fields of light*
>> Guillevic
>> from Phil Cousineau's
>> *The Soul of the World*

One final way of taking control of your life is to take very good care of yourself: physically, emotionally, socially, intellectually, spiritually, and financially. Of all the things that women have trouble with, taking good care of themselves seems to be the most difficult. This just happens to be the subject of the next chapter.

But before we go on, how about another Break? This time it's a Making Life Simpler Break.

MAKING LIFE SIMPLER BREAK

If you haven't used something or worn something in a year, give it away.

When traveling by plane to a destination for three or fewer days, use the formula "If you can't carry it, leave it home."

Teach your children (and, if necessary, your husband) to pick up after themselves.

Before an emergency develops, know exactly where to find home main water switch (and water wrench), main gas switch (and gas pipe wrench), electrical and fuse boxes, fire extinguisher, first aid kit, tool box, candles, matches, flashlights and extra batteries, important papers and documents, emergency phone numbers.

Sharpen your scissors by cutting a piece of sandpaper two or three times.

Get specific directions (or a map) for where you're going before you go.

Keep a stock of wonderful cards and inexpensive gifts on hand (buy them when you're on vacation).

Remember, just because the phone rings doesn't mean that you have to answer it.

Develop the art of doing nothing.

For almost all screws, know that left is loose and right is tight.

Always keep a wonderful book in your purse or briefcase just in case you have to wait for somebody or something.

Duct tape will fix almost anything, temporarily.

Remember, life will go on if your glasswear isn't spotless, floors cleaner than clean, clothes whiter than white, or furniture polished brighter than bright.

Buy only quality or what you really like.

Stop watching TV.

Every once in a while, spend a whole weekend at home with no social or family commitments.

When you're about to buy something, ask yourself, "Is this going to simplify or enhance my life?"

CHAPTER 14

Taking Better Care of Yourself

Let's make a commitment to take care of ourselves
so that we can live the lives we deserve.

And let's make a further commitment
that we will not leave our daughters a legacy of
invisibility . . .

In order to stop being invisible,
we must be seen and heard,
and we must see and hear ourselves.
We must become "self"-centered.

Let us redefine our role as caretakers.
We have always taken this role to mean
that we put ourselves last on the list,
meeting everyone else's needs
before we look to our own.

I am proposing that
we cannot meet the needs of others,
much less our own,
unless we start by taking care of ourselves.

Eileen Hoffman, M.D.
Our Health, Our Lives[1]

I t wasn't very long ago that notions of what women could be and do were
remarkably narrow. How easy it is to forget that before the 1970s—*and
even the 1980s*—there were many things women weren't allowed to be
or do.

THE WAY IT USED TO BE

I know from personal experience that until recent years, women had great difficulty getting admitted to Ph.D. programs and professional schools. When I was finishing a master's degree and inquired about continuing on for a doctorate, I was told by my adviser that I would never be accepted into a Ph.D. program because I would waste the degree when I got married and became a mother. Ph.D. slots were set aside for men.

Similarly, it was hopeless for women to expect to join any top law, business, architectural, or engineering firm. Supreme Court Justice Sandra Day O'Connor, after graduating from Stanford Law School (at the top of her class and having made law review), found that none of the large California law firms would hire a woman, so she got a job as a deputy county attorney.[2] Twenty-five years ago women rarely were hired by and almost never received tenure at colleges and universities. It wasn't until 1975 that a woman received a college athletic scholarship. For years women weren't allowed to run in the Boston Marathon or other marathons because the race organizers thought women's bodies "weren't up to it." Unbelievably, some of the first women marathoners wore nurses' shoes because women's running shoes did not exist.[3]

What's most astonishing, though, is that only during *the last twenty-five years* have women—working alongside sympathetic men—been able to challenge and remove most of the legal, educational, occupational, and other barriers that have kept them from becoming all that they might be and do.

How far we have come

While often the salaries and titles of women are not yet equal to those of men, think about all the accomplishments women have made. How about the thirteen women who in 1978 climbed Annapurna, one of the world's highest and most dangerous mountains? How about Libby Riddles, who in 1985 became the first woman to win the Alaskan Iditerod (thousand-mile dogsled race)? How about Mae Jameson, who in 1992 became the first African American woman to fly in space? How about the 1993 American Women's Trans-Antarctic Expedition, the first team of women to get to the South Pole without dogs? How about the women on the 1995 *America3*, the first ever all-women's boat to compete for the America's Cup?

Some of what women have done

Of course, millions of ordinary women have shown enormous courage in pushing the envelope for what is seen as appropriate female behavior. Women have torn down gender barriers, crashed through so-called "glass ceilings," and opened up new female turf. How about Sandra Day O'Connor and Ruth Bader Ginsburg, the first women to sit on the Supreme Court? Or Janet Reno, the first woman attorney general? Or Madeleine Albright, the first woman secretary of state? Or Antonia Novella, the first woman and first Hispanic surgeon general?

How about Oprah Winfrey, and Katharine Graham (publisher of *The Washington Post*) and Sherry Lansing (CEO of Paramount Pictures) and Marian Wright Edelman (African American lawyer and founder of the Children's Defense Fund) and Martina Navratilova (Wimbledon champion and one of the first sports superstars to publicly acknowledge that she is a lesbian) and Kristi Yamaguchi and Michelle Kwan (the first Asian American Olympic ice skating champions) and Jean Baker Miller (Wellesley College psychiatrist who developed the new field of women's psychology) and Louise Erdrich (best-selling Chippewa writer) and Wilma Mankiller (the first woman principal chief of the Cherokee Nation) and Rosalyn Yalow (the first American woman to receive a Nobel Prize for medicine), and Maxine Hong Kingston and Amy Tan (best-selling Asian American authors), Jill Barad (president of Mattel Toys) and scores and scores of others. All I can say is:

> *A little like outlaws,*
> *much like Old West pioneers,*
> *in a mere quarter century*
> *women have crossed vast frontiers!*

THE FINAL FRONTIER

Since the mid-1970s women have made colossal leaps forward. That is why it is so troubling and ironic that within our own *internal* worlds we often have made far less progress. There is one final frontier women must conquer, and that is overcoming their inability to take good care of themselves. Remember, until we commit to taking care of ourselves, we cannot live the lives we deserve, or provide our daughters with proper legacies, or fully meet the needs of others, much less our own.

> *Everything has been figured out, except how to live.*
> Jean-Paul Sartre

Phoebe's story

Phoebe is a classic example of inordinate success on the outside and miserable chaos on the inside. She is a married thirty-something mother of three who is president of a very successful East Coast company. This is some of what she told me as I was interviewing her for this book.

Overall, I would say I'm 80 percent happy. I have a very clear and separate sense of who I am. I love what I do. And I know that I'm really good at it. I have real confidence in my ability to make good decisions and lead the company. I have that strength; I know I have what it takes. Also, I love my kids, I love my husband, and my parents are terrific.

But then there's that 20 percent of me that wants desperately to get sick—a little bit, you know, not big time. Just this morning I was in the bathroom praying, "Dear God, I haven't been sick in a long time. Let me come down with something! If I got sick, I could rest!" Then I thought I'd go to my doctor and beg him to call my husband and say, "Phoebe needs to rest," because I can't rest. I thought, "Maybe I could get into a car accident." I know it's demented, but I think about this all the time!

So what do I do to take good care of myself? Zero. I don't do anything. It's uncanny, I can't for the life of me take care of myself. I never take vacations. I don't eat well. I drink too much coffee. Aside from rushing around, I never exercise.

You want to make me happy? Leave me alone. Find me a place where my kids can go that's soundproof; take my husband off to see the Knicks or the Yankees, far away from me; and let me sit in a quiet room and read a book. Solitude is what I don't have.

The nicest thing that could happen to me is for someone to drop me in the middle of Vermont and let me sit there for a weekend. I took fifty-two hours to myself once—I can tell you exactly when—in August 1997. Sal was gone for the weekend, and I said to the nanny, "Will you please come take care of my children," and for fifty-two precious hours I was gone.

I read, I thought, I looked at the mountains, I sat in Jacuzzis, I went shopping (which I never do), I had lunch alone, and fifty-two hours later I came home. I have been living on that memory ever since! I've promised myself to do it again, but there's never a good time for me to go away.

Last week I was sobbing uncontrollably, and it got to the point where Sal really began keeping the kids away from me and letting me rest. It took that, though; it took coming to the point where he truly thought I was losing it. I had said to him for weeks before this, "You know, I never ever have even ten minutes off."

Wherever I am and whatever I'm doing, there are at least a dozen people pissed off at me. It's almost like I can feel them breathing down my neck saying, "You aren't doing what I need you to be doing." I gave two speeches last week. I could tell people thought that I was captivating, brilliant, and in control. Little did they know that I was on the verge of a collapse because I was so exhausted. I feel that way almost all the time. If I don't spend most of my time at the office, the business falls apart. If I don't get home by six, the household falls apart. I can't stop. It's just easier to keep going and doing.

It's almost become an obsession with me, thinking about the difference between successful men and successful women. I feel like it's a victory when I get even the slightest bit of control over my life; whereas for men it's exactly the opposite. They take it for granted.

If I acted as men do, I would feel extremely guilty, extremely inefficient, and as if I were cheating or wasting time. I feel as though I always have to show something for my time. As it is, I feel bad about myself, guilty about my family, guilty about my business, guilty about everything. Men are so much better at taking care of themselves. I think this is what the real glass ceiling is all about.

Phoebe is like many other successful (and not quite so successful) women today. In her professional and volunteer involvements, she is independent, responsible, powerful, and competent. She sees herself as a staunch feminist. But when it comes to taking care of herself, she is nothing less than a "basket case"—dependent, irresponsible, weak, and incompetent. A psychiatrist friend of mine, Tom Rusk, rightly calls this "being a feminist hypocrite." Phoebe needs to realize how jarringly paradoxical her behavior is.

> *We have met the enemy, and (s)he is us.*
> Pogo comic strip

Why women have trouble with self-care

Phoebe's story offers some classic examples of how women think and behave around the issue of personal care. First of all, like so many other women, she doesn't take the logical route of simply acting to care for herself. Because our female upbringing teaches us that self-care is wrong, Phoebe and most other women take an indirect route: they think they need to be ill in order to justify taking care of themselves (and that includes resting or having time alone or doing or not doing what they think they should). Can you imagine any man praying to be sick?

Second, typical of many women, Phoebe sought permission from others to take care of herself—in her case from her doctor and her husband. Women seem to think that they need physical evidence of illness in order to justify engaging in some form of self-care without feeling guilty.

Additionally, when it comes to taking care of themselves, many women engage in a strange form of procrastination. They wait until the eleventh hour and, like Phoebe, ultimately find themselves "sobbing uncontrollably for hours" or "feeling that they are working up to a nervous breakdown." As I give lectures around the country, I can't tell you the number of times a woman has approached me afterward and said, "You know, I wish I had done something for myself earlier, but I had to get cancer [or have a heart attack or lose my husband or be in a car accident or any number of tragic occurrences] before I realized what is really important in life, and that includes taking care of myself. Please tell other women not to wait until it's too late."

Fourth, when it comes to their commitments to their families and their work, many women are not only responsible but superresponsible. But for themselves, they couldn't be more irresponsible. Like so many others, Phoebe feels as if she is on "twenty-four-seven" call (twenty-four hours a day, seven days a week) and that she is utterly indispensable both to her staff and her family. Recall how she says "if I don't spend most of my time at the office, the business falls apart," and "if I don't get home by six, the household falls apart." While I am sure there are elements of truth in her statements, the reality is that Phoebe could gain more control of her life through many of the measures we talked about in the last chapter. Taking any positive action is better than doing nothing at all. In fact, doing one thing differently can have a mobilizing effect, setting in motion other positive changes.

Finally, while it may not be apparent from her story, Phoebe is also waiting for her husband to do more at home so that she can do less and, therefore, have more time to take care of herself. There are two things wrong with this thinking. To begin with, it is neither logical nor practical for Phoebe to make her self-care dependent on the actions of another person. One has nothing to do with the other. Whether or not Sal does anything at home, Phoebe and only Phoebe is responsible for taking care of herself. The second thing that's wrong with her thinking is that she is hoping and expecting that Sal will someday change his behavior so that their marriage will become more "equal." We know that expecting people to do things or change their behavior for you (and not for themselves) just doesn't work! Phoebe needs to take care of herself no matter what her husband does or does not do.

Equality demands self-care

Before I go on, there is something critical that women need to know and understand about egalitarian marriages. Equal marriages develop between partners who care about and act responsibly not only *toward each other* but *toward themselves* as well. Equality is not something that a man gives to you or does for you; equality is something you give to and do for yourself. Yes, a good man treats a woman with care, courtesy, respect, and love — but he cannot make her equal in the relationship. Only she can do that. Only confident women (and men) can enjoy equal marriages.

My heart goes out to Phoebe. It's terrible to be as exhausted and to feel as out of control as she does. I know because, as they say, "I've been there, done that." What Phoebe fails to understand, however, is that the thoughts she engages in, the decisions she makes, and the actions she takes *every single day* are what cause her exhaustion, her personal chaos, and her bad feelings. No one is doing it to her. Sure, Phoebe's life is incredibly demanding, but she has chosen her life with all of its accompanying complications and consequences. Her life is out of control mostly because she has allowed it to get out of control. Either she doesn't know that it's her responsibility to take care of herself, or she doesn't know how to begin. I suspect that it's some of both. While those truths may be difficult to accept and may trigger our rationalizations and excuse lists, they are nevertheless the bottom line — and Phoebe and each one of us knows it.

> *We must become the change we want to see.*
> Gandhi

You must make *you* your number-one priority by taking care of yourself and getting your life under control. Experiment with different actions until you find those that work for you. Then find more. If you can't make it happen on your own, get some help. Talk with a friend or pay a coach or a teacher or a counselor to help you. It will not be easy, and the people around you may not be supportive of or happy with your actions. But if you want to feel better, only you can do things to make that happen.

Remember, no one is making you answer the phone. No one is making you say yes to invitations or requests. No one is controlling what or how much you take on. No one is standing next to you with a gun to your head forcing you to see all the people who want to see you or to do everything that people expect of you. If you just begin to take care of yourself, life will get easier.

Lest you are under the impression that self-irresponsibility is typical of just one segment of women — married working mothers — let me tell you that this impression is wrong. Because they don't think that they have the same legitimate excuses of harried, married working mothers, single women, married women who have no children, stay-at-home moms, career volunteers, empty nesters, and grandmothers are as much at risk for feeling guilty about taking care of themselves and ignoring their own needs as are women such as Phoebe. Every single woman needs to take care of herself. The rest of this chapter offers suggestions as to how.

Confident women take care of themselves; they don't need or expect others to do it for them.

> Most people live . . . in a very restricted circle of their potential being. They make use of a very small portion of their possible consciousness, and of their soul's resources . . . much like a woman who, of her whole body, should . . . only use and move her little finger.
>
> William James[4]

TAKING BETTER CARE OF YOURSELF

What the experts say

The women who wrote *Our Bodies, Ourselves* remind us that "though medical care sometimes helps us when we are sick, it does not keep us healthy. To a great extent what makes us healthy or unhealthy is how we are able to live our daily lives — what we eat, how we exercise, how much rest we get, how much stress we live with."[5] In other words, to sustain good health we need to choose how we live, take care of our bodies and minds, and make positive choices in our personal habits.

Bernadine Healy, former director of the National Institutes of Health, says that "every women needs her own medical mentor. It might be your primary care doctor, a nurse or doctor associate or even a good friend . . . someone to guide you to the right place, to encourage you to seek another opinion if need be, or to be a sounding board if you are not sure what you just heard."[6]

According to Stanford Medical School's Dr. Iris Litt, one of the most important health actions you can take is to carefully choose your primary care physician for the four C's: competence, communication skills, concern for you as a person, and cost. She suggests that you use the following checklist in making your physician choice:

- How long does it take to get an appointment?
- How long do you have to wait in the waiting room before you are seen? Are explanations given if you do have to wait?
- Do you feel as if you have enough time with the doctor and are made comfortable enough to ask all the questions you have?
- Is the doctor supportive and helpful in answering your questions rather than seeming annoyed or pressed for time?
- Are you told which tests are ordered, and are you given the opportunity to question their necessity and cost? Do you receive test results and their interpretation promptly, without having to call for them?
- If you receive a prescription, are the instructions and possible side effects explained?[7]

To this list, Dr. Eileen Hoffman adds:

- Does the doctor treat you as a whole person? Is he/she up to date on women's health data?
- Does the doctor believe in preventive care? Does she/he go beyond your current status to deal with your behavior and lifestyle?
- Does the doctor have a system for tracking your care from year to year?
- Does the doctor know "you"? Does he/she seem to remember your name when you go in for an appointment?
- Does the doctor see you as a person, not just as a seeker of services?[8]

At one of the last Stanford Healthy Woman Retreats, one of the physicians, Dr. John Farquhar, said the following to women audience members:

> . . . *as a physician, it never ceases to amaze me how people in general—and women in particular—abuse their own bodies, indifferently and deliberately. Much more than their cars or even some of their household appliances, they ignore responsibility for their bodies' everyday maintenance and especially for the consequences of their actions. It's as though people assume—sometimes hopefully, sometimes arrogantly—that illness happens to everybody else, not them. Women seem to lose sight that the goal of taking good care of themselves is to be and remain as optimally healthy as they can for as long as they can.*[9]

Sometimes we don't realize that it's *never too early or too late* to start taking good care of ourselves.[10] Exercise is a good example. Researchers say the most sedentary people—young and old—have the most to gain by starting to exercise. The same can be said of all the other forms of self-care.

Taking good care of yourself:

- allows you to fulfill your personal destiny
- gives you more energy to devote to the people and activities you love
- allows you to forget about yourself
- has as its purpose having a positive influence on the world
- is both a personal and societal responsibility

GUIDELINES FOR STARTING OR RESTARTING A SELF-CARE PROGRAM

There are five guidelines to follow in starting or updating a self-care program:

Take small steps

You'll be happy to know that when you first start making positive health changes, it doesn't make sense to try to do too much. According to the Stanford healthy living experts,[11] small steps are the order of the day because they are (a) easier, (b) require less energy, (c) require less willpower, and (d) have a lower risk of failure and discouragement. I don't remember who said it, but when it comes to health changes, "Less is fine, slow is good." This means that when you begin an exercise program, or create time for solitude, or take charge of your finances, it is best to begin slowly, with maybe just ten minutes a day. You can do it. It's easy. It doesn't require much energy or willpower, and you are much more likely to gain confidence and continue.

Enjoy the process

You must enjoy what you do. No matter how good it is for you, if you dislike what you're doing, you won't do it for very long. People don't persist at things they don't like. Obviously, this doesn't mean that there won't be times when what you do is inconvenient (like getting up earlier in the morning to go out and exercise) or is not a totally orgasmic experience (well, yes, sometimes exercising doesn't feel great). To enjoy the process, you need to make sure that whatever you do involves a majority of positive elements or at least a sense that you're accomplishing something. Remember, even the smallest act can be good and constructive.

Stay positive and be good to yourself

You are more likely to take good care of yourself if you think and act positively. To use food as an example, don't think in terms of all the forbidden foods there are in the world and force yourself into a rigid diet plan. Think about and choose the most delicious, desirable, healthy, quality foods that are available, and make sure that you eat plenty of them. In other words, the crispest, juiciest, sweetest, freshest apple you can find.

Just do it

Whatever the health action is, just do it. Edward Hall, the anthropologist who wrote *The Dance of Life*, noted that "living a life is somewhat analogous to composing music, painting, or writing a poem. Each day properly approached can be either a work of art or a disaster."[12]

Get some help

If you have trouble in carrying through with your intentions, for goodness' sake, get some help! There are many situations in which someone's good information, help, or support is readily available. For example, you might go to a friend or relative or neighbor or member of the clergy. Sometimes the situation calls for professional help. Whomever you decide to consult, make sure that he or she is the best qualified, most effective, and nicest person available.

SIX WAYS OF TAKING GOOD CARE

There are six major ways that women need to care for themselves: physically, emotionally, socially, intellectually, financially, and spiritually.

Taking good physical care of yourself

> *No woman can call herself free who does not own*
> *and control her own body.*
> >   Margaret Sanger

Here are some ideas about how to approach the physical area.

While there are a thousand and one things you can do to take good physical care of yourself, two stand out as having the most wide-ranging effects on your confidence, health, and well-being. They are (1) exercising, and (2) taking time to relax.

Exercising

Nothing has made a greater health difference in my life than exercise. And without exception every confident woman I interviewed engaged in some form of exercise and for good reasons. Here are eight of those reasons:

- improved cardiovascular health
- weight gain is kept under control

- increased muscle mass and strength
- lower blood sugar
- lower blood pressure
- increased bone density

In terms of immediate, noticeable effects, the best reasons to exercise are that it

- helps you to feel psychologically healthier
- slows down the aging process[13]

Women wanting to engage in an exercise program face two major barriers: getting started and staying with it. Many women never stay with a program long enough to see or feel the benefits. For a great many, exercise feels like another thing on their list of *shoulds.*

Most health experts suggest that women engage in three kinds of exercise — aerobic exercise, weight training, and stretching. But aerobic exercise (the oxygen-using, large-muscle-group kind) is the one that is most likely to make a real difference. Examples of aerobic exercise are walking, using a treadmill, jogging, swimming, cycling, and using an exercycle, as well as various forms of exercise dancing. Aerobic exercise is *the* calorie-burner exercise.

If you have not exercised for a while, health experts recommend beginning with ten or fifteen minutes of walking a day. Increase the length of time by five minutes per week until you're walking somewhere between thirty minutes to an hour a day.

How much exercise you should do depends upon what your goal is. If, for example, you want to lose weight, it is suggested that you exercise for a longer period of time, perhaps working up to as much as an hour a day for five or six days a week. If you're at a healthy weight now, then exercising twenty or thirty minutes a day three or four times a week seems ample.

Perhaps the most effective thing I have done for myself in staying with an exercise schedule is to say to myself that "not to exercise is not an option." In other words, I don't ask myself *if* I am going to exercise today but *when,* and then I plan everything else around it.

This is different from what I used to do: because of things that would come up, I would not exercise for a couple of days, think that I'd "blown it," and then use these lapses as an excuse to stop altogether. Even the most consistent exercisers fall off the wagon every once in a while. What's important is to realize that this happens, that it's normal, and then simply pick yourself up and go back to exercising as soon as you can.

As with other priorities, time for exercise must be created, not found. For busy people such as yourself, the beginning of the day is often the best time. Some women like to exercise at the end of the day after work and before they go home. That way they can change into sweats and not worry about having to get themselves together again. Some young mothers I know put one (sometimes two) young children in special exercise strollers and then walk or run with them in tow. Still others find walking or running with older children a good way of spending quality time.

By the way, another way to increase your exercise is to increase the number of physical activities you do during your normal day: by walking (instead of driving), taking the stairs (instead of the elevator), parking at the far end of the parking lot (instead of close by), and going out with a friend for a walk (instead of meeting her for lunch).

Steps I Will Take to Exercise
  What:_____
  When:_____
  Where:_____
  Whom I will consult or where I will go for help if I need it:_____
_____

Relaxing

The bow always strung . . . will not do.
George Eliot

In case you haven't noticed, life is pretty stressful. Stress comes to us in positive forms (as in landing a new job or falling in love) and negative forms (bad traffic, financial worries, conflict with your spouse), but it is an unavoidable fact of life from the time we get up in the morning until we go to sleep at night.

Hans Selye, the late Canadian scientist who was considered the world's greatest expert on stress, said that each one of us responds differently to stressful situations and develops our own particular set of stress symptoms.[14] Whether you develop one symptom or another depends on a complex set of factors, including your genetic makeup, personality, age, job, family circumstances, socioeconomic status, personal coping style, and health.

Symptoms of Stress
In response to stressful situations people tend to develop three kinds of symptoms: physical, psychological, and interpersonal. Among the *physical symptoms* women experience, fatigue is the one I hear about the most.

Fatigue, as one woman explained it, "is not just feeling tired, or something a good night's sleep can cure. It's the feeling of being 'bone-tired' and having the stuffing knocked out of you." Other physical symptoms include headaches (including migraines), backaches, neckaches, high blood pressure, tightness in the chest, heart palpitations, stomach problems, rashes and other dermatological problems, over- and undereating, taking drugs or increasing your alcohol consumption, biting your nails or lips, and a whole host of other symptoms. (It should be noted that these symptoms also occur with organic disease. If you develop them, you should consult a physician, particularly if they are recurring.)

Among the *psychological symptoms*, women say that they feel overextended and overloaded, irritable and out of sorts, sad or depressed, tense, pressured, or anxious; they experience forgetfulness, they find it difficult to concentrate, and they are unable to keep their mind on what they're doing. Some women, such as Phoebe (from the earlier story), have even told me that they feel like "running away from home," but of course, they don't have time to do even that! Besides, if they did, they'd feel guilty.

Some of the *interpersonal symptoms* women experience with stress are: finding themselves irritated and short-tempered with spouses, children, and work colleagues; becoming more sensitive to noise or surrounding activities; working harder but with less effectiveness; feeling resentful of others for not doing "their share"; consistently getting to work or meetings or appointments late; always feeling "behind"; and not being able to concentrate or focus on your work. Sometimes we experience a combination of physical, emotional, and interpersonal symptoms for such a long time that we don't even recognize them as symptoms. We get used to them and think that they are normal. But living with chronic, low-grade stress is not natural. If you are experiencing any of the above symptoms, it is highly likely that your body and your mind are trying to tell you that something is wrong and that you can't continue living as you are.

How Many Physicians Respond to Stress Symptoms

When the symptoms we're experiencing, especially physical symptoms, get bad enough, what do we do? Go to the doctor, of course. But if your going-to-the-doctor experiences are anything like many women's, what happens is that Doctor X has you go through a tip-to-toe checkup and then pronounces "the good news": "There's nothing wrong with you." Unless you have an unusually sensitive physician, the next pronouncement is either "It's just stress" or "It's all in your head!" Translation: "What you are experiencing is bogus, not real; you're hysterical, a crank, a complainer."

The latter statement really drives women crazy because they know that something is wrong. Why else would they be feeling so bad? Stress symptoms are not imaginary. They are very real. In fact, if one lives with stress and its consequent symptoms for long enough, eventually the "good news" status will become bad news. Long-term, chronic stress can really hurt you; it can even kill you. High blood pressure over time can lead to heart attacks and strokes. Certain stomach problems such as esophageal reflux may lead over time to cancer. But most physicians are not trained to follow Dr. Eileen Hoffman's suggestion "that they treat patients as whole persons, including dealing with their behavior and lifestyle." Even if physicians wanted to do this, few today have the time or the knowledge to help patients come up with the behavioral changes necessary to alleviate the stress. As we have seen, many physicians are under tremendous stress themselves. Realistically, we have to learn to control our stress either on our own or with the expert help of someone else.

Scientists such as Hans Selye say that most modern stress develops from our emotional reactions to events, not from the events themselves. It is estimated that only about 10 percent of modern stress comes from actual physical threat. The other 90 percent comes from the perception and reactions we have to life events.[15]

Stress-Busting Actions
So what can we do to deal with stress? As we've discussed before, the first step in controlling stress is to identify where it's coming from—the specific events, activities, and people that are stressful—and then avoid or get control of them. Remember, when in doubt, eliminate, reduce, or control the negative aspects of your life.

Suppose you live in a condo next door to noisy neighbors who—in spite of your many requests—are less than respectful of you. Move someplace else. If you are in an abusive relationship and it's doubtful that the abuser is going to change his or her behavior, get out of the relationship. If your current job involves too much hassle and you find yourself experiencing migraine headaches every other day, find yourself another position. And so on. Still, no matter how much you try to control your life and avoid difficult situations, there will always be stressful times, events, and people. We might as well acknowledge stress for what it is and learn how to better deal with it.

The second thing you can do is change the way you think about the stressors. Chapters 10 and 11 offer ways to do that—that is, how to think more positively and better deal with your negative thinking. As Herbert Benson, author of *Beyond the Relaxation Response*, says, "It's how we interpret reality . . . that is important. . . . our personal powers and potential for well being are shaped by the negative or positive ways we think."[16]

Dr. Benson has focused his life's work on developing a proactive way that people can head off feeling stressed. It's called the Relaxation

Response, a technique for "relaxing on purpose." Benson says that the Relaxation Response is an "inborn capacity of the body to enter a special state characterized by lowered heart rate, decreased rate of breathing, lowered blood pressure, slower brain waves, and an overall reduction of the speed of metabolism." What's more important, when you elicit the Relaxation Response, the changes that it produces also "counteract the harmful effects and uncomfortable feelings of stress."[17]

Benson says that one can use a simple technique to bring about the Relaxation Response. (1) Find a quiet place. (2) Sit in a comfortable position. (3) Pick a favorite word or brief prayer upon which to focus, one that is rooted in your personal belief system. (4) Close your eyes and consciously relax your body's muscles. (5) Become aware of your breathing, and breathe very slowly and naturally. Simultaneously, repeat your focus word or phrase as you exhale. (6) When intrusive thoughts come into your mind (and they will), simply say to yourself, "Oh, well," and slip gently back into the repetition of your word or phrase. (7) Do this for ten to twenty minutes at least once or twice a day.

There are other forms of relaxation in which women can engage. It's important that you do one of them every day, even if it's only for a few minutes.

RELAXATION ALTERNATIVES

- resting or napping
- walking, hiking, or sitting in a beautiful natural setting
- writing in a journal
- soaking in a bathtub filled with bubble bath, or sitting in a hot Jacuzzi, or lounging in a sauna
- enjoying nature or beautiful works of art or architecture
- listening to beautiful music
- listening to the ocean, to the sounds of rain, to a stream or river water washing over rocks
- visualizing beautiful, serene scenes
- getting a massage
- reading uplifting books or poetry
- looking at, reading, or listening to something very humorous
- talking with a sympathetic, calming person
- praying
- gardening
- yoga, deep breathing, and self-hypnosis
- knitting or crocheting

Many confident women have told me that on a regular basis they take "minisabbaticals"—that is, bite-size versions of relaxing. They might include taking a few deep breaths, having a moment when you close your eyes and say your favorite word to yourself, going outside to a garden for a couple of minutes of quiet time, reading a favorite poem, or calling a favorite friend on the phone (or sending her a nice e-mail greeting). Sometimes a series of "mini's" in a day can be as effective in helping you to relax as one major sabbatical time.

Steps I Will Take to Relax
    What: _____
    When: _____
    Where: _____
    Whom I will consult or where I will go for help if I need it: _____

_____

If we are to be responsible for our own bodies, health experts say that there are some very bottom-line things we should do and not do. It turns out that what we *don't* do is as important as what we *do* do.

Some important ***don'ts*** include: don't smoke, use drugs, abuse alcohol, don't engage in unsafe or unprotected sex, don't grossly under- or overeat, don't fail to wear a seat belt every time you are in a car. And especially: don't ever allow any person to abuse you in any way.

Here are some bottom-line ***do's***: get enough sleep, use sunscreen when you know you'll be in the sun, get an annual Pap smear (starting at age eighteen), and get a mammogram once a year (starting at age fifty). All women should do breast self-exams at least once a month.

Women often tell me they want to read about what other real women do. So here is what real women have told me about taking good physical care of themselves.

> *I live by the motto, don't get too hungry, angry, lonely, or tired.*
>   Laurie Drabble
>   Ph.D. student
>   University of California, Berkeley

> *I'm liking the person I'm becoming more and more and being more accepting of who I am. I look at the mirror, and instead of seeing a lot of flaws, I say, "That's a good color lipstick you found!" As opposed to "Oh, there's a blemish." Also, I definitely eat well. Part of Palestinian cooking is that it's very fresh, lots of fruits and vegetables. So even if I don't eat a lot of food during the*

day, it's good food. I love to have wine with dinner . . . but every-thing's in moderation.

Michelle Archer
Director of development
Syd Gammons Production Company
Sony Pictures

Part of what I learned in sobriety is that life is not going to be easy because I'm sober, it's just going to be life. And life is full of challenges. But today I can face the challenges because I want to be alive. So you know what? A wheelchair is to my legs what a keyboard is to a writer. It just gets me where I want to go in an easier way. It's not a negative thing, it's a help. I take care of myself today because I want to, not because somebody says, "You need to lose weight, so you should eat this way." It's about feeling good in my body when I eat food, and when I'm tired, I lie down and rest. And when I want to be outside, I go outside and sit in the fresh air, because sometimes I just want to be outdoors and feel the sunlight on me. And I do those things today because I have the freedom to, and because I've set up my life to have the freedom to.

Ayofemi Folayan
Los Angeles wordsmith
and performance artist

I really rely a lot on physically working out. Number one, it allows me to alleviate stress. Number two, it's something that's just for me. I'm at the gym every day at five-fifteen in the morning. The alarm goes off, and I just put my feet on the floor. When I think about it, that's when I'm in trouble, so I don't even think about it. This is mine, this is my time, my environment, this is mine.

Cheryl Kendrick
Special projects development director
City of San Diego

As T. George Harris, the founder and former publisher of *Psychology Today*, says, "Health is functioning at your best, whatever it is that you do."

Taking good emotional care of yourself

She wondered if she had already had a nervous breakdown and just didn't . . . notice it.

Susan Cheever
A Woman's Life

What does it mean to take good care of yourself emotionally? From early on, parents teach children to identify *physical* hurts and report them: "My tummy hurts," "I'm dizzy," "I feel like I'm going to throw up," or "I hurt my finger." Such hurts usually get responded to with loving attention, care, and sympathy. The same cannot be said for emotional or psychological issues.

Because parents are not adept at recognizing their own emotions—let alone being comfortable with and/or doing something about them—they fail to teach their children how to effectively handle *their* emotions. If anything, parents often teach children inappropriate ways of handling negative emotions, such as anger or upset or fear. So if a young girl says, "I'm really angry at Daddy," or "I hate my teacher," or "I'm scared," these words frequently upset and frighten parents. Parents tend to want their children to deny their feelings ("Nice girls don't get angry") and try to talk their children out of the feelings ("No, you really don't hate your teacher") or try to ignore the feelings ("Stop whining, there's nothing to be scared of"). Negative emotions are often seen as bad, as not normal.

My point is not to blame parents for this. After all, the boundaries between normal emotions and emotional problems are difficult enough for medical and mental health professionals to decipher, let alone parents.

Recent national studies show that boys and girls are taught to experience emotional pain in significantly different ways. For example, boys are taught to turn outward with their pain and are more likely to engage in antisocial behaving (acting out) and in substance and alcohol abuse.[18] Women, on the other hand, are taught to turn inward with their pain and have much higher levels of depression and anxiety disorders (such as panic disorders, phobias, and obsessive/compulsive disorders). Girls and women are also ten times more likely to have eating disorders (anorexia and bulimia).[19]

What Nourishes You? Gives You Energy?

Perhaps the most important thing you can do to take care of yourself emotionally is to carve out time in your life to do whatever renourishes, re-energizes, or refuels you. What can you do that is fun? Enjoyable? Energizing? Refreshing? What, when, and with whom do you feel like laughing? Which experiences give you a sense of perspective and calm? Which places do you go to where you feel tension and worries melt away?

Steps I Will Take to Nourish Myself, Get Energy Back
    What: _____
    When: _____
    Where: _____
    Whom I will consult or where I will go for help if I need it: _____
    _____

As with the physical area, there are some commonsense *do's* and *don'ts* about taking care of yourself.

Don't focus on the negative, worry about mistakes, or wait for others to meet your needs, wants, and desires; don't do too much or work too hard or try to be everything to everybody; don't accede to the *shoulds, musts, have-tos,* and *ought-tos* in life; don't deprive yourself; don't spend time with activities, things, and people who irritate, annoy, or displease you; don't sacrifice yourself, settle for less, or postpone your life; don't allow yourself to feel hopeless, powerless, or helpless.

Do be as responsible to yourself as you are to others, act on your priorities, find and participate in energy-giving activities and work, get control of your life, take steps to be your own person and have your own identity, have a space or room of your own; know what you want to be, do, and have, and get it for yourself; love and nurture yourself, take control and direct the course of your life; be all that you can be (not what others want you to be); consciously eliminate the activities, things, and people in your life that irritate, annoy, or displease you.

Here is what women told me they think or do about taking good emotional care of themselves.

I try to buy something for myself every week. If you know what you like, what pleases you, what makes you feel good, then you take very direct steps to act on that.

Deanna D'Adarrio
Health-care designer

Every year I take five days and go away someplace with good friends. Those days are inviolate — nobody touches them. I love the women who go. We get very relaxed. I've only missed one year out of eleven.

Carol Dressler
President, Dressler Associates

There are certain types of giving and expending energy — like certain charity kinds of things — where just by doing it I get back. I don't seem to need or want a lot of other things. I love spending time, hanging out and laughing with family and friends, really simple things.

Dana Goodman
President, Multitech Properties

I think the secret is if you like what you do, you don't need to find
time for a hobby, you know what I mean?

Patricia Schroeder
Former congresswoman from Colorado

I love to laugh, I love humor—it's such a cleansing kind of thing.
I find myself seeking this more and more, looking at ways I can be
amused. I never watch television, but I find—whether it's passing
along jokes or reading or doing something that creates amusement
and irony for me—that's a real strong way of taking care of myself.

Kristie Peterson
President, K.E. Peterson and
Company

Come rain or shine, even when I had young children, I have always
taken an afternoon rest.

Anonymous

Taking good social care of yourself

Life is partly what we make it and partly what is
made by the friends we choose.

Tehyi Hsieh

Throughout the book I have spoken about the importance of women making good choices about the people with whom they spend time. Because
so many women never think of this as a choice, let me remind you one
more time:

Spend more time with people who are positive, authentic, warm,
loving, nurturing, supportive, and appreciative of you.

Limit or eliminate the time you spend with people who are
not good for you, including those to whom you are related or
married.
(In other words, stay away from negative people who attempt to con-
trol, manipulate, criticize, or depend on you.)

You owe no one your love or your time.

Steps I Will Take to Spend More Time with Good Friends
    With whom: _____
    When: _____
    Where: _____
    Whom I will consult or where I will go for help to do this: _____
    _____

Steps I Will Take to Limit Time with People Who Are Not Good for Me
    Who: _____
    When: _____
    Where: _____
    Whom I will consult or where I will go for help to do this: _____
    _____

Ralph Waldo Emerson once said, "The only way to have a friend is to be one." Most women understand that. You know you have a friend when you and another person experience that magical moment when one or the other of you says, "Wow! You feel that way, too! I thought that I was the only one." For women, real friendship is all about experiencing a sense of closeness with another person as you share thoughts, feelings, and some-times experiences with them. You also know that you have a real friend when you can be alone with her (or him), not feel the need to say or do anything with her (or him), and especially be comfortable with silence.

To develop closeness with others, we need to offer that which we want: warmth, authenticity, positive words, and regard, as well as love, support, and appreciation. Because no one is perfect, we also need to be forgiving of mistakes our friends make and remember that having expectations for them is not the job of a good friend. We also need to allow others their own space, in addition to room for personal change. And we should consciously avoid being negative with or critical of them, or attempt to control or manipulate them, or become dependent on them. As you know, it takes time and attention and sometimes practice to be and have a good friend. But as Robert Louis Stevenson said, "A friend is a present you give to your-self." There are few things in life more delicious than having a good friend.

Doing Good for Others

What's one of the best things you can do when you're feeling down? Do something good for something or someone else. Confident women do things in the world that give them a sense of strong purpose. They offer their time, often they give of themselves in service, and they also give their money. But the most meaningful type of giving is that which has personal meaning for you, no matter how big or small. It doesn't really matter for what or for whom you do good work: it might be for a friend, or a family, or a group, or a community, or a social cause, or an animal, or the environment, or even a threatened plant species. What's really important is that you feel that your work makes a difference and that what you choose is a part of your life's work.

There are some commonsense *don'ts* and *do's* about taking good social care of yourself.

Don't accede to pressures from others, don't tolerate any form of abuse (disrespect, exploitation, being treated unfairly or being used by others), don't accept demeaning or insulting words from others, don't accept any form of sexual discrimination or harassment, don't spend time with people just because they want to be with you, don't waste time trying to meet others' expectations or getting their approval or permission, don't give up, or into other's demands.

Do spend time with genuine, stimulating, interesting, fun people, surround yourself with people who applaud your thoughts, feelings, and actions, choose as partners men who are also good friends, set limits with others, say no to others and yes when it makes sense, ask others for help or delegate to them, do something that has a positive impact on the world.

So here is what women told me they do about taking good social care of themselves.

> *I make choices about the kind of people I spend time with. I have a low tolerance for whiners and complainers. It irritates me. My mother told me, "There will always be people who will be attracted to you who will just drag you down. Be nice to them, but you don't have to spend a lot of time with them."*
>
> Barbara Gosink, M.D.
> Radiologist
> University of
> California, San Diego

> *I can't be with people who are incongruent, I can just sniff them out. I make a choice not to be with them. I need to be around people who love what they're doing or feel like they're making a difference in the world. With my friends I am completely me; I don't have to be anything for them. I am who I am, and that is an incredible gift.*
>
> Vicki Halsey
> Management consultant
> Blanchard Training

Because I cannot have children, taking care of myself emotionally and socially stand together. I look around and meet kids where they are. Luckily our neighbors have children and I do things with them.

Hanné Vedsted Hansen
Air traffic controller
Copenhagen, Denmark

After being an elected official for so many years and feeling the need to spend time with anyone who wanted to be with me, finally I can say that I'm not going to do that anymore. I'm especially not going to spend time with people who are negative, who drain me, and who have nothing good to say. Life is too short for that.

Diane Watson
Former California state senator

Taking good intellectual care of yourself (using your brain!)

The brain is only three pounds of blood, dream, and electricity, and yet from that mortal stew come Beethoven's sonatas. Dizzy Gillespie's jazz. Audrey Hepburn's wish to spend the last month of her life in Somalia, saving children.

Diane Ackerman

Perhaps because for so long only limited education was available to girls and women, and perhaps because girls are encouraged to do well in elementary and middle school but then lack the support that boys receive in high school, even today women seem to question and hold back their intellectual selves. Of course, it does not help that the modern media perpetuate the notion that girls and women should define themselves not by their brains, but solely in terms of their bodies, and especially in the approval and disapproval of their appearance by men.

When I suggest that women need to take good care of themselves intellectually, what I'm referring to is the desire to become mature, alive, intellectually curious individuals, women who are anxious to develop their full capacities and feel a passion for learning.

There are many ways of taking good intellectual care of yourself. Here are three:

Know Yourself

To begin with, gather knowledge about yourself. Know what your needs, wants, capacities, values, and purposes are. Having a strong identity and ever-increasing self-knowledge is a key factor in your ability to create a healthy, satisfying, and fulfilling life.

Become as Educated as You Can Be

Education and knowledge are the currency by which women can gain power, success, and autonomy. For some women these words are scary and unfeminine. After all, magazines suggest that many women—and especially men—are turned off by those qualities in women. Jill Ker Conway, former president of Smith College, says that today, unlike male professionals, "women professionals still find it hard to claim their victories and to celebrate their achievements."[20] They continue to be witnesses rather than actors in their own lives.[21]

Confidence is not a noisy, in-your-face attitude. It is a quiet sense of self-respect and appreciation for who you are, what you can do, and what you have accomplished. Confident women don't waste their time trying to impress other people; they don't need to. Inside they know they are worthwhile. Whether they are young or old, professionals or career volunteers, artists, writers, or gourmet cooks—confident women are powerful, successful, and autonomous, each in her very own way.

Bernadine Healy, the former director of the National Institutes of Health, says, "Educated women are healthy women . . . educated teenagers have few unwanted babies. . . . the more a woman knows, the longer she lives. Educated women improve the health of entire nations."[22]

Look for Ways to Keep Intellectually Alive

Confident women seem to have a knack for "cultivating the sense of infinite possibility." They look for ways to learn and act on their curiosity and get turned on to ideas—their own and other people's. Whether you read books, or go to art galleries, or travel, or take advantage of the infinite Internet possibilities, or attend classes and workshops, or volunteer to build houses with Habitat for Humanity, or expose yourself to new situations and challenges, each of these actions is a way to keep yourself intellectually alive.

> *The more that you read,*
> *the more things you'll know.*
> *The more that you learn,*
> *the more places you'll go.*
>   Dr. Seuss
>   *I Can Read with*
>   *My Eyes Shut*

Steps I Will Take to Take Better Intellectual Care of Myself

What: _____

When: _____

Where: _____

Whom I will consult or where I will go for help if I need it: _____

_____

Here are some commonsense *don'ts* and *do's* about taking good intellectual care of yourself.

Don't waste your intellectual capacities. Abraham Maslow said that like all physical structures, unused intelligence atrophies and then dies.[23] Don't put aside challenges because you don't think you know enough or are experienced enough; don't be controlled by or diminished by mindless social prescriptions about what women should be and do; don't squash or squander yourself, abandon your potentials and possibilities; don't buy into negative belief systems.

Do find wonderful books to read, find work that is stimulating, keep on learning about whatever turns you on, use your brain, find ways of expressing your own creativity, treat your mind with respect, pursue an intelligent and authentic life, be the author of your own thoughts and actions, take a positive approach to life, develop as many personal capacities as you can, enjoy the energy that comes from being your own person, and be selective about what you choose to listen to, read, see, and hear.

When I asked women what they did to take care of themselves intellectually, this is how they responded:

> *Probably getting a master's degree and maybe study architecture.*
>
> Deanna D'Adarrio
> Health-care designer

> *Reading, traveling. After my visit to China and Taiwan, I've really gotten turned on to hearing stories and understanding more about my family, where I've come from, my background, and who I am.*
>
> Lil Huang
> Ph.D. student, University
> of California, Santa Barbara

> *I knew I was a confident woman when I got to the place where I would go to a restaurant by myself, and unselfconsciously sit there reading a book while eating my meal and love it.*
>
> Amy Blum
> Marketing consultant

Read.   —Dottie Lamm
                                   Former Colorado U.S. senatorial candidate

If you like what you're doing, studying, researching, working, that's taking good care of yourself. Everything is intellectual.
                                   Kara Johnson
                                   Ph.D. student, Cambridge University

Because I am a TV news reporter, I'm reporting to thousands of critical, sophisticated viewers, I must be accurate, look good, and deliver my stories in a credible manner. So I take care of myself by taking care of "my state of mind." Every day I meditate twice a day for 20 minutes. It clears my head and I think more clearly.
                                   Maria Valasquez
                                   News Eight, San Diego, California

Taking good financial care of yourself

Those who never think of money need a great deal of it.
                                   Agatha Christie

For aeons now, money has been a five-letter dirty word to many women. Like sex, money is difficult to talk about: it's private, too personal, even taboo. Therefore, how to make it, how to handle it, how to manage and invest it, and yes, even where to spend it are all issues that scores of women find uncomfortable topics. "Let someone else do it" is the approach many women take—until they are suddenly faced with the specter of having to support themselves.

The adage "money talks" has two meanings for women, real and psychological. In real terms money allows you to survive (and sometimes even thrive) by allowing you to (1) support yourself and/or help support your family, (2) pay for housing, (3) buy food, household necessities, and clothing, (4) engage in a variety of hobbies, vacations, and other pleasurable activities, (5) send your children to college, (6) pay for insurance, taxes, and the like, and (7) save for retirement. Having money doesn't necessarily make you happy, but it sure is nice to have around when you need to pay the bills.

In psychological terms, money is a means for acquiring autonomy and power. Any woman who earns her own money experiences a real sense of being her own person. How satisfying it is knowing that you can rely on yourself for what you need and want, not depend on "the kindness of others" — even a husband or parents — to provide for your basic needs. In her book *In Times Like This*, Nellie McClung says, "The economic dependence of women is perhaps the greatest injustice that has been done to us."

For many legitimate, very honorable reasons — being born during an era when working outside the home was considered undesirable or unnecessary, choosing to stay home to bring up children or care for elderly parents, or dedicating your life to volunteering to worthy causes — many women are not now wage earners. If you have never earned money or are not earning it now, the more knowledgeable about and involved with your personal financial matters you are, the more autonomy and power you will have. Money is spelled p-o-w-e-r when you earn your own money and/or know a great deal about and take part in managing your own or your family's personal finances.

Confident women are financially accountable.

To take good care of yourself financially, here are the bottom-line actions that financial experts say that we should take:

Prioritize Your Wants, Needs, and Dreams into Financial Goals

If you're like most women, money comes and goes. Basically you're just happy to have enough to pay the bills and the taxes. The idea of planning for what you want to do (or have) someday is kind of like a dream, something you'll do when you're a little older and there's more time to think about it. Besides, you don't have the money right now. You'll wait until you (and/or your partner) are earning more.

Beth Kobliner, author of *Get a Financial Life*, says that this is totally the wrong approach. No matter what your age, the first step to taking care of yourself financially is to figure out what your needs, wants, and dreams are and then develop some financial goals. Prioritizing your wants and needs also includes setting aside money for special purchases, holidays, and special occasions in advance rather than spending the money and deciding after the fact how to pay for them.

Know Where Your Money Is Going

People have varying degrees of knowledge about where their money goes. Some know to the penny how much comes in and goes out. Most have only a vague idea. Certainly with the advent of computer software programs such as Quicken, the job of keeping track of your finances has become much easier. Whether it's sitting down with a pencil and paper detailing how you spend your money each month and every year, or going over a Quick Reporting of your spending, getting an accurate handle on where

Taking Better Care of Yourself

309

and when your money comes in and goes out is the second step to taking good financial care of yourself.

Don't Just Spend—Plan Your Spending

Very often when people look at their finances, they find that they are spending more than they are taking in and using credit cards to make up the difference. One way to avoid this is to take a look your priorities and begin making conscious choices about spending. Beth Kobliner has some good financial rules of thumb about spending:[24]

• Debt Rule

Your total debt (all the money you owe, including unpaid student loans, credit card balances, car loans, and any other lines of credit, but not your home mortgage) should be less than 20 percent of your annual take-home pay. Some financial advisers advise not creating debt in the first place or, if you have debt, developing a plan to pay it off right now.

• Mortgage or Rent Rule

This may not be possible in cities such as San Francisco, New York, or Los Angeles, but where it is possible, spend no more than 30 percent of your monthly take-home pay on rent or mortgage payments.

Start Saving Your Money Early

Make it a priority. Save at least 10 percent of your take-home pay each month. Some experts say that you should also save another 5 percent for your retirement plan.

Learn about Money

It's necessary to know about investing, mortgages, insurance, and retirement plans. But many women approaching the financial world for the first time feel absolutely overwhelmed by it. It is easy to feel defeated, even before you get started, when you think about all there is to know and learn. But as with everything else, accumulating information in small bits or in small periods of time is a good approach. There are many ways to learn, including reading some of the books I have listed at the end of this chapter, subscribing to financial newsletters, attending seminars, listening to audiotapes, watching videos or television financial programs, and consulting with financial professionals, which just happens to be the next step.

Find Experienced, Respected, Knowledgeable Financial Professionals

Be really choosy when you look for an adviser about finances. Whether it is a stockbroker, mutual fund manager, banker, insurance person, tax attorney, tax accountant, bookkeeper, or whatever, make choices with appropriate "due diligence." Research the options, interview the candidates, and slowly put together a team of the best available with what you can afford. This is one area where you literally cannot afford to take the first person recommended or pick out someone from the yellow pages or "off the street." And of course, always be wary of quick money offers or schemes.

Have an Estate Plan

One of the first things that a financial planner will tell you is that if you don't plan your estate (no matter how small or large), when you die the government will do it for you. According to *The Wall Street Journal's Guide to Understanding Personal Finance*, "two out of three Americans die intestate — without a will."[25] Take positive action to make sure that this doesn't happen to you. It's also important to take care of minor children, if you have them. Even though it is unpleasant, an important aspect of estate planning is deciding who should take care of your children if you die. Again, if you don't decide it yourself, the courts will decide for you.

Keep Your Financial Records Organized

It's a lot easier to deal with your finances if you're organized. As I've mentioned, one way to organize is to use a computer software program. Unfortunately, that won't do the total job; there is always a lot of paperwork to keep and file. Most women I spoke with used one or a combination of three filing systems to keep track of their financial papers: file folders, three-ring binders, and large manila envelopes. The papers or records they keep include:

- all insurance items, including auto, health, dental, homeowner's, excess liability, disability, and life
- all yearly brokerage information, divided by month
- all warranties, rebates, and receipts for major purchases
- all payables divided by the month, including bills, taxes, insurance premiums, and credit card statements
- all tax-deductible items for the year, including medical expenses, mortgage interest payment slips, property tax statements, and donation receipts
- all general financial papers, including loan or rental agreements and home purchase documents
- all income information including salary, interest payments, bonuses, and the like
- tax returns

These eight steps to financial planning and care are only the tip of the iceberg, but for women who have not yet begun, they are a good place to start. For women who are already involved in planning, these steps can be used as a checklist for noting what you are already doing and what else you might want to do.

Steps I Will Initiate to Take Better Financial Care of Myself
What: _____
When: _____
Where: _____
Whom I will consult or where I will go for help if I need it: _____
_____

Here are some commonsense *don'ts* and *do's* about taking good financial care of yourself.

Don't stay ignorant of your financial affairs, don't get into debt, don't spend more than you earn, don't stop saving, and don't fail to get everything in writing.

Do take time to become financially savvy, set aside an emergency cushion through an automatic savings plan, buy what pleases you (not necessarily just what is on sale); have a regular, scheduled bill-paying system; on a regular basis get copies of your credit report; have a separate bank account of your own if you are married.

When I asked women what they did to take care of themselves financially, this is how they responded:

> *What I would like to have more of is solitude, money, and time. I already have a great job, a great husband, and great kids.*
>
> Charlotte Huggins
> President, In Wave Pictures

> *Because it makes me feel better, I choose quality in what I purchase and in what I do.*
>
> Michelle Archer
> Director of development
> Syd Gammon Productions,
> Sony Pictures

> *When I was young and poor, I just saw that a lot of people could make it. I said to myself, "Hey, they got out of poverty, they've got a home, they're doing fine, and I can do the same thing."*
> Lily Balian
> Retired Northrup Corporation executive

*Until recently I didn't pay much attention at all to where the money
was being invested. . . . I'm now in a small investment group, so I'm
paying much more attention to what's going on.*

Sharon Davidson
Management consultant

Taking good spiritual care of yourself

*There are some people who have the quality of richness and joy
in them and they communicate it to everything they touch. It is
first of all a physical quality; then it is a quality of the spirit.*

Thomas Wolfe

Whether or not they know or admit to it, everyone has a spiritual side. After
all, sooner or later who doesn't want to understand the meaning and purpose of life?

The search for meaning takes many forms. Some people seek it through
regular observance within an established religious tradition. For others
being spiritual means living by a set of higher values or ethical standards.
Still others find it through meditation or prayer. Many women have told
me that being one with nature is a spiritual experience for them. A few said
they felt touched by a sense of the eternal at moments when they were confronted with "pure" beauty (as in the presence of a magnificent piece of art
or architecture or at a rare musical performance), or with "pure" goodness
or wiseness (as in the presence of a hero or heroine such as the late Mother
Teresa), or when coming upon the "truth" (as when having an epiphanic
experience or unexpectedly finding a luminous passage in a book).

Harvard University's Herbert Benson says that through his scientific
observations he has learned that no matter what name you give the Infinite
Absolute you worship, no matter what theology you subscribe to, the results
of believing in God are the same. (Even proclaimed atheists and agnostics
hunger for and are soothed by the idea of purposefulness.)[26] When all is
said and done, "it does not matter which God you worship, nor which theology you adopt as your own. Spiritual life, in general, is very healthy."[27]

*I enjoy the silence in a church before the service
more than any sermon.*

Ralph Waldo Emerson

Perhaps because they are the mothers of the earth, women seem to have
deep souls and special spirits. But cultural and inner forces often cause

women to bury this part of themselves. In the last decade or so, women authors have been a major force in urging women to "recapture their spirit if lost; to strengthen it, if weakened; to develop it, if it's considered latent or underdeveloped."[28] Fortunately women of many colors have been a part of this movement, including the likes of Laura Esquivel, Maya Angelou, Terry McMillan, Sandra Cisneros, Mary Crow Dog, Louise Erdrich, Annie Dillard, Kaye Gibbons, Fannie Flagg, Carolyn Myss, and Linda Duerk, to name just a few.

Almost every woman with whom I spoke about this book at one time or another invoked the words of Anne Morrow Lindbergh. Her *Gift from the Sea* seems to have taken on a Bible-like quality for those of any age who are searching for their souls. Among many other things, Lindbergh advises women who are in the state of "Zerrissenheit—torn-to-pieces" to become "inwardly attentive," to seek "solitude . . . quiet time alone [for] contemplation, prayer, music, a centering line of thought or reading, of study or work."[29]

Time to Be Alone

Solitude . . . is wonderful. Because you want to be
with the person you are with: yourself.

Jennifer James

Carve out time to be alone. Of all the suggestions I make to women in therapy or in coaching, this is the one that seems most difficult for them to do. Perhaps solitude has become anathema for women because they see it as the ultimate self-indulgence.

The brilliant Oxford University psychiatrist Anthony Storr has written a provocative book about this topic. In *Solitude* he says that the West has so idealized personal relationships that many people live under the assumption that relationships are the chief, if not the only source of human happiness.[30] They could not be more wrong, he says: "Even those who have the happiest relationships with others need something other than those relationships to complete their fulfillment."[31] What's more, the world's most creative people—poets, writers, composers, painters, and sculptors—spend most of their time alone.[32]

Not only is solitude therapeutic, but "the capacity to be alone is necessary if the brain is to function at its best and if the individual is to fulfill her highest potential . . . learning, thinking, innovation, and maintaining contact with one's inner world are all facilitated by solitude."[33] Having peace of mind, experiencing the mystical, listening to your own inner voice, and being in touch with your spirit or soul rarely occur in the midst of a hurly-burly life, but it does happen when you are alone.

Steps I Will Take to Have Some Time Alone
  What: _____
  When: _____
  Where: _____
  Whom I will consult or where I will go for help if I need it: _____
  _____

Steps I Will Take to Take Better Spiritual Care of Myself
  What: _____
  When: _____
  Where: _____
  Whom I will consult or where I will go for help if I need it: _____
  _____

Here are some commonsense *don'ts* and *do's* about taking good spiritual care of yourself.

Don't ignore your spiritual self or define your spiritual life in terms of others' needs; don't allow anyone to manipulate, control, or abuse you in the name of religious principles; don't get distracted by religious labels or dogma; don't avoid being alone or experiencing silence.

Do build in everyday periods of quiet time and solitude, even if it's for a few minutes; read books and look for experiences that nourish your spiritual self; find places for spiritual renewal, enjoy the experience of doing nothing, be grateful for and celebrate your blessings, enjoy and appreciate nature and all of God's creations; know what has meaning and purpose in your life.

When I asked women what they did to take care of themselves spiritually, this is how they responded:

> *In the entertainment industry, I don't think you lose your soul unless you give it up. It depends on your soul. Are you going to be well-liked or well-respected?*
>
> Michelle Archer
> Director of development
> Syd Gammon Productions,
> Sony Pictures

> *For me the difference between religion and spirituality is that religion is your relationship to a church and spirituality is your relationship to God. What I know is, on the days when I go out and I'm*

*in the sunshine, sitting on the pier watching the ocean go by, I feel
so close to God.*

Ayofemi Folayan

*I go to the Armenian church; I even joined the parish council. We
have a lot of new Armenians coming in from Russia. (Did you know
that the largest immigration population outside of Armenia is here
in California?) I love getting to know them and welcoming them.
But I also love the music. I like the Armenian people because they're
very warm, very hospitable. If I were to go to an Armenian church
anywhere in the world today, they would welcome me. From the time
I was a little girl, that sense of community has stayed with me.*

Lily Balian

*Having days in which there is no responsibility, nothing to do, no
people, no phones, no nothing. Just wide-open time. I have a thirst
for that. It doesn't happen very often.*

Anonymous

*Certainly being quiet. I remember my grandmother and my aunt
would say, "We're going to go into the silence now." They would say
that to you because they want you to respect it. They'd just be quiet,
either take a nap or read or be quiet.*

Carolyn Owen-Towle
Unitarian minister

*Yes, I believe in God. I feel God in many places. In my garden, at
the ocean.*

Barbara Poleski
Mother, homemaker, volunteer

Reading poetry is also part of taking care of that spiritual side of me.
Lil Huang

*I think the universe conspires to help you. I don't care if you call it
God or what you call it, but I am sure that there is some force at
work . . . to make all the things that have happened — bad and
good — happen, one after the other. I am just a player in this amazing masterpiece.*

Elisabeth Eisner
Attorney and partner, Gray, Cary, Ware and Freidenrich

THE FUTURE IS YOURS TO DECIDE

As you have seen from reading this book, confidence is not simply taking good care, it is also knowing yourself and becoming more competent in the world. As you grow and develop your own confidence — "when you let your light shine," as Marianne Williamson says — what you say and what you do will be a living example to other women and young girls that there is another way.

Right now, at the beginning of this new millennium, we are at one of the most important crossroads women have ever faced. The social, economic, and political forces are in place for us to challenge the rules we live by. We can change the limiting paradigms that have defined who we are, how we think about ourselves, and what we do. You and I can change forever what it means to be a woman. Now is the time for us to finally become all that we were meant to be.

In *Alice in Wonderland*, Alice plaintively asks the Cheshire cat, "Would you tell me please, which way I ought to go from here?" After shining its infamous smile, the cat slowly replies, "That depends a good deal on where you want to go." Having read *The Confident Woman* now, the next step is up to you. Where in the world do *you* want to go?

Wherever that might be, this is my wish for you:

> *May there always be work for*
> *your hands to do.*
>
> *May your purse always hold*
> *a coin or two.*
>
> *May the sun always shine*
> *on your windowpane.*
>
> *May a rainbow be certain*
> *to follow the rain.*
>
> *May the hand of a friend*
> *always be near to you.*
>
> *May God fill your heart*
> *with gladness to cheer you.*
>
> Irish toast

SELF-HELP BOOK BREAK

PHYSICAL CARE

Herbert Benson, M.D., *Timeless Healing*

Boston Women's Health Book Collective, *Our Bodies, Ourselves for the New Century*

Bernadine Healy, *A New Prescription for Women's Health*

Eileen Hoffman, *Our Health, Our Lives*

Iris Litt, M.D., *Taking Our Pulse: The Health of America's Women*

Chris Casson Madden, *A Room of Her Own*

Kenneth Pelletier, M.D., *Sound Mind, Sound Body*

Stanford Center for Research in Disease Prevention, *Fresh Start*

EMOTIONAL CARE

Julia Cameron, *The Artist's Way*

Mihaly Csikszentmihalyi, *Finding Flow*

Edward Deci and Richard Flaste, *Why We Do What We Do*

Luise Eichenbaum and Susie Orbach, *Between Women*

Dana Crowley Jack, *Silencing the Self*

Karen Johnson, M.D., *Trusting Ourselves*

Jean Baker Miller, *Toward a New Psychology of Women*

Martin Seligman, Ph.D., *Learned Optimism; What You Can Change . . . and What You Can't*

Véronique Vienne, *The Art of Doing Nothing*

SOCIAL CARE

David P. Celani, *Illusion of Love*

Stephanie Dowrick, *Intimacy and Solitude*

Sally Helgesen, *The Female Advantage*

Eleanor Maccoby, *The Two Sexes*

Lillian B. Rubin, *Just Friends*

Deborah Tannen, *You Just Don't Understand*

INTELLECTUAL CARE

Simone de Beauvoir, *The Second Sex*

Bram Dijkstra, *Idols of Perversity*

Annie Dillard, *An American Childhood; Teaching a Stone to Talk*

Trudy Govier, *Socrates' Children*

Carolyn Heilbrun, *Writing a Woman's Life*

Henrik Ibsen, *A Doll's House*

William James, *The Varieties of Religious Experience*

Linda K. Kerber, *No Constitutional Right to Be Ladies*

Virginia Woolf, *A Room of One's Own*

FINANCIAL CARE

Marsha Bertrand, *A Woman's Guide to Savvy Investing*

Colette Dowling, *Maxing Out: Why Women Sabotage Their Financial Security*

Beth Kobliner, *Get a Financial Life*

The Wall Street Journal's Guide to Understanding Personal Finance

SPIRITUAL CARE

Phil Cousineau, *Soul Moments*

Marcia and Jack Kelly, *Sanctuaries*

Florida Scott Maxwell, *The Measure of My Days*

Thomas More, *Care of the Soul*

John Pawson, *Minimum*

M. Scott Peck, *The Road Less Traveled*

May Sarton, *At Seventy*

Anthony Storr, *Solitude*

Judith Viorst, *Necessary Losses*

Epilogue

FINAL THOUGHTS: ON RAISING
CONFIDENT DAUGHTERS

If the truth be known, when I first started thinking about writing a book about confidence, I intended to write one for girls, not for adult women. My thought was that it would be better to help build confidence in young girls and adolescents than try to address the lack of it in women. Then I began to think about who would likely build girls' confidence, and of course, mothers and other significant women were the first people who came to mind.

I decided that the best way to reach girls and young women was to educate and empower their primary teachers: mothers, older sisters, aunts, cousins, and grandmothers, as well as female coaches, friends, and educators. Ergo, *The Confident Woman* became a book about and for women.

> *The task of a teacher is not to work for the pupil nor to oblige*
> *her to work, but to show her how to work.*
> Wanda Landowska[1]

Our daughters have many more options and opportunities than we have had. Fortunately, most of the discriminatory laws and some of the negative attitudes about women have changed. Some women have even internalized the "You've come a long way, baby" advertisement and eschew any notions that there is still work to be done.

When it comes to our daughters, however, the research says that we haven't come as far as some might think. For example, no matter their particular background, adolescent girls

- are still boy-crazy and measure their worth by how popular, attractive, and cool they are, especially to members of the opposite sex[2]

- are still striving for perfection as "the perfectly good girl: someone whom everyone will promote and value and want to be with"[3]
- are still losing their "voices" (that is, being and doing for others while sacrificing themselves) as they acquiesce to the norms of Western culture, especially with regard to idealized notions of beauty, body, and romance.[4]

We have our confidence work cut out for us because of the continuing subtle and not-so-subtle negative messages our girls receive from home, from the culture at large, from their peers, through rock and rap music, and from magazines, movies, and TV programs.

It would be presumptuous for me to try to say in a few words all that could be said about raising confident daughters. That is the subject for another book. But I would like to leave you with a few thoughts about how you can be a positive influence in your daughter's life:

BECOME A CONFIDENT WOMAN YOURSELF

You can do nothing more significant to inspire, teach, and support your daughter to become a confident woman than to think and act more like one yourself. A mother who has a strong sense of herself, who takes good care of herself, who solves her own problems, who competently handles life's challenges, who chooses to spend time with loving, supportive people, who reads and is well educated, who loves her work and yet takes time for herself, cannot help but influence her daughter in important positive ways. Children learn much less from what we say than from what we do with our lives.

Women can't really hope to change the way girls think about themselves until they change the way they live their own lives.

MAKE YOUR DAUGHTER A PRIORITY

Not just in your mind but by your everyday actions, create the time to make your daughter a top priority in your life. Spend time alone with her, play with her, read to her, take her out to lunch, exercise with her, listen to her; if she needs it, help her with schoolwork, teach her how to do things, and encourage her to plan for college and a career. Don't allow unimportant people and/or events to get in the way.

USE THE OUTCOME MODEL OF PARENTING

If you are like most mothers, you want your daughter to have all the good things in life. Confidence is one of them, but I'm sure you also want her

to have a sense of purpose, meaningful relationships, health, a good education, financial security, and of course, a lot of happiness. To help your
daughter achieve those things, you might consider using what I call the
Outcome Model of Parenting. Keeping in mind that there is no such thing
as a perfect parent, this model begins with the notion that the outcome of
your parenting — what you hope your child will become — is affected by the
behaviors and attitudes you engage in as she grows up. While no one can
fully determine how a daughter will turn out — certainly there are many
forces at work other than mothering — the outcome model offers you a way
to give your words and actions some purpose.

Let's see how the model works by taking the issue of confidence as one
example. If you want your daughter to be confident, which attitudes,
words, and behaviors are most likely to encourage confidence? Likewise,
which attitudes, words, and behaviors are likely to produce the opposite of
confidence?

Actions That Encourage and Discourage Confidence

From the time she is born through words and actions:

• **Hugging, touching, kissing and smiling — help your daughter to feel
loved,** as opposed to keeping your warm feelings to yourself. Remember,
children are never spoiled by love; nor can they hear too many loving words.

• **Helping your daughter to develop a strong identity — that is, know
who she is, what she likes and wants — and encouraging her to have
dreams, as well as plans for her future,** as opposed to telling her that she
should be or do or look a certain way, or that her wants and desires are selfish or unattainable, or that her dreams are foolish.

• **Emphasizing your daughter's strengths and competencies and helping her overcome areas of difficulty,** rather than dismissing or ignoring
what is positive or emphasizing where she is deficient.

• **Encouraging and helping your daughter to do things, and to enjoy
success and achievement through her persistence and hard work,** as
opposed to doing things for her, or discouraging her from taking risks, or
acting independently.

• **Expressing your concerns through the use of "I" language when your
daughter is inappropriate or inconsiderate,** rather than criticizing, condemning, attacking, or humiliating her.

• **Respecting your daughter by listening to her opinions, negotiating differences, and taking time to resolve conflicts,** as opposed to rejecting her ideas when they differ from yours, using your power to deal with differences, and especially being mean and/or abrupt.

• **Helping your daughter to identify and express her emotions—positive and negative**—rather than discouraging or denying her strong emotions or telling her that her emotions are silly, stupid, or childish.

• **Helping your daughter find activities and issues about which she feels passionate, and encouraging her to be involved in physical activities and sports and to develop her intellect, including taking math and science classes,** as opposed to spending time shopping or hanging out at the mall, or being focused on her weight and her appearance.

• **Teaching your daughter to be a critical consumer of the media,** rather than accepting as truth everything she sees and hears.

• **Teaching your daughter the value of self-responsibility and to take good care of herself physically, emotionally, socially, intellectually, financially, and spiritually,** as opposed to assuming that somehow she will learn these things along the way.

SUPPORT YOUR HUSBAND'S EFFORT TO RAISE A CONFIDENT DAUGHTER

While you cannot "make" your husband do or say things to raise your daughter's confidence, you can certainly encourage him to be actively involved in her life. Researchers have identified that fathers are the critical achievement role model for girls. Aside from how a father treats her mother, there is nothing more important than for him to tell his daughter how much he loves her and how important she is in his life.

TEACH YOUR SONS TO TREAT GIRLS WITH RESPECT

Until we change the way we raise boys, especially how they think about and act toward girls, the task of raising confident daughters will be more difficult. Enough said.

If you don't want you daughter to have confidence, then ignore her, lecture her, order her, control her, demand obedience from her, hit her, reject her, put her down, overprotect her, withdraw from her, dominate her, leave her out, insult her, criticize her, humiliate her, and make fun of her.

If, however, you want your daughter to have confidence, then teach her, mentor her, counsel her, listen to her, reward her positive thoughts and actions, be responsive to her, respect her, be interested in her, be honest with her, admit your mistakes and apologize to her, set limits for her, believe in her, reason with her, empathize with her, understand her, accept her, delight in her, adore her, cherish her. If you want a confident daughter, then love her like crazy.

Confident women raise confident daughters.

APPENDIX 1: SYMPTOMS OF DEPRESSION[1]

Sometimes people cannot get on top of their negative thinking and/or feelings. This may mean that they are clinically depressed. The following are the symptoms of depression. If you experience five or more of the symptoms for at least two weeks, it is very important that you consult a mental health professional.

1. Feeling depressed or sad most of the day, nearly every day.
2. Losing interest in what you like to do, having difficulty feeling pleasure.
3. Significant weight loss or weight gain.
4. Having difficulty sleeping or finding yourself sleeping all the time.
5. Experiencing a sense of restlessness or slowing down.
6. Experiencing a loss of energy and/or sense of great fatigue.
7. Feeling worthless or excessively guilty.
8. Not being able to think well, concentrate, feeling indecisive.
9. Feeling sad all the time, considering suicide.

APPENDIX II: WARNING SIGNS OF PHYSICAL AND PSYCHOLOGICAL ABUSE

Are you in danger? A violent partner is dangerous. If you are in an abusive relationship, get out.

Forms of Abuse

• Physical: Actions which cause physical pain or injury, such as hitting, kicking, pushing, or punching.

• Emotional: Words that affect confidence and self-esteem, such as name calling, putting down, insulting, discounting, swearing, or criticizing. Actions that create fear, such as isolation or threats.

• Sexual: Acts of a sexual nature that are unwelcome or uncomfortable.

Behaviors Characteristic of Abusive Partners

Many abused women don't recognize when they are being abused. Here are some of the warning signs of someone being abusive to you:

✓ Jealousy
✓ Controlling behavior
✓ Unrealistic expectations
✓ Isolation
✓ Blames others for problems
✓ Blames others for feelings
✓ Hypersensitivity
✓ Cruelty to animals or children
✓ Verbal abuse
✓ Rigid sex roles
✓ Jekyll and Hyde personality
✓ Past battering

✓ Threats of violence
✓ Breaking or striking objects
✓ Use of force during an argument
✓ Constantly checking up on partner
✓ Forces sex on partner
✓ Trivializing your thoughts or ambitions
✓ Broken promises

Relationship Rights

You have the right to:

Be treated with respect
Your own body, thoughts, opinions, and property
Have your needs be as important as your partner's
Not take responsibility for your partner's behavior
Keep your friends
Grow as an individual
Change your mind
Determine how much time you want to spend with your partner
Have your own money
Assert yourself
Not be abused physically, emotionally, psychologically, or sexually
Break up, fall out of love, and leave a relationship

What Victims of Domestic Violence Need to Know

• The abuse is not your fault.
• You don't ever deserve to be abused.
• You can't change someone who is abusive.
• Staying in the relationship won't stop the abuse.
• Over time the abuse always gets worse.
• If you stay, make a plan to keep yourself safe when the abuse happens again.

If you are in an abusive relationship, find a friend or relative you can trust and tell him or her about it. Call your local community center, or contact a national organization that can link you to a local affiliate.

Abuse Resources

There is *never* an excuse for abuse. For emergencies, please call your local police at 911. For local referrals or confidential counseling, please call the National Domestic Violence Hotline at 1-800-799-SAFE (7233) or 1-800-787-3224.

Adapted from No Safe Place: Violence Against Women is made possible in part by a grant from the Albert and Elaine Borchard Foundation and the Dr. Ezekiel R. and Edna Wattis Dumke Foundation, PBS Online, KUED, Salt Lake City, http://www.pbs.org/kued/nosafeplace/

ENDNOTES

Prologue

1. Phil Cousineau, ed., *Soul Moments: Marvelous Stories of Synchronicity—Meaningful Coincidences from a Seemingly Random World* (Berkeley, Cal.: Conari Press, 1997), p. 8.
2. Ibid., pp. 20–21.

Part I: What Confidence Is All About
Introduction: Who Am I to Be Telling You What to Do?

1. Just in case you'd like to know, Iris's source was Dr. Florence Haseltine of the National Institute for Child Health and Development.

Chapter 2: Confidence Is Just Around the Corner

1. Karen Johnson, *Trusting Ourselves: The Complete Guide to Emotional Well-Being for Women* (New York: Atlantic Monthly Press, 1991), p. 174.
2. William B. Swann, Jr., *Self-Traps: The Elusive Quest for Higher Self-Esteem* (New York: W. H. Freeman, 1996), pp. 13–14.
3. Martin E. P. Seligman, Ph.D., *Learned Optimism: How to Change Your Mind and Your Life* (New York: Pocket Books, 1998), p. vii.
4. Ibid., pp. vi–vii.
5. Brad J. Bushman, Roy F. Baumeister, "Threatened egotism, narcissism, self-esteem, and direct and displaced aggression: Does self-love or self-hate lead to violence?" *Journal of Personality and Social Psychology*, vol. 75, no. 1 (July 1998), pp. 219–29.

Part II: The Mystery of Lost Confidence
Introduction: Why Women Lack Confidence

1. Bram Dijkstra, *Evil Sisters: The Threat of Female Sexuality and the Cult of Manhood* (New York: Alfred A. Knopf, 1996), pp. 4–5.
2. Susan Howatch, *Glittering Images* (New York: Fawcett, 1995), p. 236.

Chapter 3: History's "Weaker Sex" Take on Women

1. *Merriam-Webster's WWW Dictionary,* at www.m-w.com/cgi-bin/dictionary.
2. E. J. Burford and Sandra Shulman, *Of Bridles & Burnings: The Punishment of Women* (New York: St. Martin's Press, 1992), p. 10.
3. Ibid., p. 9.
4. Cullen Murphy, "The Bible According to Eve," *U.S. News & World Report,* August 10, 1998, p. 48.
5. Ibid.
6. Virginia Woolf, *A Room of One's Own* (New York: Harcourt Brace Modern Classic, 1957), pp. 46–47.
7. Antonia Fraser, *The Weaker Vessel* (New York: Alfred A. Knopf, 1984), p. 2.
8. Bram Dijkstra, *Idols of Perversity: Fantasies of Feminine Evil in Fin-de-Siecle Culture* (New York: Oxford University Press, 1986), p. 250.
9. Burford and Shulman, *Of Bridles & Burnings,* p. 202.
10. Ibid., p. 25.
11. Ibid., p. 211.
12. Dijkstra, *Evil Sisters,* p. 3.
13. Louise Bernikow, *The American Women's Almanac: An Inspiring and Irreverent Women's History* (New York: Berkley Publishing Group, 1997), p. 119.
14. Dijkstra, *Idols of Perversity,* p. 170.
15. Ibid., p. 172.
16. Ibid., p. 167.
17. Ibid., p. 120.
18. Ibid.
19. Ibid., p. 169.
20. Burford and Shulman, *Of Bridles & Burnings,* p. 51.
21. Deborah Tannen, *You Just Don't Understand* (New York: Ballantine, 1991), p. 75.
22. Burford and Shulman, *Of Bridles & Burnings,* pp. 50–53.
23. Ibid., p. 19.
24. Ibid., p. 13.
25. Ibid.
26. Bernikow, *American Women's Almanac,* p. 50.
27. Dijkstra, *Idols of Perversity,* pp. 25–27.
28. Judith Bardwick, *The Psychology of Women: A Study of Bio-Cultural Conflicts* (New York: Harper, 1971).
29. Lynn Gamwell and Nancy Tomes, *Madness in America: Cultural and Medical Perceptions of Mental Illness Before 1914* (Ithaca, NY: Cornell University Press, 1995), pp. 125–27.
30. Dijkstra, *Idols of Perversity,* p. 101.
31. Ibid., p. 102.
32. Ibid., p. 21.
33. Virginia Woolf, *Women and Writing* (New York: Peter Smith, 1911), p. 59.
34. Carol Tavris, *The Mismeasure of Woman* (New York: Simon & Schuster, 1992), p. 17.
35. Sara Evans, *Born for Liberty: A History of Women in America* (New York: Free Press, 1991), p. 22.
36. Molly Haskell, *From Reverence to Rape: The Treatment of Women in the Movies* (Chicago: University of Chicago Press, 1987).
37. Ibid.

38. Harriet Lerner, *The Dance of Anger: A Woman's Guide to Changing Patterns of Intimate Relationships* (New York: Harper, 1985), p. 5.
39. Jill Ker Conway, *When Memory Speaks: Reflections on Autobiography* (New York: Alfred A. Knopf, 1998), p. 14.
40. Geraldine Laybourne, at www.oxygen.com.

Chapter 4: Some New Truths for Women to Live By

1. Kenneth Pelletier, *Sound Body, Sound Mind: A New Model for Lifelong Health* (New York: A Touchstone Book, 1994), p. 52.
2. Edward Hoffman, ed., *Future Visions: The Unpublished Papers of Abraham Maslow* (Thousand Oaks, Cal.: Sage Publications, 1996), p. 66.
3. Pelletier, *Sound Mind, Sound Body*, p. 39.
4. Ibid., p. 60.
5. Herbert Benson, *Timeless Healing: The Power and Biology of Belief* (New York: Scribner, 1961), p. 42.
6. Sherry Glied and Sharon Kofman, "Women and Mental Health: Issues for Health Reform" (New York: The Commonwealth Fund, Commission on Women's Health, March 1995), p. 64.
7. Stephanie Dowrick, *Intimacy & Solitude: Balancing Closeness & Independence* (New York: W. W. Norton & Co, 1991).
8. Roger T. Ames, Thomas P. Kasulis, and Wimil Dissanayake, *Self As Image in Asian Theory and Practice* (New York: SUNY, 1998), p. 450.
9. Hoffman, ed., *Future Visions*, p. 113.
10. Edward Deci and Richard Flaste, *Why We Do What We Do: Understanding Self-Motivation* (New York: Penguin Books, 1995), pp. 45–46.
11. Hoffman, ed., *Future Visions*, p. 177.
12. Deci and Flaste, *Why We Do What We Do*, p. 6.
13. Pelletier, *Sound Mind, Sound Body*, p. 17.
14. Sumru Erkut, et al., *Raising Competent Girls: One Size Does Not Fit All* (Boston: Center for Research on Women, Wellesley College, 1996), p. 6.
15. Carol Gilligan, Women's Studies Department lecture, Cal State University, Fresno, March 5, 1998.

Part III: Self-inventory and Discovery
Introduction: Getting to Know You, Getting to Know All About You

1. Alexandra Stoddard, *Daring to Be Yourself* (New York: Doubleday, 1990), p. 83.

Chapter 5: Who Are You?

1. Kenneth Pelletier, *Sound Mind, Sound Body: A New Model for Lifelong Health* (New York: Simon and Schuster, 1994), p. 109.

Chapter 6: What You Want in Your Friends and Work Colleagues

1. Karen Johnson, *Trusting Ourselves: The Complete Guide to Emotional Well-Being for Women* (New York: Atlantic Monthly Press, 1991), pp. 158–68.
2. Ibid., pp. 202–204.
3. Dinah Maria Mulock Craik, "A Life for a Life (1866)," in Rosalie Maggio, *The New Beacon Book of Quotations by Women* (Boston: Beacon Press), p. 270.

Chapter 9: *What Do You Want to Be? To Do? To Have?*

1. Peter McWilliams, *You Can't Afford the Luxury of a Negative Thought* (Los Angeles: Prelude Press, 1995).

Part IV: *Developing Your Confidence*
Introduction: *Let's Get Practical*

1. Larry Dossey, M.D., "Foreword," in Ann McGee-Cooper, *Time Management for Unmanageable People* (New York: Bantam Doubleday Dell, 1994), p. x.
2. Ann McGee-Cooper, *Time Management*, p. xv.

Chapter 10: *Accentuating the Positive . . .*

1. Linda J. Sax, et al., *The American Freshman: National Norms for Fall 1998* (Los Angeles: Higher Education Research Institute, UCLA, 1998).
2. Horace Bidwell English and Ava Champney, *A Comprehensive Dictionary of Psychological and Psychoanalytical Terms* (New York: Longmans Green, 1958), p. 442.
3. *Merriam-Webster's WWW Dictionary*, at www.m-w.com/cgi-bin/dictionary.
4. *Merriam-Webster's Ninth New Collegiate Dictionary* (Springfield, Mass.: Merriam-Webster, Inc., 1985), p. 1226.
5. Peter McWilliams, *You Can't Afford the Luxury of a Negative Thought* (Los Angeles: Prelude Press, 1995), p. 9.
6. Clarence L. Barnhart and Robert K. Barnhart, *The World Book Dictionary* (Chicago: World Book–Childcraft International, Inc., 1981), p. 782.
7. *Merriam-Webster's Ninth New Collegiate Dictionary*, p. 455.
8. Bernard Beins, Alan J. Feldman, and Susan B. Gall, eds., *Gale Encyclopedia of Psychology* (Farmington Hills, Mich.: Gale Research, 1996), p. 133.
9. McWilliams, *You Can't Afford the Luxury of a Negative Thought*, p. 38.
10. Herbert Benson, M.D., and William Proctor, *Beyond the Relaxation Response: How to Harness the Healing Power of Your Personal Beliefs* (New York: Berkley Publishing Group, 1994), p. 4.
11. Ibid., p. 51.
12. Herbert Benson, *Timeless Healing: The Power and Biology of Belief* (New York: Fireside, 1997), p. 267.
13. Martin E. P. Seligman, Ph.D., *Learned Optimism* (New York: Pocket Books, 1998), p. 7.
14. Benson, *Timeless Healing*, p. 273.
15. Dr. Robert S. Ivker and Edward Zorensky, *Thriving: The Holistic Guide to Optimal Health for Men* (New York: Three Rivers Press, 1997), p. 18.
16. David Burns, *Feeling Good: The New Mood Therapy* (New York: Avon, 1992), p. 12.
17. "Positively pre-wired: Our capacity for contentment may be inborn," *San Diego Union-Tribune*, January 31, 1999, pp. 2–3.
18. Albert Bandura, *Self-efficacy: The Exercise of Control* (San Francisco: W. H. Freeman, 1997), p. 137.
19. Ibid., p. 147.
20. Ibid.
21. Ibid.

22. Anthony Lawlor, *A Home for the Soul: A Guide for Dwelling with Spirit and Imagination* (New York: Clarkson Potter, 1997), p. 15.
23. Lawlor, *Home for the Soul.*
24. Benson, *Timeless Healing,* p. 277.
25. Matt Weinstein, *Managing to Have Fun* (New York: Fireside, 1997), p. 15.
26. Bandura, *Self-efficacy,* p. 148.

Chapter 11: Eliminating the Negative

1. Dr. Robert S. Ivker and Edward Zorensky, *Thriving: The Holistic Guide to Optimal Health for Men* (New York: Three Rivers Press, 1997), p. 37.
2. Aaron Beck, preface to David D. Burns, *Feeling Good: The New Mood Therapy* (New York: Avon, 1992), p. 42.
3. Adapted from Burns, *Feeling Good.*
4. Julia Cameron, *The Artist's Way: A Spiritual Path to Higher Creativity* (Los Angeles: Jeremy P. Tarcher, 1992), p. 31.
5. Dr. Judith Rodin, *Body Traps: Breaking the Binds That Keep You from Feeling Good About Your Body* (New York: William Morrow, 1992), p. 19.
6. Ibid.
7. Harriet Lerner, *The Dance of Anger: A Woman's Guide to Changing the Patterns of Intimate Relationships* (New York: HarperCollins, 1997), p. 7.
8. Willard Gaylin, *Feelings: Our Vital Signs* (New York: Harper and Row, 1979), p. 4.
9. Lerner, *Dance of Anger,* p. 7.
10. Kenneth Pelletier, *Sound Mind, Sound Body: A New Model for Lifelong Health* (New York: Simon and Schuster, 1994), p. 21.
11. Albert Bandura, *Self-efficacy: The Exercise of Control* (San Francisco: W. H. Freeman, 1997), p. 77.
12. Daniel Wegner, *White Bears & Other Unwanted Thoughts: Suppression, Obsession, and the Psychology of Mental Control* (New York: Guilford, 1994).
13. Ibid.
14. T. D. Borkovec, et al., "Stimulus control applications to the treatment of worry," *Behavior Research and Therapy,* vol. 21 (1983), 247–51.
15. Bandura, *Self-efficacy,* p. 148.
16. Ibid., p. 149.
17. Ibid., p. 329.
18. Martin Seligman, Ph.D., *What You Can Change . . . and What You Can't* (New York: Fawcett Columbine, 1993), p. 241.

Chapter 12: Trusting Your "Gut"

1. Tom Rusk, *Instead of Therapy: Help Yourself Change and Change the Help You're Getting* (Carson, Cal.: Hay House, 1993), p. 30.
2. In the original Lagerlöf used the pronoun *he* rather than *she.*
3. Willard Gaylin, *Feelings: Our Vital Signs* (New York: Harper and Row, 1979), p. 12.
4. Ibid., p. 13.
5. Ibid.
6. Carol Tavris, *Anger: The Misunderstood Emotion* (New York: Touchstone, 1989), p. 129.

7. Gaylin, *Feelings*, pp. 4–5.
8. Albert Ellis, *How to Stubbornly Refuse to Make Yourself Miserable About Anything—Yes, Anything* (New York: Lyle Stuart, 1988), p. 45.
9. The format of these diary entries was inspired by the work of Martin Seligman, *What You Can Change...and What You Can't* (New York: Fawcett, 1993), p. 131.
10. Deborah Tannen, *That's Not What I Meant: How Conversational Style Makes or Breaks Relationships* (New York: Ballantine, 1991), p. 14.
11. Seligman, *What You Can Change . . . and What You Can't*, p. 126.
12. Ibid.
13. Ibid., pp. 120–29.

Chapter 13: Taking Control of Your Life

1. Once again I have changed the noun *man* for *woman* and the pronoun *he* for *she*. I don't think Mary Shelley would have minded.
2. Mihaly Csikszentmihalyi, *Finding Flow: The Psychology of Engagement with Everyday Life* (New York: Basic Books, 1998), p. 20.
3. Ibid.
4. Kenneth Pelletier, *Sound Mind, Sound Body: A New Model for Lifelong Health* (New York: Simon and Schuster, 1994), p. 26.
5. Judith Rodin, *Body Traps: Breaking the Binds That Keep You from Feeling Good About Your Body* (New York: William Morrow, 1992), p. 18.
6. Ibid., p. 90.
7. Ibid., p. 44.
8. Ibid., p. 51.
9. Ibid., p. 90.
10. Ibid., p. 94.
11. Ibid., p. 124.
12. Ibid., p. 250.
13. Ibid.
14. Ibid., p. 226.
15. M. Scott Peck, *The Road Less Traveled: A New Psychology of Love, Traditional Values, and Spiritual Growth*, 2nd ed. (New York: Simon and Schuster, 1998), p. 15.
16. Csikszentmihalyi, *Finding Flow*, p. 102.
17. Ibid., p. 22.
18. Martin Seligman, et al., *The Optimistic Child* (New York: Harper Perennial, 1996), p. 33.
19. David Myers, *The Pursuit of Happiness: Discovering the Pathway to Fulfillment, Well-Being, and Enduring Personal Joy* (New York: Avon, 1993), pp. 205–207.
20. Csikszentmihalyi, *Finding Flow*, pp. 22–23.
21. Ibid., p. 102.
22. Ibid., p. 116.
23. Jean Baker Miller, *The Development of Women's Sense of Self*, p. 4.
24. Pelletier, *Sound Mind, Sound Body*, p. 227.
25. Myers, *The Pursuit of Happiness*, p. 140.
26. Suzanne Kobasa, "Stressful Life Events, Personality and Health: An Inquiry into Hardiness," *Journal of Personality and Social Psychology* 37: 1–11.
27. Edward Deci and Richard Flaste, *Why We Do What We Do: Understanding Self-Motivation* (New York: Penguin, 1996), p. 200.

28. Ibid., p. 94.
29. Ibid., p. 3.
30. Ibid.
31. Ibid., p. 196.
32. Ibid., p. 95.
33. Ibid., p. 95.
34. Ibid., p. 96.
35. Ibid., p. 196.
36. Ibid., pp. 9, 59, 87.
37. David K. Reynolds, *Constructive Living* (Honolulu: University of Hawaii Press, 1984), p. 43.
38. Csikszentmihalyi, *Finding Flow*, p. 23.
39. Carol Gilligan, *In a Different Voice: Psychological Theory and Women's Development* (Cambridge, Mass.: Harvard University Press, 1993), p. 38.

Chapter 14: Taking Better Care of Yourself

1. Eileen Hoffman, M.D., *Our Health, Our Lives: A Revolutionary Approach to Total Health Care for Women* (New York: Pocket Books, 1996), pp. 395–96.
2. Kathleen Hall Jamieson, *Beyond the Double Bind: Women and Leadership* (New York: Oxford University Press, 1995), p. 199.
3. HBO (Home Box Office), *Dare to Compete: The Struggle of Women in Sports.*
4. Once again I have used the pronoun *she* instead of the original *he.*
5. The Boston Women's Health Book Collective, *Our Bodies, Ourselves for the New Century* (New York: Touchstone, 1998), p. 3.
6. Ibid.
7. Iris Litt, M.D., *Taking Our Pulse: The Health of America's Women* (Palo Alto, Cal.: Stanford University Press, 1997), p. 281.
8. Hoffman, *Our Health, Our Lives*, pp. 27–28.
9. John Farquhar, Stanford University Healthy Woman Retreat, Fallen Leaf, Cal., June 1997.
10. Stanford Center for Research in Disease, *Fresh Start: The Stanford Medical School Health and Fitness Program* (San Francisco: KQED Books, 1996), p. xv.
11. Wesley Alles and Joyce Hanna, Stanford University Healthy Woman Retreat, Fallen Leaf, Cal., June 1997.
12. Edward Hoffman, *Future Visions: The Unpublished Papers of Abraham Maslow* (Los Angeles: Sage Publications, 1996), p. xi.
13. Stanford Center for Research in Disease Prevention, *Fresh Start* (San Francisco: KQED Books, 1996), p. xiv.
14. Hans Selye, *The Stress of Life* (New York: McGraw-Hill, 1978), p. 174.
15. Website of the Medical Center of Central Georgia, http://www.mccg.org/
16. Herbert Benson and William Proctor, *Beyond the Relaxation Response: How to Harness the Healing Power of Your Personal Beliefs* (New York: Berkley Publishing Group, 1994), p. 4.
17. Ibid., p. 5.
18. Nancy Felipe Russo, "Overview: Forging research priorities for women's mental health," *American Psychologist*, vol. 45, no. 3 (March 1990), p. 370.
19. Jane Zones and Kate Karpilow, CEWAER, *Women's Mental Health in California: Inadequate Attention* (Sacramento: California Elected Women's Association for Education and Research, 1993), p. 8.

20. Jill Ker Conway, *When Memory Speaks: Reflections on Autobiography* (New York: Alfred A. Knopf, 1998), p. 50.
21. Ibid., p. 88.
22. Bernadine Healy, *A New Prescription for Women's Health: Getting the Best Medical Care in a Man's World* (New York: Penguin, 1996), p. 21.
23. Hoffman, *Future Visions*, p. 41.
24. Beth Kobliner, *Get a Financial Life: Personal Finance in Your Twenties and Thirties* (New York: Fireside, 1996), p. 39.
25. *The Wall Street Journal's Guide to Understanding Personal Finance*, p. 114.
26. Herbert Benson, *Timeless Healing: The Power and Biology of Belief* (New York: Scribner, 1996), p. 200.
27. Ibid., p. 212.
28. Barbara Hils Carlile, "Portraits and Metaphors: Spirit of Women in Life and Literature," unpublished paper, p. 2.
29. Anne Morrow Lindbergh, *Gift from the Sea* (New York: Vintage, 1991).
30. Anthony Storr, *Solitude: A Return to the Self* (New York: Ballantine, 1989), p. ix.
31. Ibid., p. 75.
32. Ibid., p. ix.
33. Ibid., p. 28.

Epilogue: Final Thoughts: On Raising Confident Daughters

1. Once again I have taken the liberty of changing the pronoun *him* to *her.*
2. Judy Mann, *The Difference: Growing Up Female in America* (New York: Warner Books, 1994), p. 14.
3. Carol Gilligan, Annie G. Rogers, and Deborah L. Tolman, eds., *Women, Girls and Psychotherapy: Reframing Resistance* (New York: Harrington Park Press, 1991), p. 24.
4. Christine Renee Robinson, "Working with adolescent girls: Strategies to address health status," in ibid., p. 241.

Appendix I: Symptoms of Depression

1. *Desk Reference to the Diagnostic Criteria from DSM-IV* (Washington, D.C.: American Psychiatric Association Press, 1994), p. 162.

BIBLIOGRAPHY

Abuse, Violence

Barnett, Ola W., and Alyce D. La Violette. *It Could Happen to Anyone: Why Battered Women Stay*. London: Sage Publications, 1993.

Celani, David P. *The Illusion of Love: Why the Battered Woman Returns to Her Abuser*. New York: Columbia University Press, 1994.

Evans, Patricia. *The Verbally Abusive Relationship: How to Recognize It and How to Respond*. Holbrook, Massachusetts: Bob Adams, Inc., 1992.

Kirkwood, Catherine. *Leaving Abusive Partners: From the Scars of Survival to the Wisdom for Change*. London: Sage Publications, 1993.

Assertiveness Training and "I" Language

Adams, Linda, with Elinor Lenz. *E.T.W.: Effectiveness Training for Women*. New York: A Perigee Book, 1979.

Bower, Sharon Anthony, and Gordon H. Bower. *Asserting Yourself: A Practical Guide for Positive Change*. Reading, Massachusetts: Addison-Wesley Publishing Company, 1980.

Jeffers, Susan, Ph.D. *Feel the Fear and Do It Anyway*. New York: Fawcett Columbine, 1987.

Ury, William. *Getting Past No: Negotiating with Difficult People*. New York: Bantam Books, 1991.

Beauty and Body Image

Hansen, Vikki, and Shawn Goodman. *The Seven Secrets of Slim People*. New York: Harper Paperbacks, 1997.

Rodin, Dr. Judith. *Body Traps: Breaking the Binds That Keep You from Feeling Good About Your Body*. New York: Quill, 1992.

Stoddard, Alexandra. *Daring to Be Yourself*. New York: Doubleday, 1990.

Business

Bennis, Warren. *On Becoming a Leader.* Reading, Massachusetts: Addison Wesley, 1989.

Drucker, Peter F. *The Effective Executive.* New York: HarperBusiness, 1967.

Heim, Pat, Ph.D., with Susan K. Golant. *Hardball for Women: Winning at the Game of Business.* Los Angeles: Lowell House, 1992.

Helgesen, Sally. *The Female Advantage: Women's Ways of Leadership.* New York: Doubleday Currency, 1990.

Hesselbein, Frances, Marshall Goldsmith, and Richard Beckhard, editors. *The Leader of the Future.* San Francisco: Jossey-Bass Publishers, 1996.

James, Jennifer. *Thinking in the Future Tense: Leadership Skills for a New Age.* New York: Simon & Schuster, 1996.

Josefowitz, Natasha. *Paths to Power: A Woman's Guide from First Job to Top Executive.* Reading, Massachusetts: Addison-Wesley Publishing Company, 1980.

O'Neil, John R. *The Paradox of Success: When Winning at Work Means Losing at Life: A Book of Renewal for Leaders.* New York: Jeremy P. Tarcher/Putnam Book, 1993.

Senge, Peter M. *The Fifth Discipline: The Art & Practice of The Learning Organization.* New York: Doubleday Currency, 1990.

Weinstein, Matt. *Managing to Have Fun: How Fun at Work Can Motivate Your Employees, Inspire Your Co-Workers, Boost Your Bottom Line.* New York: Simon Schuster, 1996.

Winston, Stephanie. *The Organized Executive: New Ways to Manage Time, Paper and People.* New York: W. W. Norton & Company, 1983.

Career and Life Planning

Bolles, Richard Nelson. *The 1999 What Color Is Your Parachute: A Practical Manual for Job-Hunters & Career Changers.* Berkeley, California: 10 Speed Press, 1999.

Edwards, Paul and Sarah. *Finding Your Perfect Work: The New Career Guide to Making a Living, Creating a Life.* New York: Jeremy P. Tarcher/Putnam Book, 1996.

McGee-Cooper, Ann. *Time Management for Unmanageable People.* New York: Bantam Books, 1994.

Emotional Health

Briggs, Dorothy Corkille. *Celebrate Your Self: Enhancing Your Own Self-Esteem.* New York: Doubleday & Company, 1977.

Burns, David D., M.D. *Feeling Good: The New Mood Therapy.* New York: Avon Books, 1992.

Csikszentmihalyi, Mihaly. *Finding Flow: The Psychology of Engagement with Everyday Life.* New York: Basic Books, 1997.

Csikszentmihalyi, Mihaly. *Flow.* New York: HarperCollins, 1991.

Deci, Edward L., and Richard Flaste. *Why We Do What We Do: Understanding Self-Motivation.* New York: Penguin Books, 1996.

Gawain, Shakti. *Creative Visualization.* New York: Bantam Books, 1982.

Gaylin, Willard, M.D. *Feelings: Our Vital Signs.* New York: Ballantine Books, 1979.

Johnson, Karen, M.D. *Trusting Ourselves: The Complete Guide to Emotional Well-being for Women.* New York: The Atlantic Monthly Press, 1991.

Miller, Jean Baker, M.D. *Toward a New Psychology of Women.* Boston: Beacon Press, 1986.

Myers, David G., Ph.D. *The Pursuit of Happiness: Discovering the Pathway to Fulfillment, Well-being, and Enduring Personal Joy.* New York: Avon Books, 1992.

Reynolds, David K. *Constructive Living.* Honolulu: University of Hawaii Press, 1984.

Selye, Hans, M.D. *The Stress of Life.* New York: McGraw-Hill Companies, 1984.

Storr, Anthony. *Solitude: A Return to the Self.* New York: The Free Press, 1988.

Swann, William B., Jr. *Self-Traps: The Elusive Quest for Higher Self-Esteem.* New York: W. H. Freeman and Company, 1996.

Thoele, Sue Patton. *The Courage to Be Yourself: A Woman's Guide to Growing Beyond Emotional Dependence.* New York: MJF Books, 1988.

Finances

Bertrand, Marsha. *A Woman's Guide to Savvy Investing.* New York: Amacom, 1998.

Dowling, Colette. *Maxing Out: Why Women Sabotage Their Financial Security.* Boston: Little, Brown & Company, 1998.

Kobliner, Beth. *Get a Financial Life.* New York: Fireside Books, 1996.

Girls

Briggs, Dorothy Corkille. *Your Child's Self-esteem: Step-by-Step Guidelines for Raising Responsible, Productive, Happy Children.* New York: Doubleday & Company, 1975.

Brown, Lyn Mikel. *Raising Their Voices: The Politics of Girls' Anger.* Cambridge, Massachusetts: Harvard University Press, 1998.

Brown, Lyn Mikel, and Carol Gilligan. *Meeting at the Crossroads: Women's Psychology and Girls' Development.* Cambridge, Massachusetts: Harvard University Press, 1992.

Maccoby, Eleanor E. *The Two Sexes: Growing Up Apart, Coming Together.* Cambridge, Massachusetts: The Belknap Press of Harvard University Press, 1998.

Mann, Judy. *The Difference: Growing Up Female in America.* New York: Warner Books, 1994.

Orenstein, Peggy. *School Girls: Young Women, Self-esteem, and the Confidence Gap.* New York: Doubleday, 1994.

Pipher, Mary. *Reviving Ophelia: Saving the Selves of Adolescent Girls.* New York: Grosset/Putnam Book, 1994.

Rimm, Sylvia. *See Jane Win: The Rimm Report on How 1000 Girls Became Successful Women.* New York: Crown Publishers, 1999.

Seligman, Martin E. P., Ph.D. *The Optimistic Child.* New York: Harper Perennial, 1996.

Negative Thinking

Bandura, Albert. *Self-Efficacy: The Exercise of Control.* New York: W. H. Freeman and Company, 1997.

Seligman, Martin E. P., Ph.D. *Learned Optimism.* New York: Pocket Books, 1992.

Seligman, Martin E. P., Ph.D. *What You Can Change . . . and What You Can't.* New York: Fawcett Columbine, 1993.

Wegner, Daniel M. *White Bears & Other Unwanted Thoughts: Suppression, Obsession, and the Psychology of Mental Control.* New York: Viking, 1989.

Pure Enjoyment

Bond, Marybeth. *Gutsy Women: Travel Tips and Wisdom for the Road.* San Francisco: Travelers' Tales, Inc., 1996.

Kelly, Marcia and Jack. *Sanctuaries: A Guide to Lodgings in Monasteries, Abbeys, and Retreats of the United States.* New York: Bell Tower, 1992.

Lawlor, Anthony. *A Home for the Soul: A Guide for Dwelling with Spirit and Imagination.* New York: Clarkson Potter/Publishers, 1997.

Madden, Chris Casson. *A Room of Her Own: Women's Personal Spaces.* New York: Clarkson Potter/Publishers, 1997.

Vienne, Véronique. *The Art of Doing Nothing: Simple Ways to Make Time for Yourself.* New York: Clarkson Potter/Publishers, 1998.

Spiritual Matters

Cameron, Julia. *The Artist's Way: A Spiritual Path to Higher Creativity.* New York: Jeremy P. Tarcher/Putnam Book, 1992.

Cousineau, Phil. *Soul Moments: Marvelous Stories of Synchronicity.* Berkeley, California: Conari Press, 1997.

James, William. *The Varieties of Religious Experience.* New York: Touchstone Book, 1997.

Moore, Thomas. *Care of the Soul: A Guide for Cultivating Depth and Sacredness in Everyday Life.* New York: HarperCollins, 1992.

Peck, M. Scott, M.D. *The Road Less Traveled: A New Psychology of Love, Traditional Values and Spiritual Growth.* Touchstone Books, 1978.

Women

Bateson, Mary Catherine. *Composing a Life.* New York: Plume Book, 1990.

Belenky, Mary Field, Blythe Clinchy, Nancy Golderger, and Jill Tarule. *Women's Ways of Knowing: The Development of Self, Voice and Mind.* New York: Basic Books, 1986.

Cheever, Susan. *A Woman's Life: The Story of an Ordinary American and Her Extraordinary Generation.* New York: William Morrow and Company, Inc., 1994.

Dowrick, Stephanie. *Intimacy & Solitude: Balancing Closeness and Independence.* New York: W. W. Norton & Company, 1991.

Gabor, Andrea. *Einstein's Wife: Work and Marriage in the Lives of Five Great Twentieth-Century Women.* New York: Viking, 1995.

Heilbrun, Carolyn G. *Writing a Woman's Life.* New York: Ballantine Books, 1988.

Jack, Dana Crowley. *Silencing the Self: Women and Depression.* Cambridge, Massachusetts: Harvard University Press, 1991.

Lerner, Harriet Goldhor. *The Dance of Anger: A Woman's Guide to Changing the Patterns of Intimate Relationships.* New York: HarperCollins, 1985.

Lerner, Harriet Goldhor. *The Dance of Deception: Pretending and Truth-Telling in Women's Lives.* New York: HarperCollins, 1993.

Lindbergh, Anne Morrow. *Gift From the Sea.* New York: Pantheon Books, 1955.

Rubin, Lillian B. *Just Friends: The Role of Friendship in Our Lives.* New York: Harper & Row, 1985.

Tavris, Carol. *Anger: The Misunderstood Emotion.* New York: Touchstone Book, 1989.

Tavris, Carol. *The Mismeasure of Woman: Why Women Are Not The Better Sex, The Inferior Sex, or The Opposite Sex.* New York: Simon Schuster, 1992.

Vanzant, Iyanla. *In the Meantime . . . Finding Yourself and the Love That You Want.* New York: Simon & Schuster, 1998.

Wollstonecraft, Mary. *A Vindication of the Rights of Women* (1792). Buffalo, New York: Prometheus Books, 1989.

Woolf, Virginia. *A Room of One's Own.* New York: Harcourt Brace & Company, 1991.

Women's Health

Benson, Herbert, M.D. *Beyond the Relaxation Response.* New York: Berkley Books, 1985.

Benson, Herbert, M.D. *Timeless Healing: The Power and Biology of Belief.* New York: Scribner, 1996.

Borysenko, Joan, Ph.D. *Minding the Body, Mending the Mind.* New York: Bantam Books, 1988.

Boston Women's Health Book Collective. *Our Bodies, Ourselves for the New Century.* New York: Touchstone Book, 1998.

Caplan, Paula J. *They Say You're Crazy: How the World's Most Powerful Psychiatrists Decide Who's Normal.* Reading, Massachusetts: Addison-Wesley Publishing Company, 1995.

Cousins, Norman. *Anatomy of an Illness.* New York: Bantam Books, 1985.

Hoffman, Eileen, M.D. *Our Health, Our Lives: A Revolutionary Approach to Total Health Care for Women.* New York, Pocket Books, 1995.

Laurence, Leslie, and Beth Weinhouse. *Outrageous Practices: The Alarming Truth About How Medicine Mistreats Women.* New York: Fawcett Columbine, 1994.

Litt, Iris, M.D. *Taking Our Pulse: The Health of America's Women.* Stanford, California: Stanford University Press, 1997.

Nolen-Hocksema, Susan. *Sex Differences in Depression.* Stanford, California: Stanford University Press, 1990.

Pelletier, Kenneth. *Sound Mind, Sound Body: A New Model for Lifelong Health.* New York: A Fireside Book, 1994.

Sheehy, Gail. *The Silent Passage: Menopause.* New York: Random House, 1992.

Stanford Center for Research in Disease Prevention. *Fresh Start: The Stanford Medical School Health and Fitness Program.* San Francisco, California: KQED Books, 1996.

Women's History

Bell, Susan Groag, and Karen M. Offen. *Women, the Family, and Freedom: The Debate in Documents.* Stanford, California: Stanford University Press, 1983.

Dijkstra, Bram. *Evil Sisters: The Threat of Female Sexuality in Twentieth-Century Culture.* New York: Owl Book, 1996.

Dijkstra, Bram. *Idols of Perversity: Fantasies of Feminine Evil in Fin-de-siecle Culture.* New York: Oxford University Press, 1986.

Haskell, Molly. *From Reverence to Rape: The Treatment of Women in the Movies.* Chicago: The University of Chicago Press, 1987.

Kerber, Linda K. *No Constitutional Right to Be Ladies: Women and the Obligations of Citizenship.* New York: Hill and Wang, 1998.

PERMISSIONS

Grateful acknowledgment is made to the following for permission to reprint previously published material:

Random House, Inc.: Excerpt from "Phenomenal Woman" from *And Still I Rise* by Maya Angelou, copyright © 1978 by Maya Angelou; excerpt from *I Can Read With My Eyes Shut* by Dr. Seuss, TM and copyright © 1978 by Dr. Seuss Enterprises, L.P. Reprinted by permission of Random House, Inc.

Graywolf Press: Excerpt from "Gnostics on Trial," copyright © 1981 by Linda Gregg. Reprinted from *Too Bright to See* by Linda Gregg with the permission of Graywolf Press, Saint Paul, Minnesota.

New Directions Publishing Corporation: Excerpt from *Selected Poems* by Eugene Guillevic. Copyright © 1969 by Denise Levertov Goodman and Eugene Guillevic. Reprinted by permission of New Directions Publishing Corporation.

Weatherhill Publishers: Excerpt from *Zen Mind, Beginner's Mind,* by Eihei Dogen, Zenji, translated by Shunryu Suzuki-roshi, copyright © 1970. Reprinted by permission of Weatherhill Publishers.

Prof. Dieter Rams: Excerpt from "The Sixteen Commandments" by Prof. Dieter Rams. Copyright © by Prof. Dieter Rams. Reprinted by permission of the author.

Susan Polis Schutz: Excerpt from *To My Daughter with Love* by Susan Polis Schutz, copyright © 1986 by Susan Polis Schutz. Reprinted by permission of the author.

To protect the privacy of the people with whom I have worked, no case study or anecdote in this book refers to any specific individual. While illustrative material is presented, names and occupations, as well as identifying details, have been added, deleted, or rearranged. These composites of personal stories represent material collected by the author in her experience as a marriage and family therapist, executive coach, consultant, colleague, and friend.

ACKNOWLEDGMENTS

I am fortunate to have family and friends who make my life extraordinarily full and rich. I thank them for their forbearance while I was writing *The Confident Woman*, and especially for accepting e-mail relationships for longer than we all thought.

Because family members were particularly patient, they all get the PUM Award (Putting Up with Marjorie). The PUM goes to my parents, Bob and Evelyn Hansen, and the rest of the family in Fresno, the Becks, Kitty Jensen and the Sirmans. It also goes to Barbara Hansen and Dann Parks; to Erica and John Huggins in L.A. and to Jonathon Shaevitz and Karen Blumberg in New York.

Of course, many thanks go to my husband, Mort, for putting up with take-out food, vacations and social occasions endlessly put on hold, keeping the cash flow going, expert advice, and especially for getting me back on track when I strayed into irrelevant ideas and unnecessary tangents. My children, Geoff and Marejka, were unfailingly there for whatever I asked (and even for what I didn't). To them, thank you for all that you did, your loving encouragement, great ideas, sense of humor and wit, and the flowers that just showed up.

Some friends were helpful in vital ways, including reading and commenting on parts of drafts, giving examples from their own experience, and sending me their ideas. Many thanks to Susan Polis Schutz for her support, wisdom, and enduring friendship; Carol Obermeier for her warm smile, generous time, and deft editing hand; Christine Forester for her one-of-a-kind suggestions and aesthetic touch; Iris Litt for being a major motivating force to write the book; Stanford University's Institute for Research on Women and Gender, especially Laura Carstenson, for untold resources, friendships, and ideas and much more; the California Office of Women's Health for amazing health information and involvement with remarkable Council members; and the California Commission on the Status of Women for a decade of warm Commission friendships and up-to-the minute information on what's happening with women. Thanks, too, to Shawn Goodman for her generous time in telling me the way it really is. Tom Rusk deserves special recognition for his challenge to me a few years ago to become a more confident woman. Without it, this book might never have been written.

The amazing staff at the Institute for Family and Work Relationships, Dianne Schultz, Shannon Minniss, and Alina Mitchell, must be acknowledged for their above-and-beyond-the-call-of-duty assistance whenever I needed it. Dora Cruz provided special personal help, as did Sidney Ayers. Thanks to Jacque Hansen who introduced me to the resources of the University of California, San Diego, library and then to my research assistants, Tammy Elliot and Sara Waller. Thanks, T and S. Thanks also go to Kirsten Woo for her research help. Attorney Elisabeth Eisner not only consented to be interviewed for the book, but gave me her astute legal advice.

Thank you also to Olivia Heffler Bantz, David Brown, Ken Majer, Arlene Sacks, Marjorie Schneider, Donna Sevilla, Dale Steele and Kim Weiss for your friendship and special contributions along the way.

I am particularly grateful to my agent, Sandy Dijkstra, and her staff for helping me re-enter the publishing world, and especially for introducing me to my editor, Shaye Areheart. Shaye was given the LMP "Editor of the Year" award while she was editing this book; now I know why. She not only edits well, but has been an unflagging source of enthusiasm and encouragement. Thank you, Shaye, and everyone else at Harmony Books, including Dina Siciliano, Katherine Beitner, Kim Robles, David Tran, Steve Weissman, and Patricia Flynn.

A number of authors and researchers were important to me at various stages of my writing the book. I feel indebted to them and their ideas. They include: Dr. Karen Johnson and Dr. Eileen Hoffman, two founders of the women's health movement; the researchers at the Wellesley College Stone Center for Research on Women; Dr. Kenneth Pelletier of Stanford University; Harvard University's Dr. Herbert Benson; the University of Chicago's Dr. Mihaly Csikszentmihalyi; Dr. Martin Seligman of the University of Pennsylvania; Dr. Edward Deci at the University of Rochester; Stanford's Dr. Albert Bandura; Dr. Bram Dijkstra of the University of California, San Diego; and Oxford University's Dr. Anthony Storr.

Finally, there is no adequate way to thank the women whom I interviewed. Without them, this would be much less of a book. While some wished to remain anonymous, here are those who did not: Deanna D'Adarrio, Michelle Archer, Lily Balian, Amy Blum, Margaret Dalton, Sharon Davidson, Laurie Drabble, Carol Dressler, Ayofemi Folayen, Dana Goodman, Iris Goodman, Shawn Goodman, Dr. Barbara Gosink, Vicki Halsey, Barbara Hansen, Hanne Vedsted Hansen, Charlotte Huggins, Kimberly Jameson, Kitty Jensen, Kara Johnson, Vicky Jordan, Natasha Josefowitz, Lilian Huang, Kate Karpilow, Cheryl Kendrick, Ellen Kirkendall, Dottie Lamm, Tracy Lau (and her daughters Maya and Erin), Jing Lyman, Jain Malkin, Reiko Mayeno, Adrienne Newell, Reverend Carolyn Owen-Towle, Kristie Peterson, Barbara Poleski, June Polis, Leah Rabin, Louise Rosenberg, former Congresswoman Pat Schroeder, Margo Smith, Kathy Tschirin, Maria Valasquez, Senator Diane Watson, Dr. Kim Yeager, and Pat Zigarmi. Thank you one, thank you all.

I also want to acknowledge my clients over the years, whom I cannot name, for the many confidence lessons they taught me. Many other people have enriched my life. Necessarily their names are not noted here, but they are in my head and my heart.

INDEX

ABOUT THE AUTHOR

Marjorie Hansen Shaevitz, director of the Institute for Family & Work Relationships in La Jolla, California, holds a master's degree from Stanford University and is a practicing marriage and family therapist. She is the immediate past Chair of the National Advisory Panel for Stanford's Institute for Research on Women and Gender at Stanford University, as well as the California Commission on the Status of Women. Best known for her best-selling book, *The Superwoman Syndrome*, Marjorie Hansen Shaevitz not only coined the phrase in our culture's vocabulary, she helped to make it an everyday word. Named "Woman of the Year" by the California Senate and recognized with the "Women's Health Advocacy Achievement Award" by the National Association of Women Health Professionals, she has appeared on *Oprah*, with Letterman and Regis, as well as on the national morning shows. Magazines and newspapers around the country have written about Hansen Shaevitz's work including *USA Today*, *Prevention*, *The Wall Street Journal*, *Cosmo*, and *Working Mother*.